# John Ireland

*A Catalogue, Discography, and Bibliography*

# John Ireland

*A Catalogue, Discography, and Bibliography*

«»

Compiled by
STEWART R. CRAGGS
With an introduction by
GEOFFREY BUSH

CLARENDON PRESS · OXFORD
1993

Oxford University Press, Walton Street, Oxford OX2 6DP
Oxford New York Toronto
Delhi Bombay Calcutta Madras Karachi
Kuala Lumpur Singapore Hong Kong Tokyo
Nairobi Dar es Salaam Cape Town
Melbourne Auckland Madrid
and associated companies in
Berlin Ibadan

Oxford is a trade mark of Oxford University Press

Published in the United States
by Oxford University Press Inc., New York

© Stewart R. Craggs 1993

All rights reserved. No part of this publication may be reproduced,
stored in a retrieval system, or transmitted, in any form or by any means,
without the prior permission of Oxford University Press.
Within the UK, exceptions are allowed in respect of any fair dealing for the
purpose of research or private study, or criticism or review, as permitted
under the Copyright, Designs and Patents Act, 1988, or in the case of
reprographic reproduction in accordance with the terms of the licences
issued by the Copyright Licensing Agency. Enquiries concerning
reproduction outside these terms and in other countries should be
sent to the Rights Department, Oxford University Press,
at the address above

British Library Cataloguing in Publication Data
Data available

Library of Congress Cataloging in Publication Data
John Ireland: a catalogue, discography, and bibliography/
compiled by Stewart R. Craggs; with an introduction
by Geoffrey Bush.
Includes index.
1. Ireland, John, 1879–1962—Bibliography. 2. Ireland, John,
1879–1962—Discography. I. Title.
ML 134.I75C7  1993   016.78'092—dc20   92-21552
ISBN 0-19-816317-7

Typeset by Joshua Associates Ltd., Oxford
Printed in Great Britain
on acid-free paper by
Bookcraft (Bath) Ltd.,
Midsomer Norton

Dedicated to
the memory of my parents
Roger and Mary Craggs

# Contents

⟨◊⟩

|  | Page |
|---|---|
| Introduction *by Geoffrey Bush* | ix |
| Acknowledgements | xiii |
| Chronology | xiv |
| Compiler's note | xvii |
| THE CATALOGUE | 1 |
| Bibliography | 123 |
| Appendices: | |
|   1: Recordings: John Ireland as conductor, performer, and speaker | 133 |
|   2: Alphabetical list of compositions | 135 |
|   3: Classified list of compositions | 141 |
|   4: Works and Sketches, Lost or Undated | 147 |
|   5: Index of Song Titles and First Lines | 149 |
| General index | 153 |

# INTRODUCTION
## By GEOFFREY BUSH

《 》

In the first letter that John Ireland wrote to me—it was in response to a bundle of my juvenile compositions sent to him by our school chaplain—he emphasized the 'thorough and efficient' course of study undergone by Schoenberg, Bartók, and Hindemith. 'All the composers I have mentioned (and of course one could add Stravinsky) have undoubtedly been through a protracted and severe course . . . of training before blossoming out into what may at first sight appear to be without rhyme or reason.' Ireland could with justice have added his own name to that list. He began to learn the piano at the age of 8 under a teacher whose recipe for discouraging wrong notes was to rap the offender's knuckles with a ruler. Just before his fourteenth birthday he enrolled—on his own initiative—at the Royal College of Music, where he continued his piano studies under Frederick Cliffe. The era of knuckle-rapping was over, but Cliffe once sent Ireland back to his digs in disgrace to practise for three hours because his weekly lesson had been inadequately prepared. (He later recalled in a radio talk that his lapses—and their consequences—always seemed to occur when the set task was a piece by Beethoven in the key of G.) Parallel with his piano studies he learnt to play the organ, to such effect that he passed his FRCO just before his sixteenth birthday, becoming the youngest person (at that time) to gain this major diploma.

In spite of his rapid progress as an executant, however, his chief ambition was to be accepted as one of Stanford's composition students. Sir Charles Stanford was without doubt the greatest composition teacher of his day; the roll-call of his pupils reads like a history of early twentieth-century British music—besides Ireland himself there were Bliss, Boughton, Bridge, Goossens, Holst, Howells, Hurlstone, Gordon Jacob, Moeran, Coleridge-Taylor, and (rather rebelliously) Vaughan Williams. The lesson he taught Ireland, and which Ireland in turn passed on to Benjamin Britten and his other pupils, was that 'nothing but the best would do'. There are many stories of his ruthless pursuit of excellence; the first composition which Ireland showed to the man who he hoped would accept him as a student, a string quartet, was greeted with the words 'Dull as ditchwater, my boy'. The sequel reveals a rather different side to Stanford; he organized a performance of the quartet in College so that the Principal (Parry) could hear it, with the result that the boy was awarded a composition scholarship on the spot. Ireland never forgot what he and his contemporaries owed to 'that great man, Stanford', not least because instead of imposing his own personality on them (like all too many teachers), he encouraged them to find their own.

It was indeed high time that British music emancipated itself; thanks to an obsession with Germany dating back to the accession of the Hanoverians, it had allowed itself to be overshadowed first by Handel, then by Mendelssohn, and finally by the great bearded figure of Brahms. Stanford, scenting danger where the young Ireland's music was concerned—'It's all Brahms and water, my boy, and more water than Brahms'—took the drastic step of putting him on a year's rigorous course of Palestrina counterpoint, for the benefits of which Ireland in later life was profoundly grateful. The ultimate inspiration for his self-discovery, however, came from a different and rather unexpected quarter. To borrow a term from Britten, Ireland 'Mediterraneanized' his music under the liberating influence of Debussy and Ravel. (Salvation through the rediscovery of England's musical heritage—folksong, the Tudor masters, Purcell—was not for him, as it had been for Holst and Vaughan Williams.) There was never, of course, any question of directly imitating his two favourite living French composers; it was rather that his admiration for their work released him from subservience to middle European models and enabled him to find his own individual voice. (There could be no better illustration of what I mean than the Fantasy Sonata for clarinet and piano, the crown of his chamber music.)

Mention of his chamber music reminds me of the central part played by this branch of composition in Ireland's creative life. In the Sextet for clarinet, horn, and string quartet written at the age of 18 for—though not entirely approved by—Stanford ('The finale is not organic, my boy') we catch our first glimpse of the mature Ireland. His professional career was launched when his First Trio and First Violin Sonata won second and first prizes in successive years in the competitions for new chamber works sponsored by W. W. Cobbett. His reputation was finally established in 1917, when the morning after the première of his Second Violin Sonata Ireland 'woke up to find himself famous'. If we exclude juvenilia, the list is completed by the Cello Sonata—an intense, virile piece—and two more trios. The trio medium, thanks to the combination of two instruments of line and one of colour, had, so the composer once told me, an especial appeal for him.

There were other, non-musical influences which had a far-reaching effect on Ireland's development. He was fortunate in being the contemporary of two poets, Hardy and A. E. Housman, whose words were ideal for setting and whose somewhat fatalistic view of the human condition chimed in exactly with Ireland's own. The two cycles to Housman's poems, *The Land of*

*Lost Content* and *We'll to the Woods no more*, are not only among his finest musical achievements but catch the inner spirit of the words with extraordinary fidelity. (The latter cycle—consisting, uniquely, of two songs and a piano piece—is such a poignant expression of grief for the sufferings of World War I that in later years the composer could not bear to listen to it.) Another profound literary influence was that of Arthur Machen, whose *House of Souls* Ireland happened to find on a station bookstall in 1906. Machen is little read nowadays—though perhaps the publication of an anthology of his work edited by Christopher Palmer (Gerald Duckworth & Co.) may restore his reputation—so it may be helpful to indicate two themes which recur in his work and which had a particular attraction for Ireland: the immanence of the past (impinging on the present) and the immanence of the supernatural (impinging on everyday life). A typical Machen short story tells of a reporter in wartime visiting a blacked-out seaside town. Emerging from his inn just before midnight he is astonished to see a procession of joyful children who, though bearing the marks of ancient wounds, are 'singing with the rapture and exaltation of them that sing in the woods in springtime'. When on his return to the inn he tells the landlord what he has seen, the man is 'sick and shuddering with terror; he drew away from me as though I was a messenger from the dead'. What the reporter had seen was a vision of the Holy Innocents, come to celebrate Childermas in the town's old abbey. Ireland's piano piece 'The Secret Ceremonies' from the cycle *Decorations* is headed by a quotation from Machen, and *Legend* for piano and orchestra is dedicated to him—appropriately, for it was partly inspired by a Machen-like experience of Ireland's own. Picknicking one day near Chanctonbury Ring he was suddenly conscious of some children dancing in front of him. 'He at first thought they were real, but then he noticed their archaic clothing. He glanced away for an instant, and when he looked back the children had vanished . . .' (No wonder that, although he did not care for the works of Stravinsky's neo-classical period, he had a profound admiration for *The Rite of Spring*.)

The other inspiration behind *Legend* was the Sussex Downland, as it also was for the suite of that name and, among the piano music, *Amberley Wild Brooks* and *Equinox*. Places and their associations, particularly if those associations went back to ancient civilizations and even prehistory, played a very important part in Ireland's creative processes. He first visited the Channel Islands in 1900, when it was decided that members of his choir at Holy Trinity, Sloane Street, should take their annual summer holiday there; thereafter he became a regular visitor. 'The Island Spell' was written there in two successive years; two, because after his return to London inspiration deserted him. It was only when he revisited Jersey that the missing final section came into his mind spontaneously. In the late 1930s, lured by an invitation to become organist and choirmaster at St Stephen's, St Peter Port, he decided to become a permanent resident of Guernsey; he had not been long in his post before he was forced to flee from the German invasion, escaping with the manuscript of *Sarnia* on the last boat to leave the Islands before the Occupation. In the years of his retirement he returned to Sussex, a chance visit by motor car having led, almost as if by a miracle, to the purchase of a converted windmill opposite Chanctonbury Ring which he had long coveted. During his working life, however, his headquarters were in Chelsea, where for over twenty years he was in charge of the music at the Parish Church of St Luke. Even this relatively mundane, metropolitan scene was a source of inspiration to Ireland; thanks to this we have the London Overture for orchestra and the *London Pieces* for piano (including 'Chelsea Reach', which of all the solo piano works has good claim to be his masterpiece). His studio was in Gunter Grove and the nearest bus stop was a magically named pub, the World's End; at least it seemed magical to me when I used to go and see him during the school holidays, bringing my latest immature composition for his inspection. (As I have described in my book *Left, Right and Centre*, published by Thames Music, Ireland was as rigorously critical as Stanford, but without his caustic tongue).

Much more could be written—about his church music, about 'These things shall be', a vision of a better future described by the chorus with Elgarian fervour and reinforced by orchestral references to the 'Internationale', and about the Piano Concerto, which to my mind is the pinnacle of his achievement—but it is now time to sum up. Not that this is an easy, or even a practicable task. A roll-call of stylistic features—beauty of line, subtlety of harmony, mastery of form, unfailing craftsmanship, sensitive response to poetry, a thorough grasp of the potential of instruments either singly or in combination—however applicable it may be to Ireland's music does nothing to convey its inner character. A list of abstract qualities—strength of purpose, empathy with nature, quirky humour, profound feeling, and an even profounder reticence—is scarcely more helpful. The only way to understanding Ireland the composer is by direct contact with the music, and as a guide to that music Dr Craggs's annotated catalogue will be of invaluable assistance. It is a real pleasure to commend his 'right happy and copious industry' (no mean compliment, since it was originally applied by John Webster to his fellow playwright William Shakespeare).

# Acknowledgements

«»

My acknowledgements are principally due to Peter and Margaret Taylor, who helped me in so many ways and who welcomed me into their house so many times while I consulted the many papers and manuscripts kept under their roof. I have also been fortified by the enthusiasm and encouragement of fellow Trustee Bruce Phillips.

I would also like to thank, in particular, Simon Bailey, Archivist, University of London Library; Christopher Bornet of the Royal College of Music Library; Dr Geoffrey Bush, Musical Adviser to the John Ireland Trust; Oliver Davies, Keeper of Portraits at the Royal College of Music; Timothy Day of the National Sound Archive; Lewis Foreman; Joyce Horn of Hymn Copyright at Oxford University Press; Joan Redding of Chester Music; Arthur Searle, Curator of Music Manuscripts at the British Library; Lawrence Tagg, formerly of Newcastle City Libraries; the late Revd Kenneth Thompson and Jeff Walden of the BBC Written Archives Centre.

The following also very kindly answered questions and provided information: Mrs E. P. Arthur, ROH Archives; Dr Stephen Banfield; Harry Bramma; Geoffrey Brand; Alan and Nancy Bush; Richard Chesser, British Library; David Cousins, Reference Librarian, Canterbury Central Library; Robert Cowan, Archivist, Boosey & Hawkes Ltd.; Roy Douglas; Sheila Doyle of Durham University Library; John Dressler; the Revd Michael Garland of the Hymn Society; the late Sir Charles Groves; Anna Jackson, Andrew Kirk, and Barry Norman of the Theatre Museum, London; Andrew Kemp, Boosey & Hawkes Ltd.; R. C. F. Leach; Mrs Vivienne Longmire; Mrs Linda McGown; Mrs Jane Moore for Latin translations; music librarians at Bournemouth and Leeds City Libraries; O. W. Neighbour; Dr Stephen Roe of Sotheby's; Malcolm Smith; Dr Herbert Sumsion; P. G. Toms, British Coal; Carol Wakefield, Stainer & Bell Ltd.; Peter Ward Jones, Music Librarian, Bodleian Library, Oxford; John Whitehorn, EMI Music Publishing Ltd.; and Peter Wilson, Managing Editor of *British Bandsman*.

# Chronology

«‹›»

| | |
|---|---|
| 1879 | 13 August: born in Bowden, Cheshire, the youngest son of Alexander and Annie Ireland |
| 1893 | September: enters the Royal College of Music to study piano with Frederick Cliffe |
| | Death of Annie Ireland |
| 1894 | Death of Alexander Ireland |
| | Becomes a Fellow of the Royal College of Organists |
| 1896 | Appointed as assistant organist of Holy Trinity Church, Sloane Street |
| 1897 | Becomes a composition student of C. V. Stanford at the Royal College of Music |
| 1898 | Goes to live in Elm Park Mansions, Chelsea |
| 1900 | Appointed organist of St Jude's Church, Chelsea |
| | Visits the Channel Islands for the first time |
| 1901 | Leaves the Royal College of Music |
| 1904 | Appointed organist of St Luke's Church, Chelsea, a post he holds until 1926 |
| 1905 | Graduates from Durham University with a B.Mus. |
| 1906 | Becomes acquainted with the writings of Arthur Machen |
| 1908 | Ireland's *Phantasie-Trio* wins second prize in the Cobbett Chamber Music Competition and is published |
| | Begins his annual visits to the Channel Islands |
| 1909 | The First Violin Sonata wins first prize in the Cobbett Chamber Music Competition |
| 1912 | Composes 'The Island Spell' (*Decorations*) for piano while in Jersey. Completed the following year |
| 1913 | Purchases 'The Studio' Gunter Grove in Chelsea, his home for the next 40 years |
| | *The Forgotten Rite* |
| 1915 | The Second Violin Sonata begun |
| 1917 | 6 March: première of the Second Violin Sonata |
| 1920–1 | *Mai-Dun* inspired by Hardy's Dorset. Visits Sussex and takes up lodgings in Ashington |
| | *The Land of Lost Content* |

## Chronology

| | |
|---|---|
| 1922 | Appointed to the temporary staff at the Royal College of Music by Hugh Allen |
| 1923 | Becomes professor at the Royal College of Music, where his pupils included Arnell, Britten, Alan Bush, Moeran, and Searle |
| 1924 | Made Hon. RAM and a Fellow of the RCM |
| 1925–6 | Visits Dorset again. Several settings of words by Hardy |
| 1926 | Piano Sonatina |
| | 17 December: Marries Dorothy Phillips (aged 17), a pupil, at the Chelsea Register Office, with Arthur G. Miller as one of the witnesses |
| 1928 | 19 September: Marriage dissolved |
| 1929 | Ballade for piano |
| 1930 | Meets Helen Perkin, a student at the Royal College of Music |
| | Writes piano concerto for her |
| 1931 | *A Downland Suite* for brass band |
| 1932 | Receives an honorary D.Mus. from the University of Durham |
| 1936 | *London Overture* |
| 1937 | 'These things shall be' for King George VI's coronation |
| 1939 | June: *Concertino pastorale* |
| | Goes to Guernsey with John Longmire |
| 1940 | April: Starts to compose *Sarnia* |
| | 22 June: Evacuated because of imminent German invasion. Escapes on last boat sailing to the mainland. Goes to stay in Banbury with friends |
| | 30 November: Accepts a BBC commission for the *Epic March* |
| 1941 | March: Completes *Sarnia* |
| 1942 | Moves to Little Sampford Rectory (Essex) |
| 1945 | Returns to Chelsea |
| 1946 | 20 August: Completes *Satyricon* |
| 1946–7 | Music for the film *The Overlanders* |
| | Acquires personal assistant and companion, Mrs Norah Kirby, who remains with him until his death |
| 1949 | 10 September: 70th birthday celebrations, including a special BBC Promenade concert |
| 1953 | Contributes 'The Hills' to *A Garland for the Queen* to mark the coronation of HM Queen Elizabeth II |
| | Leaves Chelsea and goes to live in Sussex at Rock Lodge |
| 1958 | *Meditation on John Keble's Rogation Hymn* for organ |
| 1960 | John Ireland Trust founded |
| 1962 | 12 June: Dies at Rock Lodge, aged 82 |
| | 16 June: Buried at Shipley (Sussex) |
| 1963 | 22 November: Unveiling of the John Ireland memorial window in the Musicians' Chapel of the Church of the Holy Sepulchre, London |

# Compiler's note

《》

It was a great pleasure to receive the commission, from the John Ireland Trust, in the summer of 1987, for a catalogue of Ireland's music.

The present volume aims to document Ireland's works, to be a comprehensive and definitive source of musical and documentary information relating to his life and music, and to set the record straight concerning many musical matters. Unlike John Chapman's catalogue of 1968, it includes details of published and unpublished works. Several autograph manuscripts have not yet been found: research therefore continues and it is hoped that publication of this catalogue will stimulate interest and prompt further discoveries.

It is arranged chronologically; the information for each work being listed, wherever possible, in the following order:

1. The title of the work, with other relevant details.
2. The date of composition, mostly ascertained from the autograph holograph or manuscript.
3. The body or person responsible for a work's commission.
4. The instrumentation required for a work.
5. Dedication.
6. Duration.
7. First performances: all available dates, venues, and performers have been listed.
8. Publication details, including original and present publishers and dates assigned, by those publishers, to a particular work.
9. Location of autograph manuscripts.
10. Bibliography listing relevant references to a work. These references are mostly reviews of gramophone recordings and critical notices, in national newspapers and music journals, of first performances and publications, arranged alphabetically by author's name.
11. Details of recordings, arranged alphabetically by performers' names. Those prefaced by an asterisk denote 78 r.p.m. recordings. I have included as many recordings as I could trace, and found Eric Hughes's list in *Recorded Sound* (1974) most helpful in this respect. Approximate dates of recordings have also been included wherever possible.

12. Notes: commentaries about the background to a work, any commissions which did not come to fruition, and detailed biographical information drawn from original documentary sources, especially letters, about the composer, his dedicatees, and other important people in his life.

# THE CATALOGUE

## 1890s

### The Peaceful Western Wind

Song for unaccompanied mixed chorus (SATB). Text by Thomas Campion (1567–1620).
Unpublished.
**Location of manuscript:** Manuscript Collections, The British Library (Reference Division), Add. MS 52895.
**Notes:** See also under 1912. Ireland went to London in September 1893 and entered the RCM. For four years he studied piano (with Frederick Cliffe[1]) and organ (with Sir Walter Parrott[2]) and received a very thorough training in harmony and counterpoint.

## 1895

### In Those Days

For solo piano.
1. Daydream (With gentle movement)
2. Meridian (Andante con moto)

**Date of composition:** 1895/revised 1941 (Banbury).
**Dedication:** To Evelyn Howard-Jones.[3]
**Duration:** 1—3′ 30″; 2—3′ 45″.
**First performance:** London, Great Drawing Room, St James's Square (the Arts Council), 7 October 1961. Eric Parkin (piano).
**Publication:** Schott & Co. Ltd. © 1961. Also included in volume i of *The Collected Piano Works of John Ireland*, Stainer & Bell © 1976.
**Location of manuscript:** Manuscript Collections, The British Library (Reference Division), Add. MS 52889.
**Bibliography:** A. Robertson, 'Ireland: Piano Works', *Gramophone*, 48/566 (July 1970), 191–2.
**Recordings:** Alan Rowlands (piano) *in* Lyrita RCS 28 (1970).

---

[1] Frederick Cliffe (1857–1931): English pianist, organist, and composer. Appointed to the piano teaching staff at the RCM in 1883 and professor at the RAM in 1901. Organist to the Bach Choir.
[2] Walter Parrott (1841–1924): Professor of music at Oxford and at the RCM. Composer and organist at St George's Chapel, Windsor. Master of the King's Music.
[3] Evelyn Howard-Jones (1877–1951): Pianist and friend of Delius. Scholar and later teacher at the RCM.

## 1896

### Communion Service in A flat major

For boys' voices and organ.

> Responses to the Commandments (Smoothly)
> Nicene Creed (With animation and firmness)
> Sanctus (Slowly and smoothly)
> Benedictus (Slowly and with moderate movement)
> Agnus Dei (Very slowly)
> Gloria in excelsis (Not too fast)

**Date of composition:** 1896 (Ireland was, at the time, sub-organist at Holy Trinity, Sloane Square).

**Publication:** Houghton & Co. (London) and printed in Leipzig. Vocal score © 1902. Later withdrawn by Ireland. A memo dated 17 January 1924, now in the John Ireland Trust's Archive, reveals that 'stock of the Communion Service is now exhausted and the plates have been lost or damaged in Germany'.

**Notes:** In a letter to Kenneth Thompson, dated 17 July 1939, Ireland mentioned that he was thinking of revising the Service (BL Add. MS 60535).

## 1897

### Piano Piece (no title): theme

Unpublished.

**Location of manuscript:** Manuscript Collections, The British Library (Reference Division); Add. MS 52900.

### Quartet No. 1 for strings in D minor

For 2 violins, viola, and cello.

> 1. Allegro
> 2. Scherzo (Molto allegro)
> 3. Andante moderato
> 4. Finale (Vivace)

**First performance:** Unable to trace, although the venue may have been the RCM.

**Publication:** Boosey & Hawkes Ltd. Score and parts (ed. Charles Marks) © 1973 (Hawkes Pocket Scores no. 883).

**Location of manuscript:** Manuscript Collections, The British Library (Reference Division), Add. MS 52883. It is signed by the composer and dated: 6 March 1897.

**Notes:** This work is described by the composer as an RCM Scholarship Piece.

## Quartet No. 2 for strings in C minor

For 2 violins, viola, and cello.
1. Allegro moderato
2. Nocturne (Andante)
3. Scherzo (Presto)
4. Poco allegro

**First modern performance:** London, Royal Festival Hall (recital room), Wednesday 19 October 1960. The Quartet Pro Musica: Patrick Halling (violin), Ernest Scott (violin), Gwynne Edwards (viola), and Peter Halling (cello).

**Publication:** Boosey & Hawkes Ltd. Score and parts (ed. Charles Marks) © 1973 (Hawkes Pocket Scores no. 884).

**Location of manuscript:** Manuscript Collections, The British Library (Reference Division), Add. MS 52884. It is signed by the composer and dated: London 13 September 1897.

**Notes:** This work is described by the composer as an RCM Studentship Work. Surviving RCM concert programmes reveal facets of the composer's musical life at the time:

20 January 1897: playing the piano in the Brahms Trio in B major (Op. 8);
19 March 1897: playing the percussion (gong) in the college orchestra at an orchestral concert under C. V. Stanford;
27 May 1897: playing the Beethoven Violin Sonata in C minor (Op. 30 No. 2) with Kitty Woolley;
8 July 1897: playing the percussion with Thomas Dunhill in the orchestra at a concert in Queen's Hall.

In 1897, Ireland was awarded a Scholarship for Composition and became a pupil of Sir Charles V. Stanford[4] for four years.

---

[4] Charles Villiers Stanford (1852–1924): English composer and professor of composition at the RCM and Cambridge University. Conductor of the Bach Choir and the Leeds Festival, 1901–10. There is an undated/unpublished account of C. V. Stanford by Ireland in the John Ireland Trust Archive.

## 1898

### Sextet

For clarinet (in A), horn (in F), 2 violins, viola, and cello.
1. Allegro non troppo
2. Andante con moto
3. Intermezzo (Allegretto con grazia)
4. In tempo moderato

**Duration:** *c.*28'.

**First performance:** London, St James's Square, Friday 25 March 1960. Thea King (clarinet), John Burden (horn), and the Quartet Pro Musica. (A concert organized by Hampton Music Club.)

**Publication:** Augener & Co. Ltd. Score and parts © 1961. Now Stainer & Bell Ltd.

**Location of manuscript:** Manuscript Collections, The British Library (Reference Division), Add. MS 52882.

**Bibliography:** Anon., 'After Sixty Years', *The Times*, 26 Mar. 1960, p. 3.
E. Chapman, 'Music Survey', *Musical Events*, 15 (May 1960), 35.
A. W. F.-G., 'John Ireland's Sextet', *Musical Events*, 17 (Aug. 1962), 13.
C. S.-S., 'John Ireland: Sextet', *Music Review*, 24 (1963), 94–5.
E. Warr, 'Ireland', *Gramophone*, 49/588 (May 1972), 1902, 1907.

**Recordings:** Melos Ensemble *in* Lyrita SRCS 59 (1972).
Melos Ensemble *in* NSA tape 1974W.

**Notes:** This sextet was originally called 'Intermezzo' and was written while Ireland was at the RCM, studying composition with Stanford. Later in life, Ireland admitted that the music had been inspired by a performance he heard in London of the Brahms Clarinet Quintet.

### Vexilla Regis

A hymn for Passion Sunday, for soli (SATB) or semi-chorus, mixed chorus (SATB), brass, and organ. Text by Bishop Venantius Fortunatus (530–609), translated from the Latin by J. M. Neale.

**Instrumentation:** 2 trumpets in B flat, 2 tenor and 1 bass trombone, and organ.

**Duration:** *c.*11'.

**First performance:** London, Parish Church of the Holy Trinity (Sloane Square), sometime in 1899. The Parish Church Choir with Walter Alcock[5] (organ), conducted by John Ireland (unable to trace the brass players).

---

[5] Walter Alcock (1861–1947): Organist and Composer to HM's Chapels Royal, 1902–16. Assistant organist at Westminster Abbey, 1896–1916. Professor at organ at the RCM. Organist at

**Publication:** Galliard Ltd. Vocal score and parts © 1963. Now Stainer & Bell Ltd. (Piano reduction by Alan Rowlands.)
**Location of manuscript:** Manuscript Collections, The British Library (Reference Division), Add. MS 52894. It is signed by the composer and dated: London 2 December 1898.
**Bibliography:** D. Denton, 'Ireland', *Music Magazine*, 4 (Feb. 1991), 54.
T. Harvey, 'Ireland: Choral Works', *Gramophone*, 57/673 (June 1979), 93–4.
**Recordings:** Paula Bott (soprano), Teresa Shaw (contralto), James Oxley (tenor), Bryn Terfel (baritone)/London Symphony Chorus and Orchestra/Roderick Elms (organ)/Richard Hickox *in* Chandos CHAN 8879, ABTD 1492 (1990).
Worcester Cathedral Choir/Worcester Festival Choral Society/Worcester Sinfonia Brass Ensemble/Paul Trepte (organ)/Donald Hunt *in* Abbey LPB 803 (1979).
**Notes:** This work is described by the composer as an RCM Studentship Work.

## 1899

## Tritons

Symphonic prelude for full orchestra.
**Instrumentation:** 2 flutes and piccolo, 2 oboes, 2 clarinets in B flat, bass clarinet in B flat, 2 bassoons, 4 horns in F, 2 trumpets in F, 3 trombones, tuba, timpani, percussion (2 players: side-drum, cymbals), and strings.
**Duration:** 11'.
**First performance:** London, Alexandra House, Thursday 21 March 1901. RCM Student Orchestra, conducted by Charles V. Stanford. (RCM Concert no. 318.)
Unpublished.
**Location of manuscript:** Manuscript Collections, The British Library (Reference Division), Add. MS 52071A.
**Bibliography:** M. Jameson, 'Ireland: Orchestral Works', *Gramophone*, 69/825 (Feb. 1992), 35–6.
A. Robertson, 'Ireland: Orchestral Works', *Gramophone*, 48/573 (Feb. 1971), 1310, 1315.
**Recordings:** LPO/Adrian Boult *in* Lyrita SRCS 45, Musical Heritage Society 1481 (1971).
LSO/Richard Hickox *in* CHAN 8994 (1991).

---

the coronations of King Edward VII (1902) and King George V (1911). Assisted at the coronation of King George VI (1937). There is an undated/unpublished account of Walter Alcock by Ireland in the John Ireland Trust Archive.

**Notes:** In the programme for the first performance, the piece is called 'Symphonic Prelude' and the following quoted:

> At high noon, 'neath the sun, the strong surf beats,
> The free exultant sea-wind sweeps the shore;
> And Life, glad, great, tumultuous, with the sea
>   Wildly rejoices.

This work is described by the composer as an RCM Studentship Work.

## OTHER VERSIONS

**A Maritime Overture**

Arranged for military band by Norman Richardson.
**Date of composition:** 1944.
**Instrumentation:** 2 flutes (2nd doubling piccolo), 2 oboes, E flat clarinet, solo and 3 B flat clarinets, 2 bassoons, alto, tenor, and baritone saxophones, solo and 2 cornets, 2 trumpets, 4 horns, 3 trombones, euphonium, basses, and percussion.
**Dedication:** To Ralph Hawkes, Esq.[6]
**Duration:** c. 10'.
**Publication:** Boosey & Hawkes Ltd. Score © 1946 (QMB edn. no. 149).
**Location of manuscript:** Manuscript Collections, The British Library (Reference Division), Add. MS 52071B.
**Recordings:** Royal Artillery Band, Woolwich/R. Quinn, NSA tape M1763W.
**Notes:** Ireland composed the overture in short score, and it was from this condensed score (3-stave) that Norman Richardson prepared this version in 1946. Ralph Hawkes asked Ireland (and others) for a work in celebration of the approaching centenary of the first military band publication issued by the firm of Hawkes.

**A Maritime Overture**

Arranged for symphonic wind band by Norman Richardson.
**Instrumentation:** 2 concert flutes and piccolo, 2 oboes, E flat clarinet, solo B flat clarinet, 3 B flat clarinets, E flat alto clarinet, B flat bass clarinet, E flat alto saxophone, B flat tenor saxophone, E flat baritone saxophone, B flat bass saxophone and B flat contrabass clarinet, 2 bass, 4 horns in F, solo and first B flat cornet, 2nd B flat cornet, 2 B flat trumpets, 2 tenor trombones, bass trombones, euphonium (baritone), basses, string bass, timpani, and percussion.
**Publication:** R. Smith & Co. Ltd. Full score © 1988.
**Bibliography:** M. Macdonald, 'British Wind Music', *Gramophone*, 67/794 (July 1989), 189.
**Recordings:** City of London Wind Ensemble/G. Brand *in* LDR/Gamut LDRC 1001, LDRK 2001 (1989).

---

[6] Ralph Hawkes (1898–1950): Chairman of publishers Boosey and Hawkes. Great musical 'talent-spotter'. Gave Benjamin Britten (Ireland's pupil at the RCM) his first publishing contract in 1936.

## 1899–1900

## Sea Idyll

For solo piano.
1. Poco andante
2. Allegro appassionata
3. Andante (Mesto—added later)

**Duration:**  1—4' 00"; 2—4' 10"; 3—3' 30".
**First performance:**  London, Alexandra House, Thursday 8 March 1900. John Ireland (piano). (RCM Concert no. 301.)
**Publication:**  J. and W. Chester Ltd. Score © 1960. The first movement was included in the Centenary Album published by the House Chester in 1960 when it was also issued as a separate piece. Also included in volume i of *The Collected Piano Works of John Ireland*, Stainer & Bell © 1976. Movements 2 and 3 remain in manuscript.
**Location of manuscript:**  Manuscript Collections, The British Library (Reference Division), Add. MS 52890. It is signed by the composer and dated: London February 1900. A further autograph manuscript of *Sea Idyll* for solo piano was sold at Sotheby's on 29 November 1985. Present whereabouts: unable to trace. It was an early version of all three movements (Poco andante, 'Song', and Mesto) with numerous autograph revisions and alterations, notated in blue ink on up to twelve staves per page, with many deletions, some corrections in pencil, some alterations on additional sheets of paper, with autograph title-page: *Sea Idyll by John Ireland*, the second and third movements dated '17 December 1899' and '5 January 1900' (sale catalogue).
**Bibliography:**  Anon., 'The John Ireland Society', *The Times*, 16 May 1962, p. 5.
A. Robertson, 'Ireland: Piano Works', *Gramophone*, 48/566 (July 1970), 191–2.
**Recordings:**  Alan Rowlands (piano) *in* Lyrita RCS 29 (1970).
**Notes:**  This work is described by the composer as an RCM Studentship Work. Ireland wrote that he was introduced to Elgar about the year 1900 at the house of his friend Bernard Nevinson. There is an undated/unpublished essay about Elgar by him in the John Ireland Trust Archive. Ireland left the RCM in 1901.

## 1902

### Berceuse

For solo violin and piano.
**Duration:** 3' 30".
**Publication:** Augener & Co. Ltd. [Score © 1903.] Now Stainer & Bell Ltd.
**Location of manuscript:** Manuscript Collections, The British Library (Reference Division), Add. MS 54411.
**Notes:** Grove 5 indicates that this piece was published in January 1903.


### Elegiac Romance

For organ.
**Dedication:** To R.H.C.
**Duration:** 9' 30".
**Publication:** R. Cocks & Co. [Novello & Co. Ltd.] © 1903 (The Recital Series of Original Compositions for the Organ no. 28, ed. E. H. Lemare). Revised edition 1958: Novello & Co. Ltd. © [1958] (Original Compositions, new series no. 301). Also included in *The Organ Music of John Ireland* (ed. Robert Gower), Novello © 1983.
**Bibliography:** M. Rochester, 'Great European Organs', *Gramophone*, 68/816 (May 1991), 2047.
  S. Walsh, 'Howells/Ireland', *Gramophone*, 57/676 (Sept. 1979), 487.
**Recordings:** Robert Gower (organ) *in* Wealden Studios WS 179 (1979).
  Jonathan Bielby (organ) *in* Priory PRCD 298 (1991).
**Notes:** Grove 5 indicates that the piece was published in August 1902. Revised by the composer in 1958.

## 1903–1904

### Orchestral Poem in A minor

For full orchestra.
**Instrumentation:** 2 flutes and piccolo, 2 oboes, 2 clarinets in A, 2 bassoons, 4 horns in F, 2 trumpets in F, 3 trombones, bass tuba, timpani, percussion (1 player: cymbals), and strings.
**Publication:** DA CAPO Music Ltd © 1993.
**Location of manuscript:** Manuscript Collections, The British Library (Reference Division), Add. MS 52872. Signed by the composer and dated: London: 26 February 1904.

**Notes:** This work is described by the composer as an RCM Studentship Work.

## 1903–1911

### Songs of a Wayfarer

Song cycle for voice and piano.
1. Memory (Con moto). Text: William Blake (1757–1827), from *Poetical Sketches* (1783).
2. When daffodils begin to peer (Allegro con moto). Text: William Shakespeare (1564–1616), from *A Winter's Tale* (1611): act III, scene iv.
3. English May (Allegretto). Text: Dante Gabriel Rossetti (1828–82), first published 1886.
4. I was not sorrowful (Andante moderato). Text: Ernest Dowson (1867–1900), 'Spleen', *Verses* (1896).
5. I will walk on the earth (Allegro). Text: James Vila Blake.

**Dedication:** To my friend Robert Radford.[7] No. 4 is marked 'For Arthur Symons'.[8]
**Duration:** 1—1' 45"; 2—1' 45"; 3—2' 45"; 4—3' 00"; 5—1' 30".
**First performance:** London, Steinway Hall, 7 March 1913. Robert Radford (baritone) and John Ireland (piano).
**Publication:** Boosey & Co. Ltd. © 1912. Also included in volume iv of *The Complete Works for Voice and Piano*, Stainer & Bell Ltd. © 1981.
**Location of manuscript:** Manuscript Collections, The British Library (Reference Division), Add. MS 52898. No. 1 was written before 1905, nos. 2 and 3 about 1905, no. 4 in 1903, no. 5 is dated 22 May 1911.
**Bibliography:** R. Fiske, 'Ireland', *Gramophone*, 52/624 (May 1975), 2005–6.
J. B. Steane, 'Songs to Shakespeare', *Gramophone*, 69/828 (May 1992), 99–100.
**Recordings:** Nos. 1–4 only:
Benjamin Luxon (baritone) and Alan Rowlands (piano) *in* Lyrita SRCS 65 (1975).
No. 2 only:
Anthony Rolfe Johnson (tenor) and Graham Johnson (piano) *in* Hyperion CDA 66480 (1992).
**Notes:** No. 4 was published separately by Boosey in 1912.

---

[7] Robert Radford (1874–1933): Concert and operatic bass. Professor of singing at the RAM.
[8] Arthur Symons (1865–1945): English poet and critic. Travelled in France and Italy and was influenced by the French Symbolists. On the staff of the *Athenaeum*, *Saturday Review*, and *Academy*. Editor of the *Savoy*.

## 1904

### Intrada

For organ.
**Duration:** 3'.
**Publication:** Ascherberg, Hopwood & Crew Ltd. © 1912. Later Chappell & Co. Ltd. Now Warner & Co. Ltd. Published as *Three Pieces for Organ* with *Menuetto-impromptu* and *Marcia popolare*. It was reissued in 1944 when the composer inserted some slight alterations and added some editorial emendations by way of registration, phrasing, etc. It formed no. 1 of the *Miniature Suite for Organ* (Ascherberg, Hopwood & Crew Ltd. © 1944). Also included in *The Organ Music of John Ireland* (ed. Robert Gower), Novello © 1983.
**Bibliography:** M. Rochester, 'Great European Organs', *Gramophone*, 68/816 (May 1991), 2047.
**Recordings:** Jonathan Bielby (organ) *in* Priory PRCD 298 (1991).
**Notes:** This composition was written when Ireland had recently been appointed organist of St Luke's Parish Church in Chelsea.

### Villanella

For organ.
**Duration:** 4'.
**Publication:** Ascherberg, Hopwood & Crew Ltd. © 1912. Later Chappell & Co. Ltd. Now Warner & Co. Ltd. Reissued and revised in 1944. It formed no. 2 of the *Miniature Suite for Organ* (Ascherberg, Hopwood & Crew Ltd. © 1944). Also included in *The Organ Music of John Ireland* (ed. Robert Gower), Novello © 1983.
**Location of manuscript:** Manuscript Collections, The British Library (Reference Division), Add. MS 52891.
**Bibliography:** C.J. ['Organ Music'], *Gramophone*, 5/11 (Apr. 1928), 460.
  M. Rochester, 'Great European Organs', *Gramophone*, 68/816 (May 1991), 2047.
**Recordings:** Jonathan Bielby (organ) *in* Priory PRCD 298 (1991).
  Frederick Boyce (organ) *in* HMV CLP 1777, CSD 1539.
  *Reginald Goss-Custard (organ), HMV C 1466 (1928) (recorded at Queen's Hall, London).
  A. Sievewright (organ) *in* APS 319, CAPS 319 (cassette).
**Notes:** At the time of its composition, Ireland was organist of both St Jude's and St Luke's Parish Churches in Chelsea.

## OTHER VERSIONS

**Villanella**

Arranged for orchestra by Leslie Bridgewater.
**Date of arrangement:** 1941.
**Instrumentation:** Flute, oboe, 2 clarinets, bassoon, 2 horns, 2 trumpets, percussion, and strings.
**Publication:** Ascherberg, Hopwood & Crew Ltd. © [1941]. Later Chappell & Co. Ltd. Now Warner & Co. Ltd. Published as *Two Salon Pieces* with *Menuetto-impromptu*.

**Villanella**

Arranged for orchestra by Ronald Binge.
**Date of arrangement:** 1949.
**Instrumentation:** 2 flutes, 2 oboes, 2 clarinets, 2 bassoons, 2 horns, 2 trumpets, 3 trombones, timpani, percussion, harp, and strings.
**Publication:** Ascherberg, Hopwood & Crew Ltd. Later Chappell & Co. Ltd. Now Warner & Co. Ltd. Piano conductor and parts © [1949].

**Villanella**

A miniature: freely transcribed for piano by the composer.
**Date of arrangement:** 1912.
**Publication:** Ascherberg, Hopwood & Crew Ltd. Score © 1912. Later Chappell & Co. Ltd. Now Warner & Co. Ltd. Revised and republished in 1950.
**Location of manuscript:** Manuscript Collections, The British Library (Reference Division), Add. MS 52891.
**Bibliography:** Anon., 'John Ireland: Villanella, a Miniature', *Musical Opinion*, 74 (Mar. 1951), 281.

# Menuetto-impromptu

For organ.
**Duration:** 5'.
**Publication:** Ascherberg, Hopwood & Crew Ltd. © 1912. Later Chappell & Co. Ltd. Now Warner & Co. Ltd. Published as *Three Pieces for Organ* with *Intrada* and *Marcia popolare*. Reissued and revised in 1944. It formed no. 3 of the *Miniature Suite for Organ* (Ascherberg, Hopwood & Crew Ltd. © 1944). Also included in *The Organ Music of John Ireland* (ed. Robert Gower), Novello © 1983.
**Bibliography:** M. Rochester, 'Great European Organs', *Gramophone*, 68/816 (May 1991), 2047.
**Recordings:** Jonathan Bielby (organ) *in* Priory PRCD 298 (1991).

OTHER VERSIONS

**Menuetto-impromptu**

Arranged for orchestra by Leslie Bridgewater.
**Instrumentation:** Flute, oboe, 2 clarinets, bassoon, 2 horns, 2 trumpets, percussion, and strings.
**Publication:** Ascherberg, Hopwood & Crew Ltd. © [1941]. Later Chappell & Co. Ltd. Now Warner & Co. Ltd. Published as *Two Salon Pieces* with *Villanella*.

## Marcia popolare

For organ.
**Publication:** Ascherberg, Hopwood & Crew Ltd. © 1912. Later Chappell & Co. Ltd. Now Warner & Co. Ltd. Published as *Three Pieces for Organ* with *Intrada* and *Menuetto-impromptu*.

## Cavatina

For violin and piano.
**Publication:** Ascherberg, Hopwood & Crew Ltd. © 1911. Later Chappell & Co. Ltd. Now Warner & Co. Ltd.

OTHER VERSIONS

**Cavatina**

Arranged for organ.
**Date of arrangement:** 1904.
**Publication:** Ascherberg, Hopwood & Crew Ltd. © 1911 and 1912. Later Chappell & Co. Ltd. Now Warner & Co. Ltd.

## Concerto for viola and orchestra

By Cecil Forsyth,[9] arranged for viola and piano by John Ireland.

1. Moderato
2. Andante un poco sostenuto
3. Allegro con fuoco

**Publication:** B. Schott (Mainz) © 1904.

---

[9] Cecil Forsyth (1870–1941): English composer and author. Educated at Edinburgh University and at the RCM under Parry and Stanford. Played the viola in the Queen's Hall Orchestra, and produced two comic operas at the Savoy and Aldwych Theatres.

## Psalm Chant

For the choir of St Luke's, Chelsea.
**Date of composition:** *c.*1904.
Unpublished.

## 1905

## Eastergate

Hymn tune for mixed chorus (SATB) and organ. Text ('Holy Father in thy mercy') by Isabella S. Stevenson.
**Publication:** OUP. Vocal score © 1906. Included in *The English Hymnal* and later in the *Methodist Hymn Book* (1933).

## Evening Service in A major

For mixed chorus (SATB) and organ. Text from the Book of Common Prayer.

Magnificat (Allegro): the melody is based on a well-known Gregorian intonation.

Nunc Dimittis (Moderato).

Unpublished.
**Location of manuscript:** Manuscript Collections, The British Library (Reference Division), Add. MS 52894.

## 1905–1906

## First Rhapsody in C sharp minor

For solo piano.
Unpublished.
**Location of manuscript:** Manuscript Collections, The British Library (Reference Division), Add. MS 52890. It is dated: London 16 January 1906.
**Notes:** Ireland's address at the time of writing appears on the manuscript as 54 Elm Park Mansions, Chelsea, SW.

## 1906

### Phantasie-Trio in A minor

For violin, cello, and piano.

   In tempo moderato
   Meno mosso, quasi andantino
   Vivace e giocoso

**Dedication:** To Sir Charles V. Stanford.
**Duration:** 12' 30".
**First performance:** London, Aeolian Hall, Tuesday 26 January 1909. The London Trio: Signor Simonetti (violin), W. E. Whitehouse (cello) and Amina Goodwin (piano).
**Publication:** Galliard Ltd. Score © 1908. Novello & Co. Ltd. [© 1909]. Augener & Co. Ltd. [© 1918]. Now Stainer & Bell Ltd.
**Bibliography:** W. W. Cobbett (ed.), 'John Ireland', in *Cobbett's Survey of Chamber Music*, ii (London, OUP, 1930: 2nd edn. 1963), 20–5.

  R. Fiske, 'Ireland', *Gramophone*, 42/501 (Feb. 1965), 384.

  —— 'Ireland', *Gramophone*, 56/670 (Mar. 1979), 1580.

  J. Ireland, 'Phantasie in A minor', undated/unpublished notes, now in the John Ireland Trust Archive.

  M. Kennedy, 'Bridge/R. Clarke/Ireland', *Gramophone*, 69/820 (Sept. 1991), 84.

  —— 'Bush/Ireland', *Gramophone*, 67/794 (July 1989), 194.

  A. Robertson, 'Ireland', *Gramophone*, 16/190 (Mar. 1939), 428.

**Recordings:** Barbican Piano Trio *in* ASV DCA 646, ZCDCA 646, CDDCA 646 (1989).

  David Martin Trio *in* Saga XID 5230 (1965).

  *Grinke Trio, Decca K899/900 (1939).

  Hartley Trio *in* Gamut Classics GAMCD 518 (1991).

  Yfrah Neaman (violin), Julian Lloyd Webber (cello), and Eric Parkin (piano) *in* Lyrita SRCS 98 (1979).

**Notes:** This trio was written for the Cobbett Chamber Music Competition, the rules of which required a chamber work in one movement with the title 'Phantasie', and gained second prize in the 1908 Cobbett Competition of the Worshipful Company of Musicians. The first prize was won by Frank Bridge with his 'Phantasy' Piano Trio.

## 1907

### Te Deum in F major

For mixed chorus (SATB) and organ.
**Dedication:** To the Venerable H. E. Bevan MA, Archdeacon of Middlesex and Rector of Chelsea.[10]
**Duration:** 7' 10".
**Publication:** Novello & Co. Ltd. Vocal score © 1907 (PCB 750). A unison part for men's voices—arranged for use with the original edition for choir and organ by John Ireland, Novello [© 1952].
**Bibliography:** T. Harvey, 'Ireland: Choral Works', *Gramophone*, 57/673 (June 1979), 93–4.
**Recordings:** Portsmouth Cathedral Choir with D. Thorne (organ)/Alan Froggatt *in* GRSP 7021, GRSC 7021 (cassette).
Worcester Cathedral Choir with Paul Trepte (organ)/Donald Hunt *in* Abbey LPB 803 (1979).
**Notes:** See also Benedictus in F (1912), Jubilate in F (1914), Magnificat and Nunc Dimittis in F (1915), Benedicite in F (1919).

### Pater Noster (The Lord's Prayer)

For unaccompanied mixed chorus (SATB). Text from the Book of Common Prayer.
**Date of composition:** *c.* 1907.
**Publication:** Novello & Co. Ltd. Vocal score © 1913.

## 1908

### Psalm 42

For soprano, contralto, tenor, and bass soli, mixed chorus (SATB), and string orchestra. Text selected from Psalm 42 (Prayer Book version).

1. Chorus: Like as the hart (In tempo moderato)
2. Soprano solo: The Lord hath granted (Allegretto)
3. Solo quartet (unaccom.): My tears have been my meat (Andantino, ma non troppo lento)
4. Introduction and Fugue: Why art thou so vexed (Allegro): I will yet thank Him

Unpublished.

---

[10] Henry E. J. Bevan (1854–1935): Archdeacon of Middlesex 1903–30 and Rector of St Luke's, Chelsea, 1902–30; Rector of Holy Trinity, Sloane Street, 1895–1902.

**Location of manuscript:** Manuscript Collection, University of Durham, Palace Green (Music Exercise 278). Manuscript Collections, The British Library (Reference Division), Add. MS 52893 (incomplete). It is signed and dated by the composer: London, 28 February 1908. A copy (presented by Devon County Library in January 1984) can also be found in Add. MS 62944.

**Notes:** This composition, written at 54 Elm Park Mansions, Chelsea, was a Mus.B. exercise and bears the declaration that the setting is Ireland's unaided work which is witnessed by two people. This is dated 21 March 1908.

## Full Fathom Five

Song for 2-part chorus (SA) and piano. Text by William Shakespeare (1564–1616).
**Date of composition:** c.1908.
**Dedication:** To Miss Ethel Mary Blyth.
**Publication:** Novello & Co. Ltd. Vocal score © 1908 (The School Music Review no. 244) (Novello's Collection of Two-Part Songs no. 150).

OTHER VERSIONS

**Full Fathom Five**

Arranged as a duet by ?Kimmins.
Unpublished.

## Spring, the Sweet Spring

Song for unaccompanied mixed chorus (SATB). Text by Thomas Nashe (1567–1601).
**Date of composition:** c.1908.
**Dedication:** To Lionel Benson Esq., and the Members of the Magpie Madrigal Society.[11]
**Duration:** 1' 45".
**Publication:** Laudy & Co. Ltd. Vocal score © 1908 (Part Songs no. 59).

## There is a garden in her face

Song for 2-part chorus (SA) and piano. Text by Richard Alison.
**Date of composition:** c.1908.

---

[11] Lionel Seymour Benson (1849–1929): Amateur conductor and musician. He founded the Magpie Singers in 1886 to give charity concerts. It was renamed the Elizabethan Madrigal Society in 1911.

**Publication:** Novello & Co. Ltd. Vocal score © 1908 (Novello's Collection of Two-Part Songs no. 151). The song also appeared in Novello's School Songs [1911] no. 1076.

## 1908–1909

## Sonata No. 1 in D minor

For violin and piano.

1. Allegro leggiadro
2. Romance (In tempo sostenuto, quasi adagio)
3. Rondo (Allegro sciolto assai—Allegro di molto)

**Date of composition:** 1908 (summer)–1909 (autumn).
**Dedication:** To F.W.W.
**Duration:** c. 28'.
**First performance:** London, Steinway Hall, 7 March 1913. Marjorie Haywood (violin) and John Ireland (piano). (A Thomas Dunhill Chamber Concert: 7th series.)
**Publication:** Goodwin & Tabb Ltd. Score © 1911. Augener & Co. Ltd. © [1915]. Augener & Co. Ltd. © 1917: 2nd edition. Augener & Co. Ltd. © [1917]: revised edition. Augener & Co. Ltd. © 1944: 3rd (revised) edition. Now Stainer & Bell Ltd.
**Bibliography:** W. R. Anderson, 'John Ireland', *Gramophone*, 25/300 (May 1948), 187.

Anon., [Ireland Violin Sonata], *Musical Times*, 51/804 (Feb. 1910), 116.

Anon., 'John Ireland: Sonata in D', *Monthly Musical Record*, 45 (July 1915), 200.

R. Fiske, 'John Ireland', *Gramophone*, 42/503 (Apr. 1965), 486–7.

B. Layton, 'Ireland', *Gramophone*, 48/571 (Dec. 1970), 1039.

E. Warr, 'Ireland', *Gramophone*, 50/593 (Oct. 1972), 717.
**Recordings:** Alan Loveday (violin) and Leonard Cassini (piano) *in* Summit LSU 3081 (1965), *in* Revolution RCB 5 (1970).

Yfrah Neaman (violin) and Eric Parkin (piano) *in* Lyrita SRCS 64 (1972).
**Notes:** This sonata was entered in 1909 for the Cobbett Chamber Music Competition and won first prize. A note in the programme of the first performance states that this was the composer's Third Sonata for violin and piano (see Appendix 3). See also Geoffrey Bush's note to the Stainer & Bell reprint of the score which gives full details of the important revisions Ireland made to the work in 1917.

## 1909

### The Frog and the Crab

Unison song for equal voices and piano. Text: early sixteenth century.
**Publication:**   The Year Book Press. Vocal score © 1909 (The Year Book Press Series of Unison and Part Songs no. 31).

### In Praise of May

Song for 2-part chorus (SA) and piano. Text by Thomas Morley (1557–1603).
**Duration:**   2' 10".
**Publication:**   Novello & Co. Ltd. Vocal score © 1909 (Novello's School Songs no. 1015).

## 1910

### Annabel Lee

Recitation for voice and piano. Text by Edgar Allan Poe (1809–49).
**Date of composition:**   *c.*1910.
Unpublished.
**Location of manuscript:** Manuscript Collections, The British Library (Reference Division), Add. MS 52897.

### A Laughing Song

Song for unaccompanied mixed chorus (SATB). Text by William Blake (1757–1827).
**Date of composition:**   *c.*1910.
Unpublished.
**Location of manuscript:** Manuscript Collections, The British Library (Reference Division), Add. MS 52895.

## 1911

### Alla marcia

For organ.
**Dedication:**   To Sir Walter Parrott, M.V.O.
**Duration:**   3'.

**Publication:** Novello & Co. Ltd. Score © 1911. Published with *Sursum Corda* in Novello's Original Compositions for the Organ no. 421. Also included in *The Organ Music of John Ireland* (ed. Robert Gower), Novello © 1983.
**Bibliography:** M. Rochester, 'Great European Organs', *Gramophone*, 68/816 (May 1991), 2047.
S. Walsh, 'Howells/Ireland', *Gramophone*, 57/676 (Sept. 1979), 487.
**Recordings:** Jonathan Bielby (organ) *in* Priory PRCD 298 (1991).
Robert Gower (organ) *in* Wealden Studios WS 179 (1979).

## Bagatelle

For violin and piano.
**Date of composition:** March 1911.
**Dedication:** To Miss Marjorie Haywood.[12]
**Duration:** *c.* 3′ 30″.
**Publication:** Novello & Co. Ltd. Score © 1913.
**Bibliography:** C. J. ['Bagatelle'], *Gramophone*, 6/64 (Sept. 1928), 152.
**Recordings:** *Marjorie Haywood (violin) and piano, HMV B 2648 (1928).

OTHER VERSIONS

**Bagatelle**

Arranged for orchestra by Leslie Bridgewater.

**Instrumentation:** Flute, oboe, 2 clarinets in B flat, bassoon, 2 horns in F, cornet, trombone, timpani, percussion (1 player: triangle), and strings.
Unpublished.

**Bagatelle**

Arranged for military band by C. F. Smyly.
**Instrumentation:** E flat flute, oboe, 2 E flat clarinets, solo, and ripieno, 2nd and 3rd clarinets in B flat, also saxophone in E flat, tenor saxophone in B flat, 2 bass, 2 cornets in B flat, 4 horns in F, 2 E flat trumpets, 2 trombones, bass trombone, B flat baritone, euphonium, basses, timpani, and percussion.
Unpublished.

---

[12] Marjorie Haywood (1886–1953): Studied under Sauret at the RAM and under Ševčik in Prague. Teacher of violin at the RAM. Best known in chamber music circles.

## Capriccio

For organ.
**Dedication:**   To H. L. Balfour Esq.[13]
**Duration:**   6'.
**Publication:**   Stainer & Bell Ltd. Score © 1911 (no. 23 of 'The Organ Recitalist'). Also included in *The Organ Music of John Ireland* (ed. Robert Gower), Novello © 1983.
**Bibliography:**   M. Rochester, 'Great European Organs', *Gramophone*, 68/816 (May 1991), 2047.
  S. Walsh, 'Howells/Ireland', *Gramophone*, 57/676 (Sept. 1979), 487.
**Recordings:**   Jonathan Bielby (organ) *in* Priory PRCD 298 (1991).
  Robert Gower (organ) *in* Wealdon Studios WS 179 (1979).

## Sursum Corda

For organ.
**Dedication:**   To Sir Walter Parrott, M.V.O.
**Duration:**   4'.
**Publication:**   Novello & Co. Ltd. Score © 1911. Published with *Alla marcia* in Novello's Original Compositions for the Organ no. 421. Also included in *The Organ Music of John Ireland* (ed. Robert Gower), Novello © 1983.
**Bibliography:**   M. Rochester, 'Great European Organs', *Gramophone*, 68/816 (May 1991), 2047.
**Recordings:**   Jonathan Bielby (organ) *in* Priory PRCD 298 (1991).

## Hope the Hornblower

Song for voice and piano. Text by Henry Newbolt (1862–1938), from *Poems New and Old* (1912).
**Duration:**   1' 40".
**First performance:**   London, Royal Albert Hall, Saturday 6 January 1912. Ivor Foster (baritone) and either S. Liddle or F. A. Sewell (piano). (46th season of the London Ballad Concerts, arranged by Boosey & Co.)
**Publication:**   Boosey & Co. Vocal score © 1911. This original edition was published in G major and A major only, with alternative simplified accompaniment in both keys. This simplified version became the new edition, published in 1921. Assigned to Augener, 1961. Now Stainer & Bell Ltd. Also included in volume v of *The Complete Works for Voice and Piano*,

---

[13] Henry L. Balfour (1859–1946): English organist and choral conductor. Studied under Sullivan and Stainer, and later in Leipzig. Appointed as organist to the Royal Choral Society in 1895. In 1902 became organist at Holy Trinity, Sloane Street.

Stainer & Bell © 1981, and in *Eleven Songs by John Ireland* (introduced by John Longmire), Stainer & Bell/Galaxy © 1970.
**Bibliography:**  R. Fiske, 'Ireland', *Gramophone*, 52/624 (May 1975), 2005–6.
**Recordings:**  Benjamin Luxon (baritone) and Alan Rowlands (piano) *in* Lyrita SRCS 65 (1975).
   *George Parker (baritone) and Sidney Twemlow (piano), BBC Sound Archive recording 6813, BBC Transcription 16761.
   *Harold Williams (baritone), Edison Bell VF 1118.

OTHER VERSIONS

**Hope the Hornblower**

Arranged for voice and orchestra by Frederick Bye (in G and A).
**Date of arrangement:**  [1930s].
**Instrumentation:**  Flute, oboe, 2 clarinets, bassoon, 2 horns, harp, and strings.
Unpublished.
**Bibliography:**  M. Kennedy, 'English Orchestral Songs', *Gramophone*, 67/800 (Jan. 1990), 1366.
**Recordings:**  Stephen Varcoe (bass-baritone) and City of London Sinfonia/R. Hickox *in* Chandos ABRD 1382, ABTD 1382, CHAN 8743 (1990).

**Hope the Hornblower**

Arranged for voice, piano, and strings by G. Stacey (in F).
Unpublished.

## Hymn to Light

Song for voice with organ accompaniment ad lib. Text by James Vila Blake.
**First performance:**  Unable to trace, although Kirkby Lunn (1873–1930), an English mezzo-soprano, may have sung this work.
**Publication:**  Chappell & Co. Vocal score © 1911. Now Warner & Co. Ltd. Three versions were published: in A flat, B flat, and C.

## When lights go rolling round the sky

Song for voice and piano. Text by James Vila Blake.
**Duration:**  2′ 45″.
**Publication:**  Chappell & Co. Ltd. Vocal score © 1911. Now Warner & Co. Ltd. 2 versions were published: in D and C major. Also included in volume v of *The Complete Works for Voice and Piano*, Stainer & Bell © 1981, and in *The Land of Lost Content and Other Songs by John Ireland* (with an introduction by John Longmire), Galliard/Stainer & Bell © 1976.

**Bibliography:**   R. Fiske, 'F. Harvey', *Gramophone*, 44/524 (Jan. 1967), 380–1.
R. Fiske, 'Ireland', *Gramophone*, 52/624 (May 1975), 2005–6.
M. Kennedy, 'A Treasury of English Song', *Gramophone*, 64/764 (Jan. 1987), 1055–6.

**Recordings:**   Frederick Harvey (baritone) and Gerald Moore (piano) *in* HMV CLP 3587, CSD 3587 (1967).

Benjamin Luxon (baritone) and Alan Rowlands (piano) *in* Lyrita SRCS 65 (1975).

*Stuart Robertson (baritone) and Gerald Moore (piano), HMV B 3042 (1929), HMV Treasury EX 290911-3, EX 290911-5 (1987).

OTHER VERSIONS

### When lights go rolling round the sky

Arranged for voice and orchestra by D. Darlow (in C).
**Instrumentation:**   3 flutes and piccolo, 2 oboes, 2 clarinets, 2 bassoons, 4 horns, 2 trumpets, 3 trombones, tuba, timpani, percussion, harp, and strings.
Unpublished.

### When lights go rolling round the sky

Arranged for voice, piano, and strings by G. Stacey (in C).
Unpublished.

## Billee Bowline

Song for voice and piano, written under the pseudonym of TURLAY ROYCE. Text by Frederick E. Weatherly.
**Publication:**   Chappell & Co. Vocal score © 1911. Now Warner & Co. Ltd. 2 versions were published: in B flat and C major.

## Love's Window

Song for voice and piano, written under the pseudonym of TURLAY ROYCE. Text by H. D. Banning.
**Publication:**   Chappell & Co. Vocal score © 12 June 1911. Now Warner & Co. Ltd. 3 versions were published: in G, A, and C major.

## Alpine Song

Unison song for equal voices and piano. Text by James Vila Blake (from the German).
**Publication:**   J. Curwen & Co. Ltd. Vocal score © 1911 (Choruses for Equal Voices no. 1322). Now Music Sales Ltd.

## At Early Dawn

Song for 2-part chorus (SA) and piano. Text by James Vila Blake (from the German).
**Publication:**   J. Curwen & Co. Ltd. Vocal score © 1911 (Choruses for Equal Voices no. 1333). Now Music Sales Ltd.

## Hillo, My Bonny

Song for voice and piano, written under the pseudonym of TURLAY ROYCE. Text by James Vila Blake.
**Date of composition:**   June 1911.
**Publication:**   Chappell & Co. Ltd. Vocal score © 1913. Now Warner & Co. Ltd.

## How Jubilant the Summer Sky

Song for equal voices and piano.
**Publication:**   J. Curwen & Co. Ltd. Vocal score © 1911. Now Music Sales Ltd.

## We hardly see the sunbeam yet

Song for equal voices and piano.
**Publication:**   J. Curwen & Co. Ltd. Vocal score © 1911. Now Music Sales Ltd.

## In Praise of Neptune

Unison song for equal voices and piano. Text by Thomas Campion (1567–1620).
**Duration:**   2' 10".
**Publication:**   The Year Book Press. Vocal score © 1911 (The Year Book Press Series of Unison Songs no. 46).
**Location of manuscript:**   The autograph manuscript was put up for sale at Sotheby's on 22 November 1989 as Lot 102 but not sold. In the catalogue it is described as marked for the printer, notated in brown ink on four systems per page, each of three staves, lacking eight bars and the final bar, with some alterations, additions, and corrections in red ink and blue pencil; together with an arrangement for chorus in four parts, lacking bars 1–4.

OTHER VERSIONS

**In Praise of Neptune**

Arranged for mixed chorus (SATB) and piano.
**Date of arrangement:** [1911].
**Publication:** The Year Book Press. Vocal score © 1911 (The Year Book Press Series of Part Songs no. 47).

**In Praise of Neptune**

Arranged for mixed chorus (SATB) and orchestra by the composer.
**Date of arrangement:** [1911].
**Instrumentation:** 2 flutes, 2 oboes, 2 clarinets in A, 2 bassoons, 2 horns in F, 2 trumpets in A, timpani, percussion (2 players: triangle, side-drum, bass drum, and cymbals), and strings.
**Publication:** Ascherberg, Hopwood & Crew Ltd. Vocal score © [1911]. Later Chappell & Co. Ltd. Now Warner & Co. Ltd.
**Location of manuscript:** Manuscript Collections, The British Library (Reference Division), Add. MS 52900.

## Greater love hath no man

A motet for Passiontide and other seasons, for treble and baritone soli, mixed chorus (SATB), and organ. Alternative title: 'Many waters cannot quench love'. Text selected from the Scriptures.
**Dedication:** To Charles Macpherson, Esq. Mus.D.[14] and the Choristers of St Paul's Cathedral.
**Duration:** 6' 50".
**Publication:** Stainer & Bell Ltd. Vocal score © 1912 (Stainer & Bell's Church Choir Library no. 146).
**Bibliography:** M. Berry, 'Favourite Anthems', *Gramophone*, 68/810 (Nov. 1990), 1038, 1042.

J. Chissell, 'Treasury of English Church Music', *Gramophone*, 44/523 (Dec. 1966), 327.

T. Harvey, 'Ireland: Choral Works', *Gramophone*, 57/673 (June 1979), 93–4.

—— '19th and 20th-Century English Choral Music', *Gramophone*, 62/735 (Aug. 1984), 258.

A. Robertson, '20th Century English Church Music', *Gramophone*, 40/478 (Mar. 1963), 434.

J. Steane, 'The English Anthem', *Gramophone*, 68/808 (Sept. 1990), 599.

—— 'Great Cathedral Anthems', *Gramophone*, 66/792 (May 1989), 1766.

---

[14] Charles Macpherson (1870–1927): Organist at St Paul's Cathedral 1916–27. Professor of harmony at the RAM. Composer of various works for church use.

S. Webb, 'Chichester Cathedral', *Gramophone*, 53/628 (Sept. 1975), 506.
—— 'Choral Works', *Gramophone*, 54/640 (Sept. 1976), 460, 465.
**Recordings:** Canterbury Cathedral Choir, Philip Jones Brass Ensemble, David Flood (organ)/Alan Wicks *in* Argo 411 714-1ZH, 411 714-4ZH (1984).
Carlisle Cathedral Choir/A. Sievewright *in* APS 318, CAPS 318.
Chichester Cathedral Choir, Richard Seal (organ)/John Birch *in* HMV CLP 3588, CSD 3588 (1966), *in* HMV HQS 1350 (1975).
Exeter Cathedral Choir, Paul Morgan (organ)/Lucien Nethsingha *in* Exon Audio EXCATH 3 (1976).
Guildford Cathedral Choir, P. Wright (organ)/Andrew Millington *in* Priory PRC 257/PRCD 257 (1989).
Kilgare Presbyterian Church Choir, Austin College, Roy Perry (organ)/Bedford, Aeolian Skinner 10:310.
St Edmundsbury Cathedral Choir and M. Cousins (organ) *in* Priory PRC 270, PRCD 270 (1989).
St John's College Choir, Cambridge, Brian Runnett (organ)/George Guest *in* Argo RG 340, ZRG 5340 (1963), PRCD 257 (1989).
St Matthew's Church Choir, Northampton, Terence Allbright (organ)/M. Nicholas *in* Abbey LPB 655.
St Paul's Cathedral Choir, Andrew Lucas (organ)/John Scott *in* Hyperion KA66374, CDA66374 (1990).
Vasari Singers, Ian Curror (organ)/J. Backhouse *in* EMI Eminence CD-EMX 2161, TC-EMX 2161 (1990).
Worcester Cathedral Choir, Paul Trepte (organ)/Donald Hunt *in* Abbey LPB 803 (1979).

## OTHER VERSIONS

**Greater love hath no man**

A motet for treble and baritone soli, mixed chorus (SATB), and orchestra.
**Date of arrangement:** May 1922, for the Sons of the Clergy Festival.
**Instrumentation:** 2 flutes, 2 oboes, 2 clarinets in A, 2 bassoons, 4 horns in F, 3 trumpets in C, 3 trombones, tuba, timpani, organ, and strings.
**First performance:** London, St Paul's Cathedral, Tuesday 30 May 1922. Unable to trace any other details.
Unpublished.
**Location of manuscript:** Unable to trace. A copy reveals that it is initialled and dated 16 May 1922.
**Bibliography:** D. Denton, 'Ireland', *Music Magazine*, 4 (Feb. 1991), 54.
**Recordings:** Paula Bott (soprano) and Bryn Terfel (baritone)/LSC/LSO/Roderick Elms (organ)/Richard Hickox *in* Chandos CHAN 8879, ABTD 1492 (1990).

## In Summer Woods

Song for 2-part chorus (SA) and piano. Text by James Vila Blake (from the German).
**Publication:**   J. Curwen & Co. Ltd. Vocal score © 1911 (Choruses for Equal Voices no. 1334). Now Music Sales Ltd.

OTHER VERSIONS

**In Summer Woods**

Arranged for chorus and orchestra by T. Widicombe.
**Date of arrangement:**   1957.
**Instrumentation:**   Flute, oboe, 2 clarinets, bassoon, 2 horns, percussion, and strings. Unpublished.

## Vesper Hymn

Hymn tune for mixed chorus (SATB) and organ ('O Lord, keep us safe') as sung at Holy Trinity, Sloane Square, SW.
**Publication:**   Novello & Co. Ltd., Brighton: J. & W. Chester Ltd. Vocal score © 1911 by John Ireland.

## Slumber Song

Unison song for equal voices and piano. Text by James Vila Blake (from the German).
**Publication:**   Novello & Co. Ltd. Vocal score © 1911. Also © 1933 (Novello's School Songs no. 1469).

## Spring

Unison song for equal voices and piano. Text by James Vila Blake (from the German).
**Publication:**   Novello & Co. Ltd. Vocal score © 1911 (School Music Review no. 235). Later reprinted in School Songs Series no. 1469 [1933].

## 1912

## A Cradle Song

Song for unaccompanied mixed chorus (SATB). Text by William Blake (1757–1827), from *Songs of Experience* (1794).

**Date of composition:** March 1912.
**Dedication:** To my friend Thomas F. Dunhill.[15]
**Duration:** 2′ 50″.
**Publication:** Stainer & Bell Ltd. Vocal score © 1914 (Choral Library no. 134).

## Aubade

Song for 2-part chorus (SA) and piano. Text by Sydney Dobell (1824–74) from 'Balder'.
**Publication:** Novello & Co. Ltd. Vocal score © 1912 (Novello's Collection of Two-Part Songs no. 164).

## Benedictus in F major

For mixed chorus (SATB) and organ. Text from the Book of Common Prayer.
**Publication:** Novello & Co. Ltd. Vocal score © 1912 (PCB no. 883).
**Notes:** See also Te Deum in F (1907), Jubilate in F (1914), Magnificat and Nunc Dimittis in F (1915), Benedicite in F (1919).

## Here's to the Ships!

Song for voice and piano. Text by P. J. O'Reilly.
**First performance:** London, Royal Albert Hall, 6 January 1912. Harry Dearth (baritone) and either S. Liddle or F. A. Sewell (piano). (46th season of the London Ballad Concerts, arranged by Boosey & Co.)
**Publication:** Boosey & Co. Ltd. Vocal score © 1912. 2 versions were published: in B flat and C major.

OTHER VERSIONS

**Here's to the Ships!**

Song arranged for voice and orchestra.
**Date of arrangement:** 1912.
**Instrumentation:** 2 flutes, oboe, 2 clarinets in B flat, 2 bassoons, 2 horns in F, 2 trumpets in B flat, 2 trombones, timpani, percussion (1 player: side-drum), and strings.
Unpublished.
**Location of manuscript:** Manuscript Collections, The British Library (Reference Division), Add. MS 52897. It is dated: 5 March 1912.

---

[15] Thomas F. Dunhill (1877–1946): English composer and writer. Contemporary of Ireland's at the RCM. Wrote many songs, a symphony, and an operetta to a libretto by A. P. Herbert.

## Evening Song

Song for 2-part chorus (SA) and piano. Text by James Vila Blake (from Friedrich Ruckert).
**Publication:**   Novello & Co. Ltd. Vocal score © 1912 (Novello's Collection of Two-Part Songs no. 162).

## See how the morning smiles

Song for 2-part chorus (SA) and piano. Text by Thomas Campion (1567–1620).
**Publication:**   Stainer & Bell Ltd. Vocal score © 1912 (Stainer & Bell's Part-Songs for Treble and Alto Voices no. 55). John Ireland Trust © 1979 (Banks & Co. Ltd., York, in the Eboracum Choral Series ECS 147).
**Notes:**   This is a different setting of the words of the song 'The Peaceful Western Wind' (1890s). Ireland left Elm Park Mansions in 1912 and went to live in Gunter Grove (the Studio).

### 1912–1913

## Decorations

For solo piano.
 1. The Island Spell (Allegretto)
 2. Moon-Glade (Poco lento)
 3. The Secret Ceremonies (Con moto)

**Dedication:**   No. 1 only: To my friend Pedro G. Morales.[16]
**Duration:**   1—4' 00"; 2—3' 30"; 3—3' 30".
**Publication:**   Augener & Co. Ltd. Vocal score © 1915. Now Stainer & Bell Ltd. Each movement was also published separately [© 1919]. Also included in volume i of *The Collected Piano Works of John Ireland*, Stainer & Bell © 1976.
**Location of manuscript:**   Manuscript Collections, The British Library (Reference Division), Add. MS 52889: no. 1. ('The Island Spell') only. According to the printed copy, each movement is dated thus: No. 1—Fauvic, Jersey: August 1912; No. 2—Chelsea: May 1913; No. 3—Chelsea: June 1913.

---

[16] Pedro G. Morales (1897–1938): Spanish violinist, composer, and musicologist. Studied music, philosophy, and arts at Seville University and the piano, violin, and viola at the RCM. Remained in London for most of his life.

**Bibliography:** Anon., 'British Piano Music', *The Times Literary Supplement*, 10 Aug. 1916, p. 380.

Anon., 'John Ireland', *Monthly Musical Record*, 45 (2 Aug. 1915), 227.

Anon., 'The Neglect of New Piano Music', *The Times*, 24 July 1915, p. 9.

M. Harrison, 'Ireland', *Gramophone*, 57/674 (July 1979), 229–30.

M. Kennedy, '20th Century British Piano Music', *Gramophone*, 68/810 (Nov. 1990), 1016.

C. Palmer, 'Ireland', *Gramophone*, 53/631 (Dec. 1975), 1082.

A. Robertson, 'Ireland', *Gramophone*, 40/477 (Feb. 1963), 391.

—— 'Ireland: Piano Works', *Gramophone*, 48/566 (July 1970), 191–2.

H. Rutland, 'The Ireland Spell', in *John Ireland: A Biographical Sketch* (London: Galliard, 1965), 5–6.

L. Salter, 'Ireland', *Gramophone*, 31/360 (June 1953), 17.

**Recordings:** Daniel Adni (piano) *in* HMV HQS 1414 (1979).

Eric Parkin (piano) *in* Argo ARS 1004, RG 4 (1953), *in* Lyrita SRCS 87 (1975).

Alan Rowlands (piano) *in* Saga XIP 7008 (1963), XID 5206, *in* Lyrita RCS 28 (1970).

No. 1 only:

Christopher Headington (piano) *in* Conifer CKCL 2017, KCLCD 2017 (1990).

Alan Schiller (piano), BBC Transcription 126 865.

**Notes:** Movements 1 and 2 are prefaced by quotations from Arthur Symons:

> I would wash the dust of the world in a soft green flood:
> Here, between sea and sea, in the fairy wood,
> I have found a delicate, wave-green solitude . . .
>
> Why are you so sorrowful in dreams?
> I am sad in the night;
> The hours till the morning are white,
> I hear the hours' flight
> All night in dreams . . .

Movement 3 is prefaced by a quote from *The House of Souls* by Arthur Machen:[17]

Then there are the Ceremonies, which are all of them important, but some are more delightful than others—there are White Ceremonies, and the Green Ceremonies, and the Scarlet Ceremonies. The Scarlet Ceremonies are the best . . .

---

[17] Arthur Machen (1863–1947): Welsh translator and short-story writer. Clerk in a London publishing house, then drifted from teaching to acting in Benson's company (1902). Joined the staff of the *London Evening News* in 1912.

## Bed in Summer

Unison song for equal voices and piano. Text by Robert Louis Stevenson (1850–94) from *A Child's Garden of Verses* (1885).
**Duration:**   1' 10".
**Publication:**   J. Curwen & Co. Ltd. Vocal score © 1915 (Choruses for Equal Voices no. 1489). Now Music Sales Ltd.

OTHER VERSIONS

**Bed in Summer**

Song arranged for voice and piano.
**Date of arrangement:**   [1912–13].
**Publication:**   J. Curwen & Co. Ltd. (Curwen edn. 2129). Vocal score © 1915. Now Music Sales Ltd. 2 versions were published: in A flat and F major. Also included in volume v of *The Complete Works for Voice and Piano*, Stainer & Bell © 1981.
**Bibliography:**   T. Harvey, 'Songs', *Gramophone*, 57/678 (Nov. 1979), 895.
**Recordings:**   Alfreda Hodgson (contralto) and Alan Rowlands (piano) *in* Lyrita SRCS 118 (1979).

## Trio in D

For clarinet in B flat, cello, and piano.

1. Allegro non troppo
2. (No dynamic marks)
3. Lento
4. Con moto

**First performance:**   London, Steinway Hall, 9 June 1914. Charles Draper (clarinet), May Muckle (cello), and John Ireland (piano). (A Thomas Dunhill Chamber Concert.)
Unpublished.
**Location of manuscript:**   Manuscript Collections, The British Library (Reference Division), Add. MS 52887: incomplete. The second movement is missing. Ireland begun composition in April 1912 and finished the trio in October 1913. It was then revised between October 1913 and February 1914.

OTHER VERSIONS

This was rewritten in 1915 and given a performance at Steinway Hall, London, on 25 March of that year. Unable to trace any original manuscript. Ireland is said to have used much of this material in the Trio of 1938 (q.v.).

## 1913

### The Almond Trees

For solo piano.
**Duration:** 4'.
**Publication:** Ascherberg, Hopwood & Crew Ltd. Score © 1920 (no. 28 in the Repertoire Series of Pianoforte Music by Modern British Composers, ed. G. H. Clutsam and T. E. Dunhill). Also included in volume i of *The Collected Piano Works of John Ireland*, Stainer & Bell © 1976.
**Bibliography:** M. Harrison, 'Ireland', *Gramophone*, 57/674 (July 1979), 229–30.
—— 'John Ireland, his Friends and Pupils', *Gramophone*, 61/724 (Sept. 1983), 375.
A. Robertson, 'Ireland: Piano Works', *Gramophone*, 48/566 (July 1970), 191–2.
**Recordings:** Daniel Adni (piano) *in* HMV HQS 1414 (1979). Eric Parkin (piano) *in* Chandos DBRD 2006, DBTD 2006 (1983).
Alan Rowlands (piano) *in* Lyrita RCS 28 (1970).
**Notes:** This piano piece was inspired by a Japanese print of an almond tree which the composer saw in the window of an art shop one Sunday evening. When he enquired about the print the following morning, he was disappointed to find that it had already been sold, and the regret remained with him for the rest of his life.

### Child's Song

Unison song for equal voices and piano. Text by Thomas Moore (1779–1852).
**Publication:** Deane/The Year Book Press. Vocal score © 1914 (The Year Book Press Series of Unison and Part Songs no. 106, ed. Martin Akerman).

### Communion Service in C major

For mixed chorus (SATB) and organ.
1. Responses to the Commandments (Moderato)
2. Responses before and after the Gospel
3. Credo (Allegro giusto)
4. Sanctus (Andante)
5. Benedictus (Andante)
6. Agnus Dei (Sostenuto)
7. Pater Noster (In tempo moderato)—unaccompanied
8. Gloria (Allegro)

**Date of composition:** May 1913.
**Publication:** Novello & Co. Ltd. Vocal score © 1914 (Short Settings of the Office for the Holy Communion no. 52). Novello & Co. Ltd. [© 1952] (PCB 1304) (included the Ninefold Kyrie for use with this service). The setting of the Lord's Prayer was published separately, Novello & Co. Ltd. © 1958 (PCB 1374).
**Recordings:** Wakefield Cathedral Choir/Jonathan Bielby *in* Priory PRCD 341 (1992).

## Marigold

Impression for voice and piano.
1. Youth's Spring-Tribute (Allegretto). D. G. Rossetti (1828–82), Sonnet 14 from *The House of Life* (1881).
2. Penumbra (Poco andante). D. G. Rossetti, 1870.
3. Spleen (Con moto moderato). Ernest Dowson (1867–1900), after Verlaine, *Decorations: In Verse and Prose* (1899). The poem is one of four translations from Verlaine, the original being 'Les roses étaient toutes rouges', Aquarelles no. 2 from *Romances sans paroles* (1874).

**Date of composition:** May–June 1913 (Chelsea).
**Duration:** 1—3' 45"; 2—5' 00"; 3—3' 05".
**Publication:** G. Schirmer Ltd. Vocal score © 1916. Reissued by the Doric Music Co., York [© 1965]. Also included in volume iv of *The Complete Works for Voice and Piano*, Stainer & Bell © 1981.
**Location of manuscript:** Manuscript Collections, The British Library (Reference Division), Add. MS 65528. This autograph manuscript was purchased by the British Library from Sotheby's on 6 May 1988 (Lot 395). No. 1 is dated: 24 May 1913: No. 2: 12 May 1913; No. 3: 3 June 1913.
**Bibliography:** R. Fiske, 'Ireland: Songs—Volume 1' *Gramophone*, 52/624 (May 1975), 2005–6.
**Recordings:** Benjamin Luxon (baritone) and Alan Rowlands (piano) *in* Lyrita SRCS 65 (1975).

OTHER VERSIONS

**Marigold: Impression**

Arranged for voice and orchestra.
**Date of arrangement:** 1913.
**Instrumentation:** 3 flutes, 2 oboes and cor anglais, 2 clarinets in B flat, bass clarinet in B flat, 2 bassoons, 4 horns in F, timpani, celesta, harp, and strings.
Unpublished.
**Location of manuscript:** Incomplete—no. 1 only: Manuscript Collections, The British Library (Reference Division), Add. MS 52898.

## The Forgotten Rite

Prelude for orchestra.

**Instrumentation:** 3 flutes and piccolo, 2 oboes and cor anglais, 2 clarinets and bass clarinet in B flat, 2 bassoons, 4 horns in F, 2 trumpets in B flat, 3 trombones, timpani, celesta, harp, and strings.

**Duration:** 9'.

**First performance:** London, Queen's Hall, 13 September 1917. The Queen's Hall Orchestra, conducted by Henry J. Wood.

**Second performance:** Bournemouth, Winter Gardens, 28 February 1918. Bournemouth Municipal Orchestra, conducted by Dan Godfrey.

**Publication:** Augener & Co. Ltd. Full score © 1918. Orchestral parts [© 1920]. Revised edition © 1949. Now Stainer & Bell Ltd.

**Location of manuscript:** Manuscript Collections, The British Library (Reference Division), Add. MS 52873. It is dated: Aug.–Nov. 1913. Another autograph manuscript of this work (and an arrangement for two pianos) was sold at Sotheby's on 29 November 1985 (present whereabouts unknown).

**Bibliography:** W. R. Anderson, 'Ireland', *Gramophone*, 27/315 (Aug. 1949), 40.

Anon., 'Queen's Hall Promenade Concerts', *Musical Times*, 58 (Oct. 1917), 465.

Anon., 'Promenade Concerts', *The Times*, 14 September 1917, p. 3.

M. Harrison, 'English Music', *Gramophone*, 62/736 (Sept., 1984), 336.

M. Jameson, 'Ireland: Orchestral Works', *Gramophone*, 69/825 (Feb. 1992), 35–6.

A. Robertson, 'Ireland', *Gramophone*, 44/520 (Sept. 1966), 157–8.

A. Sanders, 'Bax/Ireland', *Gramophone*, 69/827 (Apr. 1992), 167.

**Recordings:** *Hallé Orchestra/John Barbirolli, HMV C 3894 (1949), *in* HMV EX 290107-3, EX 290107-5 (1984), EMI CDH7 63910-2 (1992).

London Philharmonic Orchestra/Adrian Boult *in* Lyrita RCS 32, SRCS 32 (1966), Musical Heritage Society 1317.

London Philharmonic Orchestra/Adrian Boult, NSA tape M579W.

London Symphony Orchestra/Richard Hickox *in* Chandos CHAN 8994 (1992).

Philharmonia Orchestra/Adrian Boult, BBC Transcription 111118.

**Notes:** This prelude was Ireland's first important orchestral work. It was inspired by his love for the Channel Islands, especially Jersey, and his admiration for the writings of Arthur Machen.

## OTHER VERSIONS

**The Forgotten Rite**

Arranged by the composer for piano duet.
**Date of arrangement:**   1913.
**Publication:**   Augener & Co. Ltd. Score © 1918. Now Stainer & Bell Ltd.
**Location of manuscript:**   Manuscript Collections, The British Library (Reference Division), Add. MS 52873. It is dated: Aug.–Nov. 1913.

## The Echoing Green

Song for 2-part chorus (SS) and piano. Text by William Blake (1757–1827).
**Date of composition:**   September 1913.
**Dedication:**   To Gwennie, Laurie and Clarice, in Jersey.
**Publication:**   J. Curwen & Co. Ltd. Vocal score © 1914 (Choruses for Equal Voices no. 1443). Now Music Sales Ltd.

## Nurses' Song

Unison song for equal voices and piano. Text by William Blake (1757–1827) from *Songs of Innocence*.
**Publication:**   The Year Book Press. Vocal score © 1914 (The Year Book Press Series of Unison and Part-Songs no. 107). The song was later reprinted under the title of 'Sunset Play'.

## Sea Fever

Song for voice and piano. Text by John Masefield (1878–1967) from *Saltwater Ballads* (1902).
**Date of composition:**   October 1913.
**Duration:**   2' 30".
**First performance:**   Unable to trace. It may have been sung by Mischa-Léon. See also note below.
**Publication:**   Augener & Co. Ltd. Vocal score © 1915. Now Stainer & Bell Ltd. 4 versions were published: in E minor, F minor, G minor, and A minor. A voice-only part was also published with melody and tonic sol-fa by W. G. Glock, Augener & Co. Ltd. [© 1929]. Also included in volume ii of *The Complete Works for Voice and Piano*, Stainer & Bell © 1981, and in *Eleven Songs by John Ireland* (introduced by John Longmire), Stainer & Bell/Galaxy © 1970.
**Location of manuscript:**   The John Ireland Trust. 2 versions. One is initialled and dated 'October 1913', the other signed by the composer but not dated. Both are in the key of E minor.

**Bibliography:** W. A. Chislett, 'Songs', *Gramophone*, 42/504 (May 1965), 550.
—— 'Songs', *Gramophone*, 43/515 (Apr. 1966), 522.
—— 'The World of the Sea', *Gramophone*, 53/627 (Aug. 1975), 363.
C. M. Crabtree, ['Sea Fever'], *Gramophone*, 5/7 (Dec. 1927), 281.
R. Fiske, 'Ireland: Songs—Volume 1', *Gramophone*, 52/624 (May 1975), 2005–6.
M. Kennedy, 'A Treasury of English Song', *Gramophone*, 64/764 (Jan. 1987), 1055–6.
H. D. R., 'Songs', *Gramophone*, 19/225 (Feb. 1942), 149.
—— 'Songs', *Gramophone*, 20/237 (Feb. 1943), 127.
A. Robertson, 'Songs', *Gramophone* 41/484 (Sept. 1963), 148.
A. Sanders, 'Compact Disc Roundup', *Gramophone*, 65/774 (Nov. 1987), 822.
J. Steane, 'An Anthology of English Song', *Gramophone*, 69/827 (Apr. 1992), 146.
—— 'English Songs', *Gramophone*, 67/800 (Jan. 1990), 1366.
F. B. Westbrook, 'Did I Say That?', *Choir*, 54/10 (Oct. 1963), 179–80.

**Recordings:** Thomas Allen (baritone) and Roger Vignoles (piano) *in* Hyperion CDA 66165 (1987).
R. Bolton (baritone) and R. Yaro (piano), Silhouette SLP17.
*John Brownlee (baritone), HMV E 553.
*Betty Chester (contralto) and Melville Gideon (piano), HMV B 1445.
*Jack Collinge (baritone), Decca F 2243.
*Edgar Coyle (baritone), Columbia 4385.
*Fraser Gange (baritone), HMV E 3.
Roy Henderson (baritone), Columbia 5395, HMV 7009.
*Roy Henderson (baritone) and Ivor Newton (piano), Decca M 526h (1943).
Raimund Herincx (baritone) and John Constable (piano) *in* Novello/BMG NVLC 107, NVLCD 107 (1990), Gamut GAMCD 506 (1992).
*Robert Irwin (baritone) and Gerald Moore (piano), HMV B 9073 (1940), *in* HMV Treasury EX 290911-3, EX 290911-5 (1987).
Benjamin Luxon (baritone) and Alan Rowlands (piano) *in* Lyrita SRCS 65 (1975).
Benjamin Luxon (baritone) and David Willison (piano) *in* Abbey LPB 689.
Kenneth McKellar (tenor) and Denis Woolford (piano) *in* Decca LK 4663, SKL 4663 (1965), *in* Decca SPA 396 (1975).
*George Parker (baritone) and Sidney Twemlow (piano), BBC Sound Archive 6811, BBC Transcription 18757.
*Stuart Robertson (baritone) and Gerald Moore (piano), HMV B 2594 (1927).
Paul Robeson (bass) and Laurence Brown (piano), HMV B 9257 J 0157 (1942).
John Shirley-Quirk (baritone) and Viola Tunnard (piano) *in* Saga XIP 7011, XID 5211 (1963), STXID 5211 (1966), SAGA 5211, CA 5211 (cassette).

Richard Standen (baritone) and Frederick Stone (piano), Westminster WLE 103, XWN 18710.
*Conrad Thibault (baritone), Victor 1583, HMV DA 1296.

**Notes:** In a note by George Parker, written in October 1958, he writes that he saw the MS immediately after it was composed and liked it very much.

It was given a first performance by another singer who did not think a great deal of it. I had the second performance with John Ireland at the pianoforte at the Three Arts Club in Marylebone Road. This was from the MSS. Before it was ever published I sang it a great deal, particularly to the soldiers in the 1914–1918 war in France and England. (Sold at Sotheby's in 1989 and now in the archives of the John Ireland Trust.)

## OTHER VERSIONS

### Sea Fever

Arranged for voice and orchestra.
Unpublished.
**Bibliography:** K. K., ['Sea Fever'], *Gramophone*, 3/8 (Jan. 1926), 391–2.
**Recordings:** *Frederick Harvey (baritone) and orchestra, HMV B 10233, *in* 7EG 8370.
*Stuart Robertson (baritone) and Mackenzie-Rogan SO, Duophone B 5098 (1926).

### Sea Fever

Arranged for bass solo, chorus, and orchestra by G. Williams (in D, E, F, and G minor).
**Instrumentation:** Flute, oboe, 2 clarinets, bassoon, 2 horns, 3 trumpets, 3 trombones, timpani, percussion, and strings.
Unpublished.

### Sea Fever

Arranged for voice and small orchestra.
**Instrumentation:** Flute, timpani, accordion, guitar, and strings.
Unpublished.

### Sea Fever

Arranged for voice and military band.
Unpublished.
**Bibliography:** W. A. Chislett, 'Spirit of England', *Gramophone*, 51/604 (Sept. 1973), 567.
—— and A. Lamb, 'Rule Britannia', *Gramophone*, 51/607 (Dec. 1973), 1265–6.
**Recordings:** M. Burchill (baritone) and Band of the Royal Corps of Signals/K. R. R. Boulding *in* Indigo GOLP-7003 (1973).
John Lawrenson (baritone) and Band of the Royal Marines *in* Polydor 2383 231 (1973).

**Sea Fever**

Arranged as a unison song for equal voices and piano.
Unpublished.

**Sea Fever**

Arranged for baritone solo, male choir, and piano by Mansel Thomas.
**Publication:** Stainer & Bell Ltd. Vocal score © 1915, 1989 (Stainer & Bell Male Voice W179).
**Recording:** Ivor Lewis (baritone) and Brymbo Male Choir/G. Hughes *in* Qualiton SQUAD 109.

## Song from o'er the Hill

Song for voice and piano. Text by P. J. O'Reilly.
**Duration:** 1' 45".
**Publication:** Leonard & Co. Ltd. Vocal score © 1913. 3 versions were published: in A flat major, C major, and B flat major. Also included in volume v of *The Complete Works for Voice and Piano*, Stainer & Bell © 1981.

## Three Dances

For solo piano.
   1. Gypsy Dance (Allegro non troppo)
   2. Country Dance (Allegretto)
   3. Reapers' Dance (Allegro)

**Dedication:** 1—To Josephte; 3—To Marjorie.
**Duration:** 1—2' 00"; 2—2' 00"; 3—2' 00".
**Publication:** J. Curwen & Co. Ltd. Score © 1913 (part of Curwen's Pianoforte Series). Now Music Sales Ltd. Also included in volume i of *The Collected Piano Works of John Ireland*, Stainer & Bell © 1976.
**Bibliography:** M. Harrison, 'Ireland', *Gramophone*, 57/674 (July 1979), 229–30.
**Recordings:** Daniel Adni (piano) *in* HMV HQS 1414 (1979).
**Notes:** Each dance was also published separately. They were also originally known as *Three Rustic Dances*.

## Porto Rico

Song for voice and piano, written under the pseudonym of TURLAY ROYCE. Text by Frederick E. Weatherly.
**Publication:** Boosey & Co. Ltd. Vocal score © 1913.

## 1913–1915

## Preludes

For solo piano.
1. The Undertone (Poco sostenuto)
2. Obsession (Allegretto con moto)
3. The Holy Boy (Andante tranquillo)
4. Fire of Spring (Animato)

**Duration:** 1—4' 00"; 2—3' 00"; 3—3' 00"; 4—2' 00".
**Publication:** Winthrop Rogers Ltd. Score 1—© 1918; 2—© 1917; 3—© 1917; 4—© 1917. Now Boosey & Hawkes Ltd. Also included in volume i of *The Complete Piano Works of John Ireland*, Stainer & Bell © 1976. No. 3 ('The Holy Boy') is included in *20th Century Classics* (volume ii), arranged for solo piano, Boosey & Hawkes Ltd. © 1989.
**Location of manuscript:** No. 2: 'Obsession'—Manuscript Collections, The British Library (Reference Division), Add MS 52890. According to the printed copy, each movement is dated thus: No. 1: Chelsea, January 1914; No. 2: 1915; No. 3: Chelsea, December 1913; No. 4: Chelsea, April 1915.
**Bibliography:** Anon., 'Reviews: Piano Music', *Musical Times*, 59 (June 1918), 258.

E. Austin, 'About Two "Things of Beauty": (1) John Ireland's Undertone', *Musical Times*, 59/908 (Oct. 1918), 444–5.

M. Harrison, 'Ireland', *Gramophone*, 57/674 (July 1979), 229–30.

—— 'Piano Recital', *Gramophone*, 50/596 (Jan. 1973), 1370.

C. Palmer, 'Ireland: Piano Works', *Gramophone*, 53/631 (Dec. 1975), 1082.

A. Robertson, 'Ireland', *Gramophone*, 40/497 (Feb. 1963), 391.

—— 'Ireland: Piano Works', *Gramophone*, 48/566 (July 1970), 191–2.

**Recordings:** Eric Parkin (piano) *in* Lyrita SRCS 87 (1975).

Alan Rowlands (piano) *in* Lyrita RCS 28 (1970).

Frank Merrick (piano), FM Society FMS3, Rare Recorded Editions SRRE 129 (1973).

No. 3 only:

Daniel Adni (piano) *in* HMV HQS 1414 (1979).

John Ogdon (piano) *in* CFP 4514, TC-CFP 4514.

Alan Rowlands (piano) *in* Saga XIP 7008 (1963), XID 5206.

**Notes:** As can be seen from the above, the first piece to be written was 'The Holy Boy' on Christmas Day 1913, but this was also inspired by a young chorister in Ireland's choir at St Luke's Church, Chelsea, where he was organist and choirmaster 1904–26. Bobby Glasby, the son of a sculptor, was a great favourite of Ireland (he also inspired the piano piece 'February's Child'), and after Bobby's father's death Ireland acquired the

Glasby home in Gunter Grove, Chelsea, where he lived for over forty years. In an early printed version, 'Obsession' came first, 'Spleen' ('The Undertone') was second, 'Carol' ('The Holy Boy') was third, and 'Rosebud' ('Fire of Spring') last.

## OTHER VERSIONS

**The Holy Boy: A Carol of the Nativity**

Arranged for string orchestra by the composer.
**Date of arrangement:** 1941.
**Instrumentation:** Violins I and II, violas, cellos, and double basses.
**Duration:** *c.*2′ 30″.
**Publication:** Boosey & Hawkes Ltd. Full score © 1941.
**Bibliography:** D. Denton, 'Ireland', *Music Magazine*, 4 (Feb. 1991), 54.
  E. Greenfield, '20th Century English Music', *Gramophone*, 49/587 (Apr. 1972), 1723.
  T. Harvey, 'English Idyll', *Gramophone*, 58/693 (Feb. 1981), 1095.
  M. Macdonald, 'Bridge/Ireland', *Gramophone*, 62/739 (Dec. 1984), 736.
  M. Oliver, 'A Christmas Garland', *Gramophone*, 64/763 (Dec. 1986), 941.
  A. Robertson, 'Ireland', *Gramophone*, 44/520 (Sept. 1966), 157–8.
  A. Sanders, 'Bridge/Ireland', *Gramophone*, 65/768 (May 1987), 1546, 1550.
**Recordings:** *Boyd Neel Orchestra/Boyd Neel, Decca M 595.
  ECO/David Garforth *in* Chandos ABRD 1112, ABTD 1112 (1984), CHAN 8390 (1987).
  English Sinfonia/Neville Dilkes *in* HMV CSD 3705 (1972), *in* HMV Greensleeves ESD 7101, TC-ESD 7101 (1981).
  London Philharmonic Orchestra/Adrian Boult *in* Lyrita RCS 31, SRCS 31, Musical Heritage Society 1498 (1966).
  London Symphony Orchestra/Richard Hickox *in* Chandos CHAN 8879, ABTD 1492 (1990).
  Royal Philharmonic Orchestra/David Willcocks *in* Unicorn-Kanchana DKP 9057, DKPC 9057, DKPCD 9057 (1986).
  String Orchestra/Jay Wilbur, Boosey & Hawkes ST 2009.

**The Holy Boy**

Arranged for brass ensemble by Robert E. Stepp.
**Date of arrangement:** 1950.
**Instrumentation:** 3 trumpets in B flat, 2 horns in F, 2 trombones, euphonium (baritone), and tuba.
**Publication:** Boosey & Hawkes Ltd. (New York). Full score © 1950.
**Bibliography:** A. Sanders, 'Compact Disc Round-Up', *Gramophone*, 66/786 (Nov. 1988), 878.
**Recordings:** London Brass Virtuosi/David Honeyball *in* Hyperion H 88013, KH 88013 (1988).

### The Holy Boy

Arranged for violin and piano.
**Date of composition:** 1919.
Unpublished.

### The Holy Boy

Arranged for solo viola (by Lionel Tertis).
**Date of arrangement:** [1925].
**Bibliography:** P. P., ['The Holy Boy'], *Gramophone*, 2/10 (Mar. 1925), 388–9.
**Recordings:** *Lionel Tertis (viola), Vocalia K 05144 (1925).

### The Holy Boy

Arranged for cello and piano.
**Date of arrangement:** 1919.
**Publication:** Winthrop Rogers Ltd. Score © 1919. Now Boosey & Hawkes Ltd.
**Bibliography:** A. Robertson, 'Ireland', *Gramophone*, 16/190 (Mar. 1939), 428.
  A. Sanders, 'British Cello Music', *Gramophone*, 65/776 (Jan. 1988), 1102.
  —— 'Compact Disc Round-Up', *Gramophone*, 66/784 (Sept. 1988), 492.
**Recordings:** *Boris Hamburg (cello) and Gerald Moore (piano), HMV B 3302.
  *Florence Hooton (cello) and Ross Pratt (piano), Decca K 900 (1939).
  Julian Lloyd Webber (cello) and John McCabe (piano) *in* ASV digital DCA 592, ZCDCA 592 (1988), CDD 592 (1988).

### The Holy Boy

Arranged for flute and piano. Edited by James Galway.
**Date of arrangement:** 1987.
**Publication:** Hawkes & Co. Ltd. Score © 1987.
**Bibliography:** R. Rostron, 'Flute', *Music Teacher*, 67/9 (Oct. 1988), 35.

### The Holy Boy

Arranged for two descant recorders and piano by Geoffrey Russell-Smith.
**Date of arrangement:** [1970].
**Publication:** Boosey & Hawkes Ltd. [© 1970].

### The Holy Boy: A Carol of the Nativity

Transcribed for organ by the composer.
**Date of transcription:** 1919.
**Publication:** Winthrop Rogers. Score © 1919. Now Boosey & Hawkes Ltd. Also included in *The Organ Music of John Ireland* (ed. Robert Gower), Novello © 1983.
**Bibliography:** M. Rochester, 'Great European Organs', *Gramophone*, 68/816 (May 1991), 2047.
**Recordings:** Jonathan Bielby (organ) *in* Priory PRCD 298 (1991).

### The Holy Boy

Arranged for voice and piano, organ, or strings by the composer. Text by Herbert S. Brown.
**Date of arrangement:** 1938.
**Publication:** Hawkes & Co. Ltd. Vocal score © 1938. 2 versions were published: in E flat and F. Also included in *Sing Solo Christmas* (ed. John Carol Case), OUP © 1987.
**Location of manuscript:** Manuscript Collections, The British Library (Reference Division), Add. MS 52897 (2 versions: piano/strings). Included in Ireland's notebooks (Add. MS 52901A) is 'The Holy Boy' 'in one manifestation'. He was later to parody it in 'Adam lay ybounden' (q.v.).
**Recordings:** Clifford Hughes (tenor) and George Blackmore (organ) *in* Pilgrim KLP 35.
**Notes:** When making this version in 1938, Ireland added two bars' introduction, and made other modifications.

### The Holy Boy: A Carol of the Nativity

Arranged for unaccompanied mixed chorus (SCTB) by the composer. Text by Herbert S. Brown.
**Date of arrangement:** 1941.
**Dedication:** For Trevor Harvey[18] and the BBC Singers.
**Publication:** Hawkes & Co. Ltd. Vocal score © 1941. Reissued by Boosey & Hawkes Ltd. [© 1953] (Winthrop Rogers Church Choir Series no. 24).
**Bibliography:** T. Harvey, 'Ireland: Choral Works', *Gramophone*, 57/673 (June 1979), 93–4.
**Recordings:** Worcester Cathedral Choir/Donald Hunt *in* Abbey LPB 803 (1979).

## 1914

### Jubilate in F major

For mixed chorus (SATB) and organ. Text from the Book of Common Prayer.
**Publication:** Novello & Co. Ltd. Vocal score © 1914 (PCB 911). Unison part for men's voices—arr. for use with the original edition for choir and organ by John Ireland. Novello & Co. Ltd. [© 1959].
**Notes:** See also Te Deum in F (1907), Benedictus in F (1912), Magnificat and Nunc Dimittis in F (1915), Benedicite in F (1919). In a note, now in the Ireland Trust Archive, the composer reveals that, at the outbreak of World War I, 'I had, at the beginning, offered my services to fight for my country, and went for medical examinations several times but my health and

---

[18] Trevor Harvey (1911–89): Read music at Oxford where he was Heberden Organ Scholar and conducted productions at the Oxford University Opera Club. Assistant chorus master at the BBC, 1935–42. Freelance conductor from 1946, and formed his own chamber orchestra.

physique did not reach the standard required, and I was not accepted for any form of military service.'

## 1915

### Evening Service in F major

For mixed chorus (SATB) and organ. Text from the Book of Common Prayer.
Magnificat (Moderato)
Nunc Dimittis (Tranquillo ma non troppo lento)
**Duration:** Magnificat—3' 35"; Nunc Dimittis—2' 12".
**Publication:** Novello & Co. Ltd. Vocal score © 1915 (PCB 916). Unison part for men's voices—arr. for use with the original edition for choir and organ by John Ireland. Novello & Co. Ltd. [© 1959].
**Bibliography:** T. Harvey, 'Ireland: Choral Works', *Gramophone*, 57/673 (June 1979), 93–4.
**Recordings:** Worcester Cathedral Choir with Paul Trepte (organ)/Donald Hunt *in* Abbey LPB 803 (1979).
**Notes:** See also Te Deum in F (1907), Benedictus in F (1912), Jubilate in F (1914), Benedicite in F (1919).

### Rhapsody

For solo piano.
**Date of composition:** March 1915.
**Duration:** 8'.
**Publication:** Winthrop Rogers Ltd. Score © 1917. Now Boosey & Hawkes Ltd. Also included in volume i of *The Collected Piano Works of John Ireland*, Stainer & Bell © 1976.
**Bibliography:** M. Macdonald, 'Ireland', *Gramophone*, 42/497 (Oct. 1964), 201.
C. Palmer, 'Ireland: Piano Works', *Gramophone*, 53/631 (Dec. 1975), 1082.
**Recordings:** *Moura Lympany (piano), BBC Transcription 20441/2.
Eric Parkin (piano) *in* Argo RG 28, *in* Lyrita SRCS 87 (1975).
Alan Rowlands (piano) *in* Lyrita RCS 24 (1964).

### An Island Hymn

Anthem for unaccompanied men's voices (TTBB). Text from Isaiah 42: 10, 12.
**Date of composition:** June 1915.
**Dedication:** Composed for and dedicated to all Brave Defenders of the Realm of King George V, whether on sea, land or in the air, and especially the Men's Choir of HMS 'Achilles', somewhere in the North Sea.

**Publication:** Stainer & Bell Ltd. Vocal score © 1915 (in *12 Short Anthems for Men's Voices*).
**Notes:** One of twelve short anthems for use in church, on deck, in camp or trench, as occasion may require, the others written by Archer, Balfour, Belchamber, Hodge, Morris, Roper, Sanders, Sewell, Toms, Vinden, and Wetton.

REVISED VERSION

**Island Praise**

Anthem for unaccompanied men's voices (TTBB).
**Date of revision:** Autumn 1955.
**Publication:** E. H. Freeman Ltd. (Brighton). Vocal score © 1956 (University Part-Songs and Anthems). Now EMI Music Publishing Ltd.

## 1915–1917

## Sonata No. 2 in A minor

For violin and piano.

1. Allegro
2. Poco lento quasi adagio
3. In tempo moderato—Con brio

**Date of composition:** October 1915–January 1917.
**Dedication:** To Albert Sammons.[19]
**Duration:** c.26'.
**First performance:** London, Aeolian Hall, 6 March 1917. Albert Sammons (violin) and William Murdoch (piano).
**Publication:** Winthrop Rogers Ltd. Score © 1917. Now Boosey & Hawkes Ltd.
**Bibliography:** Anon., 'A Prize Sonata', *The Times*, 7 Feb. 1917, p. 2.
Anon., 'Messrs. Sammons and Murdoch's Recital', *The Times*, 7 Mar. 1917, p. 9.
Anon., 'Aeolian Hall', *Musical Times*, 58/890 (Apr. 1917), 168.
J. Ireland, 'Notes on Sonata No. 2 in A minor', unpublished, 1950, now in the John Ireland Trust Archive.
A. Robertson, 'Ireland', *Gramophone*, 40/477 (Feb. 1963), 391.
E. Warr, 'Ireland', *Gramophone*, 50/593 (Oct. 1972), 717.

---

[19] Albert Sammons (1886–1957): English violinist. Leader of the Beecham Orchestra, 1908–13, and the Philharmonic Orchestra. Also composed, and was professor of violin at the RCM. There is an undated/unpublished tribute to Sammons by Ireland in the John Ireland Trust Archive.

**Recordings:** *Arthur Catterall (violin) and William Murdoch (piano), Columbia L1322/3.
*Eda Kersey (violin) and Kathleen Long (piano), BBC Sound Archive 6734–7, BBC Transcription 18202/8.
Yfrah Neaman (violin) and Eric Parkin (piano) in Lyrita SRCS 64 (1972).
Tessa Robbins (violin) and Alan Rowlands (piano) in Saga XIP 7008 (1963), XID 5206.

## 1916

## Two Songs

For voice and piano. Text by Eric Thirkell Cooper from *Soliloquies of a Subaltern*.

1. Blind (Steady and sustained)
2. The Cost (Hurried and impassioned)

**Date of composition:** November 1916.
**Duration:** 1—1' 30"; 2—1' 15".
**First performance:** 'The Cost'—London, Wigmore Hall, 12 June 1917. Muriel Foster (soprano) and John Ireland (piano).
**Publication:** Winthrop Rogers Ltd. Vocal score © 1917. Now Boosey & Hawkes Ltd. Also included in volume v of *The Complete Works for Voice and Piano*, Stainer & Bell © 1981.
**Bibliography:** J. B. Steane, 'The Flowering of English Song', *Gramophone*, 68/810 (Nov. 1990), 1038.
**Recordings:** Philip Frohnmayer (baritone) and Logan Skelton (piano) in Centaur/Gamut CRC 2075 (1990).
**Notes:** 'The Cost' is subtitled 'Song of a Great War'.

## A Garrison Churchyard

Song for voice and piano. Text by Eric Thirkell Cooper.
Unpublished.
**Location of manuscript:** Manuscript Collections, The British Library (Reference Division), Add. MS 52897. It is signed and dated by the composer: 11 December 1916.

## 1917

## Trio [No. 2] in E

For violin, cello, and piano.
**Duration:** 14'.
**First performance:** London, Wigmore Hall, 12 June 1917. Albert Sammons (violin), C. Warwick-Evans (cello), and John Ireland (piano).
**Publication:** Augener Ltd. Score © 1918. Now Stainer & Bell Ltd.
**Location of manuscript:** Manuscript Collections, The British Library (Reference Division), Add. MS 52885. It is dated: Chelsea: June 1917.
**Bibliography:** Anon., 'Mr Ireland's Music', *The Times*, 14 June 1917, p. 9.
R. Fiske, 'Ireland', *Gramophone*, 42/501 (Feb. 1965), 384.
—— 'Ireland', *Gramophone*, 56/670 (Mar. 1979), 1580.
**Recordings:** Kamaran Trio, NSA tape M607W.
David Martin Trio *in* Saga XID 5230 (1965).
Yfrah Neaman (violin), Julian Lloyd Webber (cello), and Eric Parkin (piano) *in* Lyrita SRCS 98 (1979).

## The Heart's Desire

Song for voice and piano. Text by A. E. Housman (1859–1936) from *A Shropshire Lad* (1896): no. x ('March'), omitting the first two stanzas.
**Duration:** 2'.
**First performance:** London, Wigmore Hall, 12 June 1917. Muriel Foster (soprano) and John Ireland (piano).
**Publication:** Winthrop Rogers Ltd. Vocal score © 1917. Now Boosey & Hawkes Ltd. 3 versions were published: in D flat major, B major, and B flat major. Also included in volume i of *The Complete Works for Voice and Piano*, Stainer & Bell © 1981.
**Bibliography:** E. Greenfield, 'Ireland', *Gramophone*, 41/492 (May 1964), 513.
T. Harvey, 'Ireland: Songs', *Gramophone*, 57/678 (Nov. 1979), 895.
—— 'A Shropshire Lad', *Gramophone*, 57/683 (Apr. 1980), 1583.
**Recordings:** John Mitchinson (tenor) and Alan Rowlands (piano) *in* Lyrita SRCS 118 (1979).
*George Parker (baritone) and Sidney Twemlow (piano), BBC Sound Archive 6812, BBC Transcription 18760.
John Shirley-Quirk (baritone) and Eric Parkin (piano) *in* Saga XIP 7015, XID 5207 (1964).
Graham Trew (baritone) and Roger Vignoles (piano) *in* Meridian E77031-2 (1980).

## 1917–1918

## Two Songs

For voice and piano. Text by Rupert Brooke (1887–1915), from *1914 and Other Poems* (1915).

    1. The Soldier (Moderato)
    2. Blow out, you bugles (Con moto)

**Dedication:**   No. 2 only—To W.L.R.
**Duration:**   1—2′ 30″; 2—2′ 35″.
**First performance:**   'The Soldier'—London, Wigmore Hall, 12 June 1917. Muriel Foster (soprano) and John Ireland (piano).
**Publication:**   Winthrop Rogers Ltd. Vocal score: 1—© 1917; 2—© 1918. Now Boosey & Hawkes Ltd. 'The Soldier' was published in F, G flat, and E flat major. Also included in volume iv of *The Complete Works for Voice and Piano*, Stainer & Bell © 1981.
**Bibliography:**   Anon., 'Mr Ireland's Music', *The Times*, 14 June 1917, p. 9.
R. Fiske, 'Ireland: Songs', *Gramophone*, 53/626 (July 1975), 227–8.
H.D.R., 'Ireland', *Gramophone*, 20/237 (Feb. 1943), 127.
**Recordings:**   No. 1:
\*Roy Henderson (baritone) and Ivor Newton (piano), Decca M526 (1943).
\*L. Watts (tenor) and N. Newby (piano), Argo R1007.
No. 2:
Benjamin Luxon (baritone) and Alan Rowlands (piano) *in* Lyrita SRCS 66 (1975).

## 1917–1920

## London Pieces

For solo piano.

    1. Chelsea Reach (Tempo di barcarole)
    2. Ragamuffin (Con moto, ma non troppo allegro)
    3. Soho Forenoons (Allegretto)

**Duration:**   1—6′ 00″; 2—3′ 00″; 3—4′ 00″.
**Publication:**   Augener Ltd. Nos. 1 and 2—score © 1918; no. 3—Score © 1920. Now Stainer & Bell Ltd. Each piece was also available separately. Also included in volume ii of *The Collected Piano Works of John Ireland*, Stainer & Bell © 1976.
**Location of manuscript:**   Manuscript Collections, The British Library (Reference Division), Add. MS 52889. All three are signed by the composer

and dated: Nos. 1 and 2: November 1917 (later changed in the printed copy to Autumn 1917); No. 3: February 1920. Also in the British Library (Add. MS 52900) is an unpublished version of *London*, scored for 3 pianos. It is described as 'an evocation of London life which combines musical pastiche with spoken narrative'. Included is an arrangement, in its entirety, of 'Ragamuffin' with verbal comment.

**Bibliography:** Anon., 'John Ireland: London Pieces', *Monthly Musical Record*, 48 (Apr. 1918), 84.

J. Noble, 'Ireland', *Gramophone*, 38/449 (Oct. 1960), 238.

C. Palmer, 'Ireland: Piano Works', *Gramophone*, 53/631 (Dec. 1975), 1082.

H. Rutland, 'Ragamuffin', in *John Ireland: A Biographical Sketch* (London: Galliard, 1965), 6–7.

L. Salter, 'Ireland', *Gramophone*, 31/360 (June 1953), 17.

**Recordings:** Eric Parkin (piano) *in* Argo ARS 1004 RG 4 (1953), *in* Lyrita SRCS 87 (1975).

Alan Rowlands (piano) *in* Lyrita RCS 15 (1960).

**Notes:** The original title of these pieces was *London: Impressions for Piano*, but this is crossed out in the original manuscripts of nos. 1 and 2. Also crossed out is the original title of the first piece: 'The River.' Benjamin Britten quoted from 'Ragamuffin' in the third of his *Three Character Pieces for piano* (1930). See *Letters from a Life*, vol. i, ed. Donald Mitchell and Philip Reed (London, Faber, 1991), 270.

## 1918

### Earth's Call (A Sylvan Rhapsody)

Song for voice and piano. Text by Harold Munro (1879–1932), from 'Weekend' in *Collected Poems* (1933).

**Date of composition:** February 1918.
**Duration:** 4' 45".
**Publication:** Winthrop Rogers Ltd. Vocal score © 1918. Now Boosey & Hawkes Ltd. Doric Music Co. Vocal score © 1966. Also included in volume iv of *The Complete Works for Voice and Piano*, Stainer & Bell © 1981.
**Bibliography:** T. Harvey, 'Ireland: Songs', *Gramophone*, 57/678 (Nov. 1979), 895.

J. B. Steane, 'The Flowering of English Song', *Gramophone*, 68/810 (Nov. 1990), 1038.

**Recordings:** Ellen Frohnmayer (soprano) and Logan Skelton (piano) *in* Centaur/Gamut CRC 2075 (1990).

Alfreda Hodgson (contralto) and Alan Rowlands (piano) *in* Lyrita SRCS 118 (1979).

## Spring Sorrow

Song for voice and piano. Text by Rupert Brooke (1887–1915), from *Poems 1911–1914* (1914).
**Date of composition:** April 1918.
**Duration:** 1' 45".
**Publication:** Winthrop Rogers Ltd. Vocal score © 1918. Now Boosey & Hawkes Ltd. 2 versions were published: in F and A flat major. Also included in volume iv of *The Complete Works for Voice and Piano*, Stainer & Bell © 1981.
**Bibliography:** R. Fiske, 'Ireland: Songs', *Gramophone*, 53/626 (July 1975), 227–8.
E. Greenfield, 'Ireland', *Gramophone*, 41/492 (May 1964), 513.
**Recordings:** Valerie Baulard (contralto) and Simon Wright (piano) *in* MAXS MSCB 12/13.
Benjamin Luxon (baritone) and Alan Rowlands (piano) *in* Lyrita SRCS 66 (1975).
\*Stuart Robertson (baritone) and piano, HMV B3411.
John Shirley-Quirk (baritone) and Eric Parkin (piano) *in* Saga XIP 7015, XID 5207 (1964).

## The Bells of San Marie

Song for voice and piano. Text by John Masefield (1878–1967), from *Ballads and Poems* (1910).
**Date of composition:** July 1918.
**Duration:** 2' 40".
**Publication:** Augener & Co. Ltd. Vocal score © 1919. Now Stainer & Bell Ltd. 3 versions were published: in G, C, and A minor. Also included in volume ii of *The Complete Works for Voice and Piano*, Stainer & Bell © 1981, and in *Eleven Songs by John Ireland* (introduced by John Longmire), Stainer & Bell/Galaxy © 1970.
**Bibliography:** R. Fiske, 'Ireland: Songs', *Gramophone*, 53/626 (July 1975), 227–8.
**Recordings:** Benjamin Luxon (baritone) and Alan Rowlands (piano) *in* Lyrita SRCS 66 (1975).
\*George Parker (baritone) and Sidney Twemlow (piano), BBC Transcription 18765, BBC Sound Archive 6815.

## I have twelve oxen

Song for voice and piano. Text: anon. Early English, Balliol MS 354.
**Duration:** 1' 45".

**Publication:** Winthrop Rogers Ltd. Vocal score © 1919. Now Boosey & Hawkes Ltd. 2 versions were published: in F and G major. Also included in volume v of *The Complete Works for Voice and Piano*, Stainer & Bell © 1981.
**Location of manuscript:** John Ireland Trust, London. It is signed by the composer and dated: Chelsea, July 1918.
**Bibliography:** A. Blyth, 'Peter Dawson', *Gramophone*, 61/724 (Sept. 1983), 378.
R. Fiske, 'Ireland: Songs', *Gramophone*, 53/626 (July 1975), 227–8.
E. Greenfield, 'Ireland', *Gramophone*, 41/492 (May 1964), 513.
N.P., ['I have 12 oxen'], *Gramophone*, 2/9 (Feb. 1925), 342.
A. Porter, 'Ireland', *Gramophone*, 34/397 (June 1956), 20–1.
A. Robertson, 'English Songs', *Gramophone*, 48/565 (June 1970), 85.
**Recordings:** Peter Dawson (bass-baritone) and piano (recorded 1920) *in* HMV RLS 1077053, TC-RLS 1077059 (1983).
Benjamin Luxon (baritone) and Alan Rowlands (piano) *in* Lyrita SRCS 66 (1975).
Lois Marshall (soprano) and piano *in* USSR DO 11577.
*George Parker (baritone) and Sidney Twemlow (piano), BBC Sound Archive 6811, BBC Transcription 18758.
Peter Pears (tenor) and Benjamin Britten (piano) *in* Decca LW5241 (1956), London LL1532: 5024, Eclipse ECS545 (1970).
Albert Pengelly (tenor) and Ivy Mason Whipp (piano), Pengelly AJP2.
*Stuart Robertson (baritone) and piano, HMV B3411.
John Shirley-Quirk (baritone) and Eric Parkin (piano) *in* Saga XIP 7015, XID 5207 (1964).
*Norman Williams (bass-baritone) and piano, Velvet Face 1120 (1925).

OTHER VERSIONS

### J'ai douze bœufs

Song for voice and piano. French version by Lilian Fearn.
**Date of arrangement:** 1919.
**Publication:** Winthrop Rogers Ltd. Vocal score © 1919. Now Boosey & Hawkes Ltd. Also included in *Melodies anglaises*, Boosey & Hawkes Ltd. Score © 1946.

## If there were dreams to sell

Song for voice and piano. Text by Thomas Lowell Beddoes (1803–49).
**Duration:** 1' 50".
**Publication:** Winthrop Rogers Ltd. Vocal score © 1918. Now Boosey & Hawkes Ltd. 3 versions were published: in E flat, F, and D flat major. Also included in volume v of *The Complete Works for Voice and Piano*, Stainer & Bell © 1981.

**Bibliography:**   R. Fiske, 'Ireland: Songs', *Gramophone*, 53/626 (July 1975), 227–8.
M. Kennedy, 'A Treasury of English Song', *Gramophone*, 64/764 (Jan. 1987), 1055–6.
N.P., ['If there were dreams'], *Gramophone*, 2/2 (July 1924), 60–1.
**Recordings:**   George Baker (baritone) and Mme Adami (piano), HMV B1816 (1924) *in* HMV Treasury EX 290911-3, EX 290911-5 (1987).
Benjamin Luxon (baritone) and Alan Rowlands (piano) *in* Lyrita SRCS 66 (1975).
George Parker (baritone) and Sidney Twemlow (piano), BBC Transcription 18759, BBC Sound Archive 6812.

OTHER VERSIONS

**If there were dreams to sell**

Song arranged for voice, harp, and strings by F. Bye (in F and D flat major).
Unpublished.
**Bibliography:**   M. Kennedy, 'English Orchestral Songs', *Gramophone*, 67/800 (Jan. 1990), 1366.
**Recordings:**   Stephen Varcoe (bass-baritone) and City of London Sinfonia/Richard Hickox *in* Chandos ABRD 1382, ABTD 1382, CHAN 8743 (1990).

**If there were dreams to sell**

Song arranged for voice and orchestra by E. Griffiths (in F major).
**Instrumentation:**   2 flutes, 2 oboes, 2 clarinets, 2 bassoons, 4 horns, 2 trumpets, 3 trombones, timpani, percussion, harp, and strings.
Unpublished.

## The Sacred Flame

Song for voice and piano. Text by Mary Coleridge (1861–1907), from *Poems* (1907), edited posthumously by Henry Newbolt.
**Duration:**   1' 45".
**Publication:**   Winthrop Rogers Ltd. Vocal score © 1918. Now Boosey & Hawkes Ltd. 2 versions were published: in C and B flat major. Also included in volume i of *The Complete Works for Voice and Piano*, Stainer & Bell © 1981.
**Bibliography:**   E. Greenfield, 'Ireland', *Gramophone*, 41/492 (May 1964), 513.
T. Harvey, 'Ireland: Songs', *Gramophone*, 57/678 (Nov. 1979), 895.
**Recordings:**   John Mitchinson (tenor) and Alan Rowlands (piano) *in* Lyrita SRCS 118 (1979).
John Shirley-Quirk (baritone) and Eric Parkin (piano) *in* Saga XID 7015, XID 5207 (1964).

## Leaves from a Child's Sketchbook

For solo piano.
1. By the Mere (Allegretto)
2. In the Meadow (Moderato)
3. The Hunt's Up (Con brio)

**Duration:**   1—1' 00"; 2—2' 30"; 3—1' 00".
**Publication:**   Winthrop Rogers Ltd. Score © 1918. Now Boosey & Hawkes Ltd. Reissued: Augener Ltd. Score [© 1961]. Now Stainer & Bell Ltd. Also included in volume ii of *The Collected Piano Works of John Ireland*, Stainer & Bell © 1976.
**Bibliography:**   Anon., 'Reviews: Pianoforte Music', *Musical Times*, 59 (June 1918), 258.

## Merry Andrew

For solo piano.
**Dedication:**   To William Murdoch.[20]
**Duration:**   4'.
**First performance:**   London, February 1920. York Bowen (piano).
**Publication:**   Ascherberg, Hopwood and Crew Ltd. Score © 1919 (Repertoire Series no. 2). Later Chappell & Co. Ltd. Now Warner & Co. Ltd. Also included in volume ii of *The Collected Piano Works of John Ireland*, Stainer & Bell © 1976.
**Bibliography:**   A. Kalisch, 'London Concerts', *Musical Times*, 61/925 (Mar. 1920), 177–8.
   E. Markham Lee, 'The Amateur's Repertoire', *Musical Opinion*, 52 (July 1929), 908–9.
   C. Palmer, 'Ireland: Piano Works', *Gramophone*, 53/631 (Dec. 1975), 1082.
   A. Robertson, 'Ireland: Piano Works', *Gramophone*, 48/566 (July 1970), 191–2.
**Recordings:**   York Bowen (piano), NSA Archive LP 25575.
   Eric Parkin (piano), NSA tape M619W *in* Lyrita SRCS 87 (1975).
   Alan Rowlands (piano) *in* Lyrita RCS 29 (1970).

OTHER VERSIONS

**Merry Andrew**

Arranged for small orchestra by James Brash.
**Date of arrangement:**   December 1934.

---

[20] William Murdoch (1888–1942): Pianist. Born in Australia and came to England at 17 and studied at the RCM. Made his reputation as a chamber music player, especially in association with Albert Sammons.

**Instrumentation:** Flute, oboe, clarinet in A, cor anglais, alto saxophone in E flat, tenor saxophone in B flat, 2 horns in E flat, bassoon, trombone, tuba, timpani, and strings.
Unpublished.

**Merry Andrew**

Arranged for orchestra by G. H. Clutsam.
**Instrumentation:** Flute, oboe, 2 clarinets, bassoon, 2 horns, 2 trumpets, trombone, timpani, percussion, harp, and strings.
Unpublished.

## Mother and Child

Songs for voice and piano. Text by Christina Rossetti (1830–94), from *Sing-Song: A Nursery Rhyme Book* (1873).

1. Newborn (Moderato)
2. The Only Child (Moderato)
3. Hope (Allegretto)
4. Skylark and Nightingale (Allegretto)
5. The Blind Boy (Andante moderato)
6. Baby (Allegretto)
7. Death-Parting (Moderato con moto)
8. The Garland (Poco andante)

**Dedication:** To my sister.
**Duration:** 1—1′ 00″; 2—1′ 30″; 3—0′ 50″; 4—0′ 50″; 5—1′ 00″; 6—1′ 00″; 7—1′ 50″; 8—1′ 10″.
**Publication:** Winthrop Rogers Ltd. Vocal score © 1918. Now Boosey & Hawkes Ltd. No. 1 ('Newborn') was published separately in 1918 under the title 'Your brother has a falcon'. No. 4 ('Skylark and Nightingale') was also published separately in 1918. Also included in volume ii of *The Complete Works for Voice and Piano*, Stainer & Bell © 1981.
**Bibliography:** T. Harvey, 'Ireland: Songs', *Gramophone*, 57/678 (Nov. 1979), 895.
**Recordings:** Alfreda Hodgson (contralto) and Alan Rowlands (piano) *in* Lyrita SRCS 118 (1979).

## Remember

Song for voice and piano. Text by Mary Coleridge (1861–1907), from *Not Yet in Fancy's Following* (1896).
**Duration:** 1′ 35″.
**Publication:** Winthrop Rogers Ltd. Vocal score © 1918. Now Boosey & Hawkes Ltd. 3 versions were published: in D, C, and B flat major. Also

included in volume i of *The Complete Works for Voice and Piano*, Stainer & Bell © 1981.
**Bibliography:** T. Harvey, 'Ireland: Songs', *Gramophone*, 57/678 (Nov. 1979), 895.
**Recordings:** John Mitchinson (tenor) and Alan Rowlands (piano) *in* Lyrita SRCS 118 (1979).

## A Song of March

Unison song for equal voices and piano. Text by James Vila Blake.
**Publication:** Edward Arnold Ltd. Vocal score © 1918 (Singing Music Class no. 24).

## The Towing Path

For solo piano.
**Duration:** 4' 00".
**Publication:** Augener & Co. Ltd. Score © 1919. Now Stainer & Bell Ltd. Also included in volume ii of *The Collected Piano Works of John Ireland*, Stainer & Bell © 1976.
**Location of manuscript:** Manuscript Collections, The British Library (Reference Division), Add. MS 52891. It is dated: Pangbourne, 1918.
**Bibliography:** M. Macdonald, 'Ireland', *Gramophone*, 42/497 (Oct. 1964), 201.
C. Palmer, 'Ireland: Piano Works', *Gramophone*, 53/631 (Dec. 1975), 1082.
**Recordings:** *Graham Mitchell (piano), Argo U1005.
Eric Parkin (piano) *in* Lyrita SRCS 87 (1975).
Alan Rowlands (piano) *in* Lyrita RCS 24 (1964).

## (Three) Variations on 'Cadet Rousselle'

Arrangement of the French folk song for voice and piano. Text in French.
**Dedication:** To our good friend, Edwin Evans, who suggested this collaboration.[21]
**Duration:** 3' 32".
**First performance:** London, Aeolian Hall, 6 June 1919. Raimond Collignon (soprano) and Harriet Cohen (piano). However, it may have been earlier, on 27 April 1918.
**Publication:** J. & W. Chester Ltd. Vocal score © 1920 (Repertoire Collignon no. 1).
**Recordings:** Ian Partridge (tenor) and Jennifer Partridge (piano), NSA M4674W.

---

[21] Edwin Evans (1874–1945): Music critic for the *Daily Mail*, *Liverpool Post*, and *Time and Tide*. President of the ISCM and Chairman of the British section.

**Notes:** It was at the suggestion of the music critic Edwin Evans that four of his composer friends should make arrangements of the tune for voice and piano. Frank Bridge arranged variations 1, 3, and 6; Arnold Bax arranged variations 2, 5, and 12; John Ireland arranged variations 4, 8, and 9; Eugene Goossens arranged variations 7, 10, and 11. In a note from Ireland to Edwin Evans, dated 13 June [1919], he wrote, '... please regard them as a little personal tribute to yourself and treat them as your own property' (Ireland Trust Archive).

OTHER VERSIONS

**Variations on 'Cadet Rousselle'**

Arranged for orchestra by Eugene Goossens.
**Date of arrangement:** 1930.
**Instrumentation:** 2 flutes, 2 oboes, 2 clarinets in B flat, bassoon, 2 horns in F, trumpet in C, timpani, percussion (3 players: side-drum, triangle, tambourine, glockenspiel, xylophone, tubular bells, cymbals), harp, and strings.
**Dedication:** To our good friend, Edwin Evans, who suggested this collaboration.
**Publication:** J. & W. Chester Ltd. Full score © 1931. It is dated: December 1930, Cincinnati.
**Notes:** Goossens scored ten of the twelve variations for small orchestra—nos. 9 and 10 were omitted.

## Irene

Hymn tune for mixed chorus (SATB) and organ. Text ('God of Nations') by Alfred Moss.
**Publication:** Hunter & Longhurst Ltd. Vocal score © 1918 (no. 2 of *Three Hymns for the Celebration of Peace*).

# 1918–1919

## Three Songs

For voice and piano. Text by Arthur Symons (1865–1945).

1. The Adoration (Allegretto con moto), from *The Loom of Dreams* (1901)
2. Rest: Respos (Tranquillo e sostenuto), from *The Loom of Dreams* (1901)
3. The Rat (Lento), from *Amoris victima* (1897).

**Duration:** 1—2' 30"; 2—2' 30"; 3—1' 40".
**First performance:** Unable to trace. Marguerite d'Alvarez may have sung them.
**Publication:** J. & W. Chester Ltd. Vocal score: no. 1—© 1919; 3 versions were published: in A flat minor, B minor, and F sharp minor. No. 2—

© 1920; 'Rest' also appeared as a music supplement to the *Chesterian* in February 1923 (J. & W. Chester © 1923). A French version by G. Jean-Aubry was also provided for the first and second songs. English and French versions: Chester Music [© 1980]. No. 3—© 1919. Also included in volume ii of *The Complete Works for Voice and Piano*, Stainer & Bell © 1981.

**Location of manuscript:** Manuscript Collections, The British Library (Reference Division), Add. MS 52899. No. 1 is dated: October 1918; no. 2 is dated: Chelsea: July 1920; no. 3 is signed by the composer and dated: 1918. The key signatures in the original manuscript differ from those in the printed copy:

| *Original* | *Printed copy* |
| --- | --- |
| 1. F sharp minor | B flat minor |
| 2. B flat minor | B flat minor |
| 3. A flat minor | B minor |

**Bibliography:** T. Harvey, 'Ireland: Songs', *Gramophone*, 57/678 (Nov. 1979), 895.

**Recordings:** Alfreda Hodgson (contralto) and Alan Rowlands (piano) *in* Lyrita SRCS 118 (1979).

## 1918–1920

### Sonata in E minor-major

For solo piano. In three movements:

1. Allegro moderato
2. Non troppo lento
3. Con moto moderato

**Duration:** 25'.

**First performance:** London, 12 June 1920. Frederic Lamond (piano).[22]

**Publication:** Augener & Co. Ltd. Score © 1920. Now Stainer & Bell Ltd. The printed copy is dated: Chelsea: October 1918 to January 1930 [*sic*]. Revised by the composer (1951), Augener & Co. Ltd. [© 1951]. Also included in volume v of *The Collected Piano Works of John Ireland*, Stainer & Bell © 1976.

**Location of manuscript:** Manuscript Collections, The British Library (Reference Division), Add. MS 52891.

**Bibliography:** M. Child, 'New Music', *Musical Times*, 61 (Aug. 1920), 556.

M. Harrison, 'Ireland: Piano Works', *Gramophone*, 54/647 (Apr. 1977), 1573–4.

A. Kalisch, 'London Concerts', *Musical Times*, 61/929 (July 1920), 462–3.

---

[22] Frederick Lamond (1868–1948): Studied piano with von Bülow and Liszt, and was a composer of symphonies, overtures, trios, and sonatas. He was later a professor at the Scottish National Academy of Music.

F. Lamond, 'Some Remarks on John Ireland's New Sonata', *Monthly Musical Record*, 50 (Aug. 1920), 170–2.

M. Macdonald, 'Ireland', *Gramophone*, 42/497 (Oct. 1964), 201.

A. Robertson, 'Ireland', *Gramophone*, 41/492 (May 1964), 523.

L. Salter, 'Ireland', *Gramophone*, 31/360 (June 1953), 17.

**Recordings:** Frank Merrick (piano), Frank Merrick Society FMS 8 (1964).
Eric Parkin (piano) *in* Argo ARS 1004 RG 4 (1953), *in* Lyrita SRCS 88 (1977).
Alan Rowlands (piano) *in* Lyrita RCS 24 (1964).

## 1919

## May Flowers

Song for 2-part chorus (SS) and piano. Text by Christian Rossetti (1830–94).
**Date of composition:** January 1919.
**Dedication:** For Lillian.
**Publication:** Edward Arnold & Co. Ltd. Vocal score © 1919 (Singing Class Music no. 136).

## Benedicite in F major

For mixed chorus (SATB) and organ. Text from the Book of Common Prayer.
**Publication:** J. Curwen & Co. Ltd. Vocal score © 1920 (Church Choralist no. 586). Now Music Sales Ltd. Novello & Co. Ltd. Vocal score © 1942 (PCB 1254).
**Notes:** See also Te Deum in F (1907), Benedictus in F (1912), Jubilate in F (1914), Magnificat and Nunc Dimittis in F (1915).

## Love Unknown

Hymn tune for mixed chorus (SATB) and organ. Text ('My song is love unknown') by Samuel Crossman (*c.* 1624–64).
**Duration:** *c.* 3' (five verses).
**Publication:** *The Public School Hymn Book*, edited by a committee of the Headmasters' Conference © 1920. Later included in the first edition of *Songs of Praise* (OUP, 1925).
**Bibliography:** T. Harvey, 'Ireland: Choral Works', *Gramophone*, 57/673 (June 1979), 93–4.
**Recordings:** Rodney Christian Fellowship Choir/G. Bennson (organ)/R. Smith-Bishton *in* HMV CLP 3638, CSD 3638.
Royal School of Church Music Choir, 1965 in RM1/2, RS1/2.

Worcester Cathedral Choir/Worcester Festival Choral Society/Paul Trepte (organ)/Donald Hunt *in* Abbey LPB 803 (1979).

OTHER VERSIONS

**Love Unknown**

Hymn tune arranged for mixed chorus (SATB), orchestra, and organ by Robert Stewart.
**Commissioned by:** The BBC for *Songs of Praise*.
**First performance:** Rochester, Cathedral Church of Christ and the Blessed Virgin Mary, 1 December 1988. Local schools' orchestras, conducted by Paul Hale. This recording was subsequently shown on BBC1, 19 March 1989 (Palm Sunday).
Unpublished.

**My song is love unknown**

Hymn anthem for solo soprano, mixed chorus (SATB), and piano, arranged by Betty Pulkingham.
**Date of arrangement:** 1975.
**Publication:** Celebration Services (International) Ltd. Vocal score © 1975.

**My song is love unknown**

Hymn tune arranged for 21 bells (3 octaves) by John Folkening.
**Publication:** John Ireland Trust (Tune) © 1989/Concordia Publishing House, St Louis © 1989, in *Ten Hymn Accompaniments for Handbells*, Set 2, by John Folkening.

## Hawthorn Time

Song for voice and piano. Text by A. E. Housman (1859–1936), from *A Shropshire Lad* (1896), no. xxxix.
**Duration:** 1' 30".
**Publication:** Winthrop Rogers Ltd. Vocal score © 1919. Now Boosey & Hawkes Ltd. 2 versions were published: in C and B flat major. Also included in volume i of *The Complete Works for Voice and Piano*, Stainer & Bell © 1981.
**Bibliography:** T. Harvey, 'Ireland: Songs', *Gramophone*, 57/678 (Nov. 1979), 895.
**Recordings:** John Mitchinson (tenor) and Alan Rowlands (piano) *in* Lyrita SRCS 118 (1979).

## Mighty Father

Hymn tune for mixed chorus (SATB) and organ. Text ('Mighty Father, thou whose aid') based on a hymn by Charles Wesley.

**Publication:** *The Public School Hymn Book*, edited by a committee of the Headmasters' Conference © 1920.

## Summer Evening

For solo piano.
**Duration:** 5'.
**Publication:** Ascherberg, Hopwood & Crew Ltd. Score © 1920 (Repertoire Series no. 13). Later Chappell & Co. Ltd. Now Warner & Co. Ltd. Also included in volume ii of *The Collected Piano Works of John Ireland*, Stainer & Bell © 1976.
**Bibliography:** M. Harrison, 'Ireland: Piano Works', *Gramophone*, 54/647 (Apr. 1977), 1573–4.
A. Robertson, 'Ireland: Piano Works', *Gramophone*, 48/566 (July 1970), 191–2.
**Recordings:** Eric Parkin (piano) *in* Lyrita SRCS 88 (1977).
Alan Rowlands (piano) *in* Lyrita RCS 28 (1970).

## Fraternity

Hymn tune for mixed chorus (SATB) and organ. Text ('These things shall be') by J. A. Symonds. Written at the request of Geoffrey Shaw.
**Publication:** Stainer & Bell Ltd. Vocal score © 1919 (in USA). Also included in volume i of the official publication of the League of the Arts for National and Civic Ceremony, *The Motherland Song Book*, for unison and mixed voices.

### 1920

## Two Songs

For voice and piano.
  1. The Trellis (Moderato). Text by Aldous Huxley (1894–1963), from *Oxford Poetry* (1918).
  2. My true love hath my heart (Con anima ma non troppo mosso). Text by Sir Philip Sydney (1554–86), from *The Countess of Pembroke's Arcadia* (1580).

**Duration:** 1—3' 00"; 2—1' 40".
**Publication:** Augener & Co. Ltd. Now Stainer & Bell Ltd. Vocal score: 1— © 1920; 2—© 1921. 2 versions were published of each: 1—in A flat and F major; 2—in E and G major. Also included in volume i of *The Complete Works for Voice and Piano*, Stainer & Bell © 1981, and in *Eleven Songs by John Ireland* (introduced by John Longmire), Stainer & Bell/Galaxy © 1970.

**Location of manuscript:** Manuscript Collections, The British Library (Reference Division), Add. MS 52899. Ireland records at the end of each manuscript that the music was 'completed' in January 1920 (1) and February 1920 (2).
**Bibliography:**   R. Fiske, 'Ireland', *Gramophone*, 42/498 (Nov. 1964), 239.
  T. Harvey, 'Ireland: Songs', *Gramophone*, 57/678 (Nov. 1979), 895.
**Recordings:**   No. 1:
  Peter Pears (tenor) and Benjamin Britten (piano) *in* Argo RG 418, ZRG 5418 (1964).
  Complete:
  John Mitchinson (tenor) and Alan Rowlands (piano) *in* Lyrita SRCS 118 (1979).

## The Darkened Valley

For solo piano.
**Duration:**   4'.
**Publication:**   Augener Ltd. Score © 1921. Now Stainer & Bell Ltd. Also included in volume ii of *The Collected Piano Works of John Ireland*, Stainer & Bell © 1976.
**Location of manuscript:** Manuscript Collections, The British Library (Reference Division), Add. MS 52889. It is dated: May 1920. The original version is written in A flat minor and marked 'Allegretto poco sostenuto'. However, this was altered to G minor for the printed copy, which is marked 'Allegretto sostenuto'.
**Bibliography:**   Anon., 'Reviews of New Publications', *Monthly Musical Record*, 51 (Nov. 1921), 254.
  M. Harrison, 'Ireland: Piano Works', *Gramophone*, 54/647 (Apr. 1977), 1573–4.
  M. Macdonald, 'Ireland', *Gramophone*, 42/497 (Oct. 1964), 201.
**Recordings:**   Eric Parkin (piano) *in* Lyrita SRCS 88 (1977).
  Alan Rowlands (piano) *in* Lyrita RCS 24 (1964).
**Notes:**   The music is prefaced by a quotation from William Blake (1757–1827):

> Walking along the darkened valley
> With silent melancholy.

## When May is in his prime

Song for unaccompanied mixed chorus (SATB). Text by Richard Edwardes (1523–66).
**Date of composition:**   1920 ('Southwater').

**Publication:** Novello & Co. Ltd. Vocal score © 1920 (*Novello's Part-Song Book*, 2nd series: no. 1384).

## The East Riding

Song for voice and piano. Text by Eric Chilman.
**Duration:** 1' 30".
**Publication:** Enoch & Sons Ltd. Vocal score © 1920. 3 versions were published: in C, A, and G minor. Also included in volume i of *The Complete Works for Voice and Piano*, Stainer & Bell © 1981.
**Bibliography:** T. Harvey, 'Ireland: Songs', *Gramophone*, 57/678 (Nov. 1979), 895.
**Recordings:** John Mitchinson (tenor) and Alan Rowlands (piano) *in* Lyrita SRCS 118 (1979).

## The Journey

Song for voice and piano. Text by Ernest Blake.
**Duration:** 1'.
**Publication:** Enoch & Sons Ltd. Vocal score © 1920. 3 versions were published: in C, D, and B flat major. Also included in volume v of *The Complete Works for Voice and Piano*, Stainer & Bell © 1981.
**Bibliography:** R. Fiske, 'Ireland: Songs', *Gramophone*, 53/626 (July 1975), 227–8.
**Recordings:** Benjamin Luxon (baritone) and Alan Rowlands (piano) *in* Lyrita SRCS 66 (1975).

## The Three Ravens

Arranged for voice and piano. Text and melody traditional.
**Duration:** 3' 30".
**Publication:** Winthrop Rogers & Co. Ltd. Vocal score © 1920. Now Boosey & Hawkes Ltd. 2 versions were published: in F and G minor. Also included in volume v of *The Complete Works for Voice and Piano*, Stainer & Bell © 1981.
**Bibliography:** T. Harvey, 'Ireland: Songs', *Gramophone*, 57/678 (Nov. 1979), 895.
**Recordings:** Alfreda Hodgson (contralto) and Alan Rowlands (piano) *in* Lyrita SRCS 118 (1979).

## 1920–1921

## The Land of Lost Content

Song cycle for voice and piano. Text by A. E. Housman (1859–1936), from *A Shropshire Lad* (1896).

| | |
|---|---|
| 1. The Lent Lilly (Andantino con moto) | no. XXIX |
| 2. Ladslove (Poco sostenuto) | no. LI |
| 3. Goal and Wicket (Vivace) | no. XVII |
| 4. The Vain Desire (In tempo moderato) | no. XXXIII |
| 5. The Encounter (Allegro alla marcia) | no. XXII |
| 6. Epilogue (Allegretto con moto—Sostenuto, con moto moderato in the manuscript) | no. LVII |

**Duration:** 1—2' 15"; 2—2' 10"; 3—1' 05"; 4—2' 15"; 5—1' 15"; 6—1' 25".

**Publication:** Augener & Co. Ltd. Vocal score © 1921. Now Stainer & Bell Ltd. 2 versions of each song were published: 1—D and E minor; 2—F and A flat major; 3—C sharp and E minor; 4—F sharp and A minor; 5—A and C major; 6—B flat and D flat major. All numbers were published separately, Augener & Co. Ltd. [© 1922]. Also included in volume i of *The Complete Works for Voice and Piano*, Stainer & Bell © 1981, and in *The Land of Lost Content and Other Songs by John Ireland* (with an introduction by John Longmire), Galliard/Stainer & Bell © 1976.

**Location of manuscript:** Manuscript Collections, The British Library (Reference Division), Add. MS 52898. No. 3 is dated: 22 November 1920; no. 4 is dated: Dies Irae. 8 January 1921; no. 6 is dated: October 1920–January 1921.

**Bibliography:** Anon., 'Reviews of New Publications', *Monthly Musical Record*, 51 (Nov. 1921), 255.

R. Fiske, 'English Songs', *Gramophone*, 53/632 (Jan. 1976), 1229.

—— 'Ireland', *Gramophone*, 42/498 (Nov. 1964), 239.

T. Harvey, 'Ireland: Songs', *Gramophone*, 57/678 (Nov. 1979), 895.

**Recordings:** John Mitchinson (tenor) and Alan Rowlands (piano) *in* Lyrita SRCS 118 (1979).

Peter Pears (tenor) and Benjamin Britten (piano) *in* Argo RG 418, ZRG 5418 (1964).

Peter Pears (tenor) and Benjamin Britten (piano), BBC Transcription 101167.

Peter Pears (tenor) and John Ireland (piano) (from the composer's collection), NSA tape M608W.

Anthony Rolfe Johnson (tenor) and David Willison (piano) *in* Polydor Select 2460 258 (1976).

**Notes:** This song cycle was composed for Gervase Henry Elwes, but never performed by him, owing to his death in January 1921.

## Mai-Dun

For full orchestra.
**Instrumentation:** 3 flutes and piccolo, 2 oboes and cor anglais, 2 clarinets in A, bass clarinet in A, 2 bassoons, 4 horns in F, 3 trumpets in C, 3 trombones, tuba, timpani, percussion (3 players: side-drum, cymbals, triangle, tambourine, glockenspiel), and strings.
**Duration:** 13'.
**First performance:** London, Queen's Hall, Monday 12 December 1921. The Goossens Symphony Orchestra, conducted by Eugene Goossens.
**Second performance:** London, Queen's Hall, 27 September 1922. The New Queen's Hall Orchestra, conducted by Henry Wood.
**Publication:** Augener & Co. Ltd. Full score and parts © 1923. Miniature score © 1930. Now Stainer & Bell Ltd.
**Location of manuscript:** Manuscript Collections, The British Library (Reference Division), Add. MS 52874. It is initialled and dated: J.I. 1920–1921.
**Bibliography:** M. Harrison, 'English Music', *Gramophone*, 62/736 (Sept. 1984), 336.
R. Layton, 'Ireland', *Gramophone*, 64/764 (Jan. 1987), 1022.
M. Oliver, 'Ireland', *Gramophone*, 64/760 (Sept. 1986), 376.
E.R., 'Orchestral', *Monthly Musical Record*, 79 (Jan.–Apr. 1949), 162.
A. Robertson, 'Ireland', *Gramophone*, 44/520 (Sept. 1966), 157–8.
L. Salter, 'Ireland', *Gramophone*, 29/341 (Oct. 1951), 99.
**Recordings:** *Hallé Orchestra/John Barbirolli, HMV DB 9651/2 (1951), *in* HMV EX 290107-3, EX 290107-5 (1984).
London Philharmonic Orchestra/Adrian Boult *in* Lyrita RCS 32, SRCS 32 (1966), Musical Heritage Society 1317.
London Philharmonic Orchestra/Bryden Thomson *in* Chandos ABRD 1174, ABTD 1174 (1986), CHAN 8461 (1987).
**Notes:** According to a programme note (p. 15) written by Ireland for the third performance in Leeds Town Hall on 7 October 1922 by the London Symphony Orchestra, conducted by Albert Coates, this 'Symphonic Rhapsody' (as it was first called) was sketched in October 1920 and completed in November 1921.

## OTHER VERSIONS

### The Vagabonds

Ballet in three scenes:

1. The Journey to the Encampment
2. The Encampment
3. The Aftermath

The music of *Mai-Dun* and the 'Threnody' from *Concertino pastorale* (1939) was used.

**First performance:** London, Sadler's Wells Theatre, 29 October 1946. The Sadler's Wells Theatre Ballet (director: Ninette de Valois). Cast included June Brae, Alan Carter, Leo Kersley, and Pamela Chrimes. John Cranko and Kenneth Macmillan are mentioned in the programme as Vagabond Men. Choreography: Anthony Burke; Décor: Vivienne Kernot; Costumes: Mathilda Etches; Musical Director: Harry Platts.

Synopsis: Two couples are travelling to the encampment for the night. There is rivalry between the two men for the vagabond girl. A fight ensues in which her lover kills his rival. The gypsies turn upon him, try him and kill him. The girl is left insane with remorse and dies. She and her lover are united in death.

**Bibliography:** Anon., 'Sadler's Wells Ballet', *The Times*, 30 Oct. 1946, p. 6.
Anon., 'The Vagabonds', *Dancing Times* (Dec. 1946), 116–18.
R. Hill, 'Mediocre, but not very', *Daily Mail*, 30 Oct. 1946, p. 3.

### Mai-Dun

Arranged for piano duet by the composer.
**Date of arrangement:** [1931].
**Publication:** Augener & Co. Ltd. Score © 1931. Now Stainer & Bell Ltd.
**Location of manuscript:** Manuscript Collections, The British Library (Reference Division), Add. MS 52874.

# 1921

# Two Pieces

For solo piano.

1. For Remembrance (Andantino con moto)
2. Amberley Wild Brooks (Con moto moderato, quasi allegro comodo)

**Duration:** 1—4'; 2—3'.
**Publication:** Augener & Co. Ltd. Score © 1921. Now Stainer & Bell Ltd. Also included in volume ii of *The Collected Piano Works of John Ireland*, Stainer & Bell © 1976.
**Location of manuscript:** Manuscript Collections, The British Library (Reference Division), Add. MS 52891. No. 1 is dated: February 1921; no. 2 is dated: June 1921.

**Bibliography:** Anon., 'Two Pieces', *Monthly Musical Record*, 51 (Nov. 1921), 254.
M. Harrison, 'Ireland: Piano Works', *Gramophone*, 54/647 (Apr. 1977), 1573–4.
E. Markham Lee, 'The Amateur's Repertoire', *Musical Opinion*, 52 (July 1929), 908–9.
A. Robertson, 'Ireland', *Gramophone*, 41/483 (Aug. 1963), 111–12.
—— 'Ireland: Piano Works', *Gramophone*, 48/560 (July 1970), 191–2.
**Recordings:** No. 1:
John Clegg (piano) *in* Alpha DB148C.
Alan Rowlands (piano) *in* Lyrita RCS 23 (1963).
No. 2:
John Clegg (piano) *in* Alpha DB148C.
*Graham Mitchell (piano), Argo U1004.
Eric Parkin (piano) *in* Argo RG 28, *in* Lyrita SRCS 88 (1977).
Alan Rowlands (piano) *in* Lyrita RCS 29 (1970).
Phyllis Sellick (piano), BBC Sound Archive T30897.

## Love is a sickness full of woes

Song for voice and piano. Text by Samuel Daniel (*c.*1562–1619), from *Hymen's Triumph* (1615), act i, scene v.
**Duration:** 1′ 45″.
**Publication:** Winthrop Rogers Ltd. Vocal score © 1921. Now Boosey & Hawkes Ltd. 3 versions were published: in G flat major, F major, and E flat major. Also included in volume i of *The Complete Works for Voice and Piano*, Stainer & Bell © 1981.
**Location of manuscript:** Manuscript Collections, The British Library (Reference Division), Add. MS 52898. It is in E flat major and dated: July 1921.
**Bibliography:** T. Harvey, 'Ireland: Songs', *Gramophone*, 57/678 (Nov. 1979), 895.
**Recordings:** John Mitchinson (baritone) and Alan Rowlands (piano) *in* Lyrita SRCS 118 (1979), *in* ZRG 898, KZRC 898 (1979).

## The Merry Month of May

Song for voice and piano. Text by Thomas Dekker (*c.*1570–*c.*1641), from *The Shoemaker's Holiday* (1600), 'The First Three-Man's Song'.
**Date of composition:** July 1921.
**Duration:** 1′ 30″.
**Publication:** Winthrop Rogers Ltd. Vocal score © 1921. Now Boosey & Hawkes Ltd. 3 versions were published: in E major, G major, and D major.

Also included in volume v of *The Complete Works for Voice and Piano*, Stainer & Bell © 1981.
**Bibliography:** R. Fiske, 'Ireland: Songs', *Gramophone*, 53/626 (July 1975), 227–8.
E. Greenfield, 'Ireland', *Gramophone*, 41/492 (May 1964), 513.
**Recordings:** Benjamin Luxon (baritone) and Alan Rowlands (piano) *in* Lyrita SRCS 66 (1975).
John Shirley-Quirk (baritone) and Eric Parkin (piano) *in* Saga XID 7015, XID 5207 (1964).

## The Ferry

Unison song for equal voices and piano. Text by Christina Rossetti (1830–94).
**Publication:** Edward Arnold & Co. Ltd. Vocal score © 1921 (Singing Class Music no. 45).

## Fain would I change that note

Song for unaccompanied mixed chorus (SATB). Text by Tobias Hume (?–1645), from *The First Part of Airs* (1605).
**Duration:** 2' 10".
**Publication:** Novello & Co. Ltd. Vocal score © 1921. This song appeared as a supplement of the *Musical Times*, 62/941 (July 1921).

## 1922

## On a Birthday Morning

For solo piano.
**Date of composition:** 1922.
**Dedication:** Pro amicitia [for friendship].
**Duration:** 4'.
**Publication:** Augener & Co. Ltd. Score © 1922. Now Stainer & Bell Ltd. Also included in volume ii of *The Collected Piano Works of John Ireland*, Stainer & Bell © 1976.
**Location of manuscript:** Manuscript Collections, The British Library (Reference Division), Add. MS 52890. It is dated: 22 February 1922.
**Bibliography:** Anon., 'On a Birthday Morning', *Monthly Musical Record*, 52 (Aug. 1922), 189.
M. Harrison, 'Ireland: Piano Works', *Gramophone*, 54/647 (Apr. 1977), 1573–4.
J. Noble, 'Ireland', *Gramophone*, 38/449 (Oct. 1960), 328.

**Recordings:** Eric Parkin (piano) *in* Lyrita SRCS 88 (1977).
Alan Rowlands (piano) *in* Lyrita RCS 15 (1960).
**Notes:** This piece is the first in a series of piano works and songs which Ireland wrote annually during the 1920s to commemorate the birthday (on 22 February) of his friend Arthur G. Miller (A.G.M.). Miller was the son of a Chelsea antique dealer from whose shop Ireland bought several items of furniture. A chorister at St Luke's Church, where Ireland was organist and choirmaster, Miller became such a valued friend that in about 1932 the composer made a will leaving all his estate to him. It was only in the last years of his life that he changed the will to make Mrs Norah Kirby, his companion, his legatee.

## The Vagabond

Song for voice and piano. Text by John Masefield (1879–1967), from *Saltwater Ballads* (1902).
**Duration:** 1' 45".
**Publication:** Augener & Co. Ltd. Vocal score © 1922. Now Stainer & Bell Ltd. 4 versions were published: in B flat major, A flat major, G major, and F major. Also included in volume ii of *The Complete Works for Voice and Piano*, Stainer & Bell © 1981, and in *Eleven Songs by John Ireland* (introduced by John Longmire), Stainer & Bell/Galaxy © 1970.
**Location of manuscript:** Manuscript Collections, The British Library (Reference Division), Add. MS 52899. It is dated: February, 1922.
**Bibliography:** R. Fiske, 'Ireland: Songs', *Gramophone*, 53/626 (July 1975), 227–8.
**Recordings:** Benjamin Luxon (baritone) and Alan Rowlands (piano) *in* Lyrita SRCS 66 (1975).

## Soliloquy

For solo piano.
**Duration:** 3'.
**Publication:** Augener & Co. Ltd. Score © 1922. Now Stainer & Bell Ltd. Also included in volume ii of *The Complete Piano Works of John Ireland*, Stainer & Bell © 1976.
**Location of manuscript:** Manuscript Collections, The British Library (Reference Division), Add. MS 52890. It is dated: March 1922.
**Bibliography:** Anon., 'Soliloquy', *Monthly Musical Record*, 52 (Aug. 1922), 189.
M. Harrison, 'Ireland: Piano Works', *Gramophone*, 54/647 (Apr. 1977), 1573–4.
J. Noble, 'Ireland', *Gramophone*, 38/449 (Oct. 1960), 238.

**Recordings:** *Graham Mitchell (piano), Argo U1005.
Eric Parkin (piano) *in* Lyrita SRCS 88 (1977).
Alan Rowlands (piano) *in* Lyrita RCS 15 (1960).

## Twilight Night

Song for unaccompanied mixed chorus (SATB). Text by Christina Rossetti (1830–94).
**Date of composition:** 3 September 1922.
**Duration:** 2′ 35″.
**Publication:** Novello & Co. Ltd. Vocal score © 1923. This song appeared as a supplement of the *Musical Times*, 64/964 (June 1923).

## Equinox

For solo piano.
**Date of composition:** 1922.
**Duration:** 2′ 30″.
**Publication:** Augener & Co. Ltd. Score © 1923. Now Stainer & Bell Ltd. Also included in volume ii of *The Collected Piano Works of John Ireland*, Stainer & Bell © 1976.
**Location of manuscript:** Manuscript Collections, The British Library (Reference Division), Add. MS 52889. It is dated: Autumn, 1922.
**Bibliography:** Anon., 'Equinox', *Monthly Musical Record*, 53 (July 1923), 202–3.
M. Harrison, 'Ireland: Piano Works', *Gramophone*, 54/647 (Apr. 1977), 1573–4.
J. Noble, 'Ireland', *Gramophone*, 38/449 (Oct. 1960), 238.
**Recordings:** Eric Parkin (piano) *in* Lyrita SRCS 88 (1977).
Alan Rowlands (piano) *in* Lyrita RCS 15 (1960).

## 1923

## Sonata in G minor

For cello and piano.
  1. Moderato e sostenuto
  2. Poco largamente
  3. Con moto e marcato

**Duration:** *c.* 22′.
**First performance:** London, Aeolian Hall, 4 April 1924. Beatrice Harrison (cello) and Evelyn Howard-Jones (piano).

**Publication:** Augener & Co. Ltd. Score © 1924. Now Stainer & Bell Ltd. The composer later made some revisions which were incorporated in the printed copy, Augener & Co. Ltd. [© 1940/1].

**Location of manuscript:** Manuscript Collections, The British Library (Reference Division), Add. MS 52888. It is dated: December 1923. A movement from an unpublished Cello Sonata can also be found in Add. MS 52900.

**Bibliography:** R. Anderson, 'Ireland', *Musical Times*, 112/1660 (June 1981), 388.

Anon., 'Miss Beatrice Harrison', *Musical Opinion*, 47/560 (May 1924), 789.

J. Brooke, ['Cello Sonata'] in *The Goose Cathedral* (London, Bodley Head, 1950), 92.

R. Fiske, 'Ireland', *Gramophone*, 42/503 (Apr. 1965), 486–7.

M. Harrison, 'Ireland', *Gramophone*, 58/696 (May 1981), 1486.

K.K., ['Cello Sonata'], *Gramophone*, 7/76 (Sept. 1929), 159.

R. Layton, 'Ireland', *Gramophone*, 48/571 (Dec. 1970), 1039.

B.V., 'New Chamber Music', *Musical Times*, 65/978 (Aug. 1924), 716.

E. Warr, 'Ireland', *Gramophone*, 49/588 (May 1972), 1902, 1907.

**Recordings:** André Navarra (cello) and Eric Parkin (piano) *in* Lyrita SRCS 59 (1972).

Derek Simpson (cello) and Leonard Cassini (piano) *in* Summit LSU 3081 (1965), Revolution RCB5 (1970).

Julian Lloyd Webber (cello) and John McCabe (piano) *in* ASV ACA 1001, ZCACA 1001 (1981).

**Notes:** Later printed copies also reveal metronome marks as revised by the composer in 1948. The composer also played the sonata with Thelma Reiss and Antonio Sala (1893–1945), who also recorded the work—see Appendix 1.

From 1923 to 1939, Ireland was a teacher of composition, and a professor of composition at the RCM. Amongst his pupils were Benjamin Britten (1913–76): see *Letters from a Life*, vol. i, ed. Donald Mitchell and Philip Reed (London, Faber, 1991), 146–7, 191, 211, and 229; Alan Bush (1900–   ); Ernest J. Moeran (1894–1950); and Humphrey Searle (1915–82).

## OTHER VERSIONS

### Sonata in G minor for cello and piano

Cello part arranged for viola by Lionel Tertis.

**Date of arrangement:** 1941.

**First performance:** Bedford, BBC Studios, 14 December 1942. Lionel Tertis (viola) and John Ireland (piano). (Broadcast in the BBC Home Service.)

**Publication:** Augener & Co. Ltd. Score © 1941. Now Stainer & Bell Ltd. The

composer later made some revisions which were incorporated in the printed copy, Augener & Co. Ltd. [© 1948].
**Location of manuscript:** Manuscript Collections, The British Library (Reference Division), Add. MS 54432.
**Bibliography:** R. Hill, 'Two First Performances', *Radio Times*, 11 Dec. 1942, p. 4.

## 1924

## Prelude in E flat major

For solo piano.
**Duration:** 5'.
**Publication:** Augener & Co. Ltd. Score © 1925. Now Stainer & Bell Ltd. Also included in volume iii of *The Collected Piano Works of John Ireland*, Stainer & Bell © 1976.
**Location of manuscript:** Manuscript Collections, The British Library (Reference Division), Add. MS 52890. It is dated: 22 February 1924.
**Bibliography:** Anon., 'Prelude in E♭', *Monthly Musical Record*, 55 (Mar. 1925), 78.
C. Palmer, 'Ireland: Piano Works', *Gramophone*, 53/631 (Dec. 1975), 1082.
A. Robertson, 'Ireland: Piano Works', *Gramophone*, 48/566 (July 1970), 191–2.
**Recordings:** Eric Parkin (piano) *in* Argo RG 28 (1970), *in* Lyrita SRCS 87 (1975).
Alan Rowlands (piano) *in* Lyrita RCS 28.
**Notes:** This piece's original title was *Penumbra*.

## When I am dead, my dearest

Song for voice and piano. Text by Christina Rossetti (1830–94), from 'Song' in *Goblin Market and Other Poems* (1862).
**Dedication:** To A.G.M.: Cerne Abbas, June 1925 [A.G.M. was Arthur G. Miller].
**Duration:** 2'.
**Publication:** OUP. Vocal score © 1928. Also included in volume ii of *The Complete Works for Voice and Piano*, Stainer & Bell © 1981.
**Location of manuscript:** Manuscript Collections, The British Library (Reference Division), Add. MS 52899. It is dated: 16 July 1924.
**Bibliography:** R. Fiske, 'Ireland', *Gramophone*, 53/626 (July 1975), 227–8.
**Recordings:** Benjamin Luxon (baritone) and Alan Rowlands (piano) *in* Lyrita SRCS 66 (1975).
  *George Parker (baritone) and Sidney Twemlow (piano), BBC Sound Archive 6814, BBC Transcription 11876.

OTHER VERSIONS

### When I am dead, my dearest

Arranged for voice and string quartet.
**Date of arrangement:** 1924.
**Instrumentation:** Violins I and II, viola, and cello.
**Publication:** OUP. Hire only.
**Location of manuscript:** Manuscript Collections, The British Library (Reference Division), Add. MS 52899.

## What are you thinking of?

Song for voice and piano. Text by Christina Rossetti (1830–94), from *Mother and Child* (published 1896).
**Duration:** 3'.
**Publication:** Stainer & Bell Ltd. Vocal score © 1976. Also included in volume ii of *The Complete Works for Voice and Piano*, Stainer & Bell © 1981, and in *The Land of Lost Content and Other Songs by John Ireland* (with an introduction by John Longmire), Galaxy/Stainer & Bell © 1976.
**Location of manuscript:** Manuscript Collections, The British Library (Reference Division), Add. MS 52899. It is dated: September 1924.
**Bibliography:** T. Harvey, 'Ireland: Songs', *Gramophone*, 57/678 (Nov. 1979), 895.
**Recordings:** Alfreda Hodgson (contralto) and Alan Rowlands (piano) *in* Lyrita SRCS 118 (1979).

## They told me, Heraclitus

Quartet for unaccompanied men's voices (TTBB). Text by William Cory (1823–92), from *Ionica*.
**Dedication:** To Herbert Hughes,[23] and written for the De Reszke Singers.
**Duration:** 2' 15".
**Publication:** Boosey & Co. Ltd. Vocal score © 1924 (Boosey's Modern Festival Series no. 316).

## Chelsea

Hymn tune for mixed chorus (SATB) and organ. Text ('Sing brothers, sing and praise your king') by C. A. Alington.
**Publication:** OUP. This tune was written for *Songs of Praise* (1925) but not included. It did however appear in the *Enlarged Songs of Praise* in 1931.

---

[23] Herbert Hughes (1882–1937): Irish critic and composer. Studied at the RCM. One of the founders of the Irish Folksong Society. Music critic of the *Daily Telegraph*.

# 1925

## Two Pieces

For solo piano.
1. April (Allegretto quasi andantino)
2. Bergomask (Allegro non troppo)

**Duration:** 1—4′ 30″; 2—4′ 00″.
**Publication:** Augener & Co. Ltd. Score © 1925. Now Stainer & Bell Ltd. Also included in volume iii of *The Collected Piano Works of John Ireland*, Stainer & Bell © 1976.
**Location of manuscript:** Manuscript Collections, The British Library (Reference Division), Add. MS 52891. No. 1 is dated: 1925; no. 2 is dated: for 22 February 1925.
**Bibliography:** M. Harrison, 'Ireland: Piano Works', *Gramophone*, 54/647 (Apr. 1977), 1573–4.
—— 'Ireland: Piano Works', *Gramophone*, 57/674 (July 1979), 229–30.
K.K., ['April'], *Gramophone*, 7/76 (Sept. 1929), 159.
A. Robertson, 'Ireland: Piano Works', *Gramophone*, 48/566 (July 1970), 191–2.
**Recordings:** No. 1:
Daniel Adni (piano) *in* HMV HQS 1414 (1979).
John Ogdon (piano) *in* CFP 41514, TC-CFP 4514.
Eric Parkin (piano) *in* Lyrita SRCS 88 (1977).
No. 2:
Alan Rowlands (piano) *in* Lyrita RCS 28 (1970).

## Great Things

Song for voice and piano. Text by Thomas Hardy (1840–1928), from *Moments of Vision* (1917).
**Dedication:** To Alfred Read.
**Duration:** 2′.
**Publication:** Augener & Co. Ltd. Vocal score © 1935. Now Stainer & Bell Ltd. 2 versions were published: in C major and D major. Also included in volume iii of *The Complete Works for Voice and Piano*, Stainer & Bell © 1981, and *Eleven Songs by John Ireland* (introduced by John Longmire), Stainer & Bell/Galaxy © 1970.
**Location of manuscript:** Manuscript Collections, The British Library (Reference Division), Add. MS 52897.
**Bibliography:** R. Fiske, 'Ireland: Songs', *Gramophone*, 53/626 (July 1975), 227–8.
E. Greenfield, 'Ireland', *Gramophone*, 41/492 (May 1964), 513.

**Recordings:** Benjamin Luxon (baritone) and Alan Rowlands (piano) *in* Lyrita SRCS 66 (1975).

John Shirley-Quirk (baritone) and Eric Parkin (piano) *in* Saga XIP 7015, XID 5207 (1964).

## Santa Chiara (Palm Sunday; Naples)

Song for voice and piano. Text by Arthur Symons (1865–1945), from *Images of Good and Evil* (1899).

**Duration:** 2′ 35″.

**Publication:** Augener & Co. Ltd. Vocal score © 1925. Now Stainer & Bell Ltd. 3 versions were published: in G minor, C minor, and A minor. Also included in volume ii of *The Complete Works for Voice and Piano*, Stainer & Bell © 1981, and *Eleven Songs by John Ireland* (introduced by John Longmire), Stainer & Bell/Galaxy © 1970.

**Location of manuscript:** Manuscript Collections, The British Library (Reference Division), Add. MS 52898.

**Bibliography:** R. Fiske, 'Ireland: Songs', *Gramophone*, 53/626 (July 1975), 227–8.

E. Greenfield, 'Ireland', *Gramophone*, 41/492 (May 1964), 513.

**Recordings:** Benjamin Luxon (baritone) and Alan Rowlands (piano) *in* Lyrita SRCS 66 (1975).

*George Parker (baritone) and Sidney Twemlow (piano), BBC Sound Archive 6813, BBC Transcription 18762.

Peter Pears (tenor) and Viola Tunnard (piano), NSA tape 965W.

John Shirley-Quirk (baritone) and Eric Parkin (piano) *in* Saga XIP 7015, XID 5207 (1964).

## Three Songs to Poems by Thomas Hardy

For voice and piano. Text from *Late Lyrics and Earlier* (1922).

1. Summer Schemes (Comodo)
2. Her Song (Rather slowly)
3. Weathers (Allegretto pastorale)

**Duration:** 1—2′ 00″; 2—2′ 25″; 3—2′ 00″.

**Publication:** J. B. Cramer & Co. Ltd. Vocal score © 1925. No. 1—2 versions were published: in A flat major and G major; no. 2—3 versions were published: in D minor, F minor, and E minor; no. 3—3 versions were published: in C major, E major, and D major. Also included in volume iii of *The Complete Works for Voice and Piano*, Stainer & Bell © 1981.

**Bibliography:** T. Harvey, 'Ireland: Songs', *Gramophone*, 57/678 (Nov. 1979), 895.

A. Robertson, 'Ireland', *Gramophone*, 41/489 (Feb. 1964), 378–9.

J. B. Steane, 'An Anthology of English Song', *Gramophone*, 69/826 (Mar. 1992), 109.

**Recordings:** Alfreda Hodgson (contralto) and Alan Rowlands (piano) *in* Lyrita SRCS 118 (1979).

No. 2:

Janet Baker (mezzo-soprano) and Martin Isepp (piano) *in* Classics Club X541, *in* Saga XIP 7013, XID 5213 (1964), STXID 5213 (1963), SAGA 5313, CA 5213, SCD 9012 (1992).

Valerie Baulard and Simon Wright (piano) *in* MAXS MSCB 12/13.

Helen Watts (contralto) and Frederick Stone (piano), NSA tape 064W.

## 1926

## Five Poems by Thomas Hardy

For baritone and piano.

1. Beckon to me (with moderate movement), from *Human Shows* (1925)
2. In my Sage Moments (Deliberate), from *Human Shows* (1925)
3. It was what you bore with you, woman (With gracious movement), from *Late Lyrics and Earlier* (1922)
4. The Tragedy of that Moment (Slowly), from *Human Shows* (1925)
5. Dear, think not that they will forget you (Deliberate), from *Late Lyrics and Earlier* (1922)

**Dedication:** To John Goss.[24]

**Duration:** 1—2′ 00″; 2—3′ 05″; 3—1′ 10″; 4—2′ 00″; 5—2′ 15″.

**Publication:** OUP. Vocal score © 1927. Also included in volume iii of *The Complete Works for Voice and Piano*, Stainer & Bell © 1981.

**Location of manuscript:** Manuscript Collections, The British Library (Reference Division), Add. MS 52897. No. 2 is incomplete.

**Bibliography:** R. Fiske, 'Ireland: Songs', *Gramophone*, 52/624 (May 1975), 2005–6.

E. Greenfield, 'Ireland', *Gramophone*, 41/492 (May 1964), 513.

**Recordings:** Benjamin Luxon (baritone) and Alan Rowlands (piano) *in* Lyrita SRCS 65 (1975).

John Shirley-Quirk (baritone) and Eric Parkin (piano) *in* Saga XIP 7015, XID 5207 (1964).

---

[24] John Goss (1894–1953): English baritone. Also active as a music editor.

## A Graduation Song

Unison song for equal voices and piano. Text by John Drinkwater (1882–1937).
**Dedication:** To Sir Holburt Waring, Vice Chancellor of London University.[25]
**First performance:** London, Royal Albert Hall, 12 May 1926, on the occasion of the annual presentation of graduates for degrees (Presentation Day). It appears to have been sung in unison by all those present, accompanied on the organ by Dr Charles Macpherson, organist at St Paul's Cathedral. It was also sung at the same occasion in subsequent years until 1931 (from 1929 by a soloist), but its use was then discontinued.
**Publication:** J. Curwen & Co. Ltd. Vocal score © 1926 (Choruses for Equal Voices no. 1691). Now Music Sales Ltd.
**Bibliography:** Anon., 'Presentation of Graduates for Degrees', *London University Gazette*, 2 June 1926, 149–51.
**Notes:** Letters, now in the University of London's Archive, show that Holst, Elgar, and Rutland Boughton were also approached as possible composers of this work.

## Three Songs

For voice and piano.
1. Love and Friendship (With moderate movement). Text by Emily Brontë (first published 1850).
2. Friendship in Misfortune (Sustained and fervent). Text: Anon.
3. The One Hope (Rather slowly). Text by Dante Gabriel Rossetti from Sonnet 101, the last in *The House of Life* (1881, first published 1870).

**Dedication:** No. 1 only: To AGM for 22 February 1926.
**Duration:** 1—2' 15"; 2—1' 55"; 3—4' 15".
**Publication:** Augener & Co. Ltd. Vocal score © 1928. Now Stainer & Bell Ltd. Also included in volume v of *The Complete Works for Voice and Piano*, Stainer & Bell © 1981, and in *Eleven Songs by John Ireland* (introduced by John Longmire), Stainer & Bell/Galaxy © 1970.
**Location of manuscript:** Manuscript Collections, The British Library (Reference Division), Add. MS 52899.
**Bibliography:** R. Fiske, 'Ireland: Songs', *Gramophone*, 52/624 (May 1975), 2005–6.

E. Greenfield, 'Ireland', *Gramophone*, 41/492 (May 1964), 513.

---

[25] Holburt J. Waring (1866–1953): Consulting surgeon, St Bartholomew's Hospital, Metropolitan Hospital, and the Royal Dental Hospital. Vice-Chancellor of London University 1922–4, and Dean of the Faculty of Medicine. Wrote many books on medicine.

**Recordings:** Complete:
Benjamin Luxon (baritone) and Alan Rowlands (piano) *in* Lyrita SRCS 65 (1975).
Peter Pears (tenor) and Benjamin Britten (piano) *in* Argo RG 418, ZRG 5418 (1964).
No. 1:
George Parker (baritone) and Sidney Twemlow (piano), BBC Sound Archive 6814, BBC Transcription 18763.
Nos. 1 and 2:
John Shirley-Quirk (baritone) and Eric Parkin (piano) *in* Saga XIP 7015, XID 5207 (1964).

## 1926–1927

## Sonatina

For solo piano.
1. Moderato
2. Quasi lento
3. Rondo (Ritmico, non troppo allegro)

**Date of composition:** June 1926–October 1927.
**Dedication:** To Edward Clark.[26]
**Duration:** 12'.
**First performance:** London, BBC Studios, 19 April 1928. John Ireland (piano). (Broadcast by the BBC.)
**Publication:** OUP. Score © 1928. Also included in volume iii of *The Collected Piano Works of John Ireland*, Stainer & Bell © 1976.
**Bibliography:** Anon., 'New Music', *Musical Times*, 69 (Sept. 1928), 801.
Anon., 'Reviews', *Monthly Musical Record*, 58 (Oct. 1928), 306.
F. Dawes, 'Ireland', *Musical Times*, 116/1588 (June 1975), 543.
M. Harrison, 'Ireland: Piano Works', *Gramophone*, 56/661 (June 1978), 86.
J. Noble, 'Ireland', *Gramophone*, 38/449 (Oct. 1960), 238.
J. Warrack, 'English Piano Works', *Gramophone*, 52/619 (Dec. 1974), 1187.
**Recordings:** John McCabe (piano) *in* Decca Ace of Diamonds SDD 444 (1974).
Eric Parkin (piano) *in* Lyrita SRCS 89 (1978).
Alan Rowlands (piano) *in* Lyrita RCS 15 (1960).
No. 3:
*William Murdoch (piano), Columbia 4944.

---

[26] Edward Clark (1888–1962): English conductor. Studied in Paris, Vienna, and in Berlin with Schoenberg. Led the orchestra for Diaghilev's London seasons (1924–6) and with the BBC (1927–36). Elected president of the ISCM in 1947. Married to Elisabeth Lutyens.

**Notes:** The third movement, Rondo, was published separately by OUP (© 1928). Ireland played the Sonatina at the 7th ISCM Festival in Geneva, 7 April 1929.

## We'll to the Woods no more

Song cycle for voice and piano. Text by A. E. Housman (1859–1936), from *Last Poems* (1922).

1. We'll to the Woods no more (Rather slowly; marked Poco lento in the manuscript). This is the introductory poem to Housman's *Last Poems*.
2. In Boyhood (At speaking pace)
3. Spring will not wait: [Epilogue for piano] (Moderato sostenuto)

**Dedication:** To Arthur [printed copy only]. In the manuscript, the dedication appears as: 'To Arthur: in memory of the darkest days'.
**Duration:** 1—2' 05"; 2—1' 35"; 3—4' 00".
**Publication:** OUP. Vocal score © 1928. Also included in volume iii of *The Complete Works for Voice and Piano*, Stainer & Bell © 1981. Each was issued separately by OUP (© 1928), no. 3 in The Clarendon Piano Series no. 13. This was republished in [1975]. Also included in volume iii of *The Collected Piano Works of John Ireland*, Stainer & Bell © 1976.
**Location of manuscript:** Manuscript Collections, The British Library (Reference Division), Add. MS 52899. Nos. 1 and 2 are dated: February 1927; no. 3 is initialled and dated: February 1927. Also added is 'for AGM: February 22 1927'.
**Bibliography:** R. Fiske, 'Ireland: Songs', *Gramophone*, 52/624 (May 1975), 2005–6.

A. Robertson, 'Ireland: Piano Works', *Gramophone*, 48/566 (July 1970), 191–2.
**Recordings:** Complete:
Benjamin Luxon (baritone) and Alan Rowlands (piano) *in* Lyrita SRCS 65 (1975).
No. 3:
Alan Rowlands (piano) *in* Lyrita RCS 29 (1970).
**Notes:** No. 3 is prefaced by a quotation from *A Shropshire Lad*:

> Spring will not wait the loiterer's time
> Who keeps so long away.

## 1927

### New Prince, New Pomp

Carol for unaccompanied mixed chorus (SATB). Text by Robert Southwell (1561?–95).
**Publication:** Mowbray & Co. Ltd. Vocal score © ? Now EMI Music Publishing Ltd. The carol was also included in *The Oxford Book of Carols* (OUP © 1928).
**Recordings:** Grailville College Singers, Audio Fidelity AFLP 1820. Scottish Junior Singers and organ, BBC Sound Archives 20097.

## 1928

### Two Songs

For voice and piano.

1. Tryst (In Fountain Court) (Very slow and sustained). Text by Arthur Symons, from *Silhouettes* (1892).
2. During Music (Moderato). Text by D. G. Rossetti (1886).

**Date of composition:** April 1928.
**Duration:** 1—3' 30"; 2—2' 45".
**Publication:** OUP. Vocal score © 1929. Also included in volume ii of *The Complete Works for Voice and Piano*, Stainer & Bell © 1981.
**Bibliography:** R. Fiske, 'Ireland: Songs', *Gramophone*, 53/626 (July 1975), 227–8.
**Recordings:** Benjamin Luxon (baritone) and Alan Rowlands (piano) *in* Lyrita SRCS 66 (1975).

## 1929

### If we must part

A valediction for voice and piano. Text by Ernest Dowson, from *Verses* (1896).
**Duration:** 1' 50".
**Publication:** Stainer & Bell & Co. Ltd. Vocal score © 1976. Also included in *The Complete Works for Voice and Piano*, Stainer & Bell Ltd. © 1981, and in *The Land of Lost Content and Other Songs by John Ireland* (with an introduction by John Longmire), Galaxy/Stainer & Bell © 1976.
**Location of manuscript:** Manuscript Collections, The British Library (Reference Division), Add. MS 52898. It is dated: for 25 July 1929.

**Bibliography:**  R. Fiske, 'Ireland: Songs', *Gramophone*, 53/626 (July 1975), 227–8.

**Recordings:**  Benjamin Luxon (baritone) and Alan Rowlands (piano) *in* Lyrita SRCS 66 (1975).

## Ballade

For solo piano.

**Duration:** 9'.

**First performance:**  Unable to trace. Arthur Alexander may have been the soloist involved.

**Publication:**  B. Schott (Mainz). Score © 1931. Also included in volume iii of *The Complete Piano Works of John Ireland*, Stainer & Bell © 1976.

**Bibliography:**  Anon., 'Reviews', *Monthly Musical Record*, 61 (Nov. 1931), 337–8.

M. Harrison, 'Ireland: Piano Works', *Gramophone*, 56/661 (June 1978), 86.

A. Robertson, 'Ireland', *Gramophone*, 41/483 (Aug. 1963), 111–12.

**Recordings:**  Eric Parkin (piano) *in* Lyrita SRCS 89 (1978).

Alan Rowlands (piano) *in* Lyrita RCS 23 (1963).

**Notes:**  2 sheets of proofs exist in the Manuscript Collections, The British Library (Reference Division), Add. MS 52900.

## 1929–1930

## Two Pieces

For solo piano.

1. February's Child (Allegretto amabile)
2. Aubade (Con moto)

**Dedication:**  1—To AGM for 22 February, 1929.

**Duration:**  1—4' 30"; 2—4' 00".

**Publication:**  B. Schott (Mainz). Score © 1931. No. 1—no. 2157; no. 2—no. 2158; each was also published separately. Also included in volume iii of *The Collected Piano Works of John Ireland*, Stainer & Bell © 1976.

**Location of manuscript:**  Manuscript Collections, The British Library (Reference Division), Add. MS 52891.

**Bibliography:**  M. Harrison, 'English Piano Music', *Gramophone*, 54/648 (May 1977), 1717.

—— 'Ireland: Piano Works', *Gramophone*, 56/661 (June 1978), 86.

A. Robertson, 'Ireland', *Gramophone*, 41/483 (Aug. 1963), 111–12.

**Recordings:**  Eric Parkin (piano) *in* Lyrita SRCS 89 (1978).

Alan Rowlands (piano) *in* Lyrita RCS 23 (1963).

No. 2:
Richard Deering (piano) *in* Saga 5445 (1977).

**Notes:** 'February's Child' may have also been inspired (as was 'The Holy Boy') by Bobby Glasby, the son of a sculptor who lived in Gunter Grove, and who was a chorister at the church of St Luke's, Chelsea, where Ireland was organist.

## 1929–1931

## Songs Sacred and Profane

Song cycle for voice and piano.

1. The Advent (Rather slowly). Text by Alice Meynell (1847–1922), from *Preludes* (1875).
2. Hymn for a Child (With movement). Text by Sylvia Townsend Warner (1893–1978), from *The Espalier* (1924).
3. My Fair (With breath). Text by Alice Meynell (1847–1922), from *Preludes* (1875).
4. The Salley Gardens (At speaking pace). Text by W. B. Yeats (1865–1939), from *Crossways* (1889).
5. The Soldier's Return (Alla marcia). Text by Sylvia Townsend Warner (1893–1978), from *The Espalier* (1924).
6. The Scapegoat (Animated). Text by Sylvia Townsend Warner (1893–1978), from *The Espalier* (1924).

**Dedication:** 1—To Mary Grundting; 2—To Helen [Perkin]; 5—To Edward Clark.
**Duration:** 1—3' 10"; 2—2' 00"; 3—3' 10"; 4—2' 00"; 5—1' 00"; 6—1' 20".
**First performance:** London, BBC Studios, 30 March 1933. John Armstrong (tenor) and John Ireland (piano). This broadcast was however postponed because of John Armstrong's illness. Subsequently the two artistes gave the first performance on 29 May 1933 and this was broadcast by the BBC.
**Publication:** Schott & Co. Ltd. Vocal score © 1934. No. 4 ('The Salley Gardens') was published separately in E minor and D minor. Also included in volume i of *The Complete Works for Voice and Piano*, Stainer & Bell © 1981.
**Location of manuscript:** Manuscript Collections, The British Library (Reference Division), Add. MS 52898. No. 1 is dated: Christmas 1931. The poem, entitled 'Meditation', is headed with a quote, in Latin, from Isaiah 45:8:

> Rorate Coeli desuper, et nubes pluent Justum
> Aperietur Terra, et germinet Salutorem.
>
> [Drop down dew from above, ye heavens, the
>   clouds shall rain down justice,
> Let the earth open and bring forth a Saviour.]

The quote can also be found in the Introit Anthem for the Mass of the 4th Sunday in Advent. No. 2 is not dated. No. 3 is initialled and dated: July 1929. No. 4 is missing. No. 5 is initialled and dated: St Andrew's Day 1931. No. 6 is initialled and dated: 7 December 1931.

**Bibliography:** A. Blyth, 'Lieder and Song Recital', *Gramophone*, 51/609 (Feb. 1974), 1595–6.

R. Fiske, 'Janet Baker', *Gramophone*, 45/530 (July 1967), 75.

—— 'Songs: Ireland', *Gramophone*, 53/626 (July 1975), 227–8.

E. Greenfield, 'Ireland', *Gramophone*, 41/492 (May 1964), 513.

J. B. Steane, 'Pageant of English Songs', *Gramophone*, 61/721 (June 1983), 75.

**Recordings:** Philip Hattey (baritone) and Paul Hamburger (piano), NSA tape M1227R.

Benjamin Luxon (baritone) and Alan Rowlands (piano) *in* Lyrita SRCS 66 (1975).

John Shirley-Quirk (baritone) and Eric Parkin (piano) *in* Saga XIP 7015, XID 5207 (1964).

No. 4:

Janet Baker (mezzo-soprano) and Gerald Moore (piano) *in* HMV HQS 1091 (1967), Angel S 36456, HMV 100642-1, TC-ESD 100642-4 (1983), HMV ASD 2929 (1974), HMV ESD 1024391, TC-ASD 1024394.

George Parker (baritone) and Sidney Twemlow (piano), BBC Sound Archive 6815, BBC Transcription 18766.

## 1930

## Concerto in E flat for piano and orchestra

1. In tempo moderato
2. Lento espressivo
3. Allegretto giocoso

**Date of composition:** Spring and summer 1930.

**Instrumentation:** 2 flutes and piccolo, 2 oboes, 2 clarinets in B flat, 2 bassoons, 4 horns in F, 2 trumpets in C, 3 trombones, bass tuba (ad lib), timpani, percussion (2 players: side-drum, cymbals, triangle, tambourine, Chinese block), and strings.

**Dedication:** [To Helen Perkin].[27]

---

[27] Helen C. Perkin (1909– ): English pianist and composer. Pupil of Ireland's at the RCM, 1926–33, where she was awarded an Octavia Hill Travelling Scholarship to study with Webern in Vienna. Became Ireland's protégée, amid much gossip, and a well-known exponent of Ireland's music. However, in 1934 she married and abandoned her career as a concert pianist. Ireland and

**Duration:** 23'–25'.

**First performance:** London, Queen's Hall, Thursday 2 October 1930. Helen Perkin (piano) and the BBC Symphony Orchestra, conducted by Henry Wood.

**Publication:** J. & W. Chester & Co. Ltd. Full score © 1932. Separate piano part © 1932.

**Location of manuscript:** Manuscript Collections, The British Library (Reference Division), Add. MS 52878. It is dated: April–September 1930.

**Bibliography:** Anon., 'Dance Orchestra Mutes for New Piano Concerto', *The Times*, 2 Oct. 1930, p. 21.

Anon., 'Mr John Ireland's Piano Concerto', *Musical Times*, 75 (Mar. 1934), 253.

Anon., 'New Music', *The Times*, 12 Mar. 1932, p. 10.

Anon., 'A Proms Favourite', *Record Times*, Aug. 1958, p. 5.

E. Blom, 'Ireland's Piano Concerto', *Monthly Musical Record*, 61 (Jan. 1931), 9–11.

A. Collins, 'Ireland's First Piano Concerto', *Chesterian*, 15 (1934), 101–3.

T. Harvey, 'Ireland', *Gramophone*, 46/545 (Oct. 1968), 538–9.

J. Ireland, 'Concerto in E♭', undated and unpublished paper, now in the John Ireland Trust Archive.

M. Kennedy, 'Ireland: Piano Concerto', *Gramophone*, 67/800 (Jan. 1990), 1321.

H. Lambert, 'John Ireland's Piano Concerto', *Sackbut* (Jan. 1931), 168–9.

R. Layton, 'Ireland', *Gramophone*, 64/764 (Jan. 1987), 1022.

—— 'Twentieth Century British Piano Concertos', *Gramophone*, 55/649 (June 1977), 67.

W. Mann, 'John Ireland: Piano Concerto in E♭', in R. Hill (ed.), *The Concerto* (Harmondsworth, Penguin Books, 1962), 413–17.

M. E. Oliver, 'Ireland', *Gramophone*, 64/760 (Sept. 1986), 376.

A. Robertson, 'Ireland', *Gramophone*, 36/423 (Aug. 1958), 102.

—— 'Ireland', *Gramophone*, 43/511 (Dec. 1965), 312–13.

A. Sanders, 'The Art of Leslie Heward', *Gramophone*, 63/747 (Aug. 1985), 249–50.

**Recordings:** Sandra Bianca (piano)/Hamburg PO/Hans-Jürgen Walther *in* MGM E 3366 (1957).

Colin Horsley (piano)/RPO/Basil Cameron *in* CLP 1182 (1958), HQM 1007 (1965), Capitol G7183, SG7183 (1959), HMV SLS 5080 (1977).

*Eileen Joyce (piano)/Hallé Orchestra/Leslie Heward, Columbia DX 1072-4 (1942), *in* EM 290462-3, 290462-5 (1985).

she never met again, and in 1950 he removed the dedication from the score. At the end of the third movement, Ireland included a violin passage, quoting from a string quartet by Helen Perkin. See J. Longmire, *John Ireland: Portrait of a Friend* (London, Baker, 1969), 26–31, and M. Searle, *John Ireland: The Man and his Music* (Tunbridge Wells, Midas Books, 1979), 76–8.

Eileen Joyce (piano)/LPO/Adrian Boult (rec. 10 Sept. 1949), BBC Sound Archive T41731, NSA tape 930W.

Eric Parkin (piano)/LPO/Adrian Boult *in* Lyrita SRCS 36 (1968), Musical Heritage Society 1429.

Eric Parkin (piano)/LPO/Bryden Thomson *in* Chandos ABRD 1174, ABTD 1174 (1986), CHAN 8461 (1987).

Katherine Stott (piano)/RPO/Vernon Handley *in* Conifer MCFC 175, CDFC 175 (1990).

Geoffrey Tozer (piano)/Melbourne SO/David Measham *in* Unicorn-Kanchana DKP 9056, DKPC 9056 (1987).

**Notes:** The concerto was taken up by several pianists including Reginald Paul (August 1934), Helen Guest, and Angus Morrison. Records show that Ireland conducted a performance in Eastbourne in March 1932. It was later performed in Moscow in January 1934, under Edward Clark, Frankfurt in February 1934, Stockholm in August 1934, Budapest (under Dohnányi) and Vienna (under Konrath) in January 1935, and South Africa in August 1935. Clifford Curzon introduced it to the United States of America in Carnegie Hall, New York, on 10 March 1939.

OTHER VERSIONS

**Concerto for piano and orchestra**

Arranged for 2 pianos.
**Publication:** J. & W. Chester & Co. Ltd. Score [© 1932].

## Ballade of London Nights

For solo piano.
**Duration:** 7'.
**First performance:** London, Broadcasting House, 6 June 1965. Alan Rowlands (piano). This recording was subsequently broadcast in the Third Programme on Friday 30 July 1965.
**Publication:** Boosey & Hawkes Ltd. Score © 1968. Also included in volume iii of *The Complete Piano Works of John Ireland*, Stainer & Bell © 1976.
**Location of manuscript:** Manuscript Collections, The British Library (Reference Division), Add. MS 52889.
**Bibliography:** M. Harrison, 'John Ireland, his Friends and Pupils', *Gramophone*, 61/724 (Sept. 1983), 375.

P. J. Pirie, 'Broadcasting', *Musical Times*, 106 (Sept. 1965), 704.

A. Robertson, 'Ireland: Piano Works', *Gramophone*, 48/566 (July 1970), 191–2.

A. Whittall, 'The Britten Connection', *Gramophone*, 69/826 (Mar. 1992), 88.

**Recordings:** Alan Goldstone (piano) *in* Gamut Classics GAMCD 526 (1992).
Eric Parkin (piano) *in* Chandos DBRD 2006, DBTD 2006 (1983).
Alan Rowlands (piano) *in* Lyrita RCS 29 (1970).
Alan Rowlands (piano), NSA tape 471W.

## 1931

## Meine Seele erhebt der Herren
## (My soul doth magnify the Lord)

Choral Prelude by J. S. Bach (1685–1750), transcribed for solo piano and included in *A Bach Book for Harriet Cohen*.
**Commissioned by:** Harriet Cohen.[28]
**Dedication:** For Harriet Cohen.
**Duration:** 3'.
**First performance:** London, Queen's Hall, Monday 17 October 1932. Harriet Cohen (piano).
**Publication:** OUP. Score © 1932.
**Location of manuscript:** O. W. Neighbour, London. It is dated: August 1931.
**Bibliography:** Anon., 'Recital of the Week', *The Times*, 21 Oct. 1932, p. 12.
H. Cohen, 'Bach Book for Harriet Cohen', in *A Bundle of Time: Memoirs* (London, Faber, 1969), 183.

## 1932

## Indian Summer

For solo piano.
**Duration:** 3'.
**Publication:** Published in *Pro musica*, 1 (1932), by the Danish firm Wilhelm Hansen (Copenhagen).
**Notes:** The piece's original title was *The Cherry Tree*.

## Tutto e sciolto

Song for voice and piano. Text by James Joyce (1882–1941), from *Pomes Penyeach* (1927).
**Commissioned by:** Herbert Hughes for *The Joyce Book*.

---

[28] Harriet Cohen (1895–1967): English pianist. Studied at the RAM and won her reputation as an exponent of early keyboard music and of modern English composers, including Bax, Vaughan Williams and Fricker.

**Duration:** 2'.

**First performance:** London, College of Nursing (Cavendish Square), Wednesday 16 March 1932. Dorothy Moulton, John Armstrong, and Sinclair Logan (singers) with William Busch (piano) (a .Contemporary Music Centre Concert).

**Publication:** OUP. Score © 1932. Also included in volume v of *The Complete Works for Voice and Piano*, Stainer & Bell © 1981.

**Bibliography:** Anon., [Recital], *The Times*, 18 Mar. 1932, p. 12.

R. Fiske, 'Ireland: Songs', *Gramophone*, 53/626 (July 1975), 227–8.

**Recordings:** Benjamin Luxon (baritone) and Alan Rowlands (piano) in Lyrita SRCS 66 (1975).

**Notes:** *The Joyce Book* was published by the Sylvan Press and OUP in 1932: 500 copies were printed, 450 put on sale. The blue silk wrappers were made of hand-woven silk from the Edinburgh Weavers, and the grey paper was mould-made in Holland. Besides Ireland, Moeran, Bax, Roussel, Hughes, Sessions, Bliss, Howells, Antheil, Edgardo Carducci, Goossens, Orr, and Van Dieren wrote songs for the project, which was edited by Herbert Hughes. William Walton and Darius Milhaud were amongst those who declined to contribute.

## A Downland Suite

For brass band.

1. Prelude (Allegro energico)
2. Elegy (Lento espressivo)
3. Minuet (Allegretto grazioso)
4. Round (Poco allegro)

**Commissioned by:** The National Brass Band Championships of Great Britain as the test piece for the 1932 contest.

**Instrumentation:** Solo cornet in B flat, soprano in E flat, ripieno and flugel-horn in B flat, 2nd and 3rd cornets in B flat, solo horn in E flat, 1st and 2nd horn in E flat, 1st and 2nd baritone in B flat, 1st and 2nd trombone in B flat, bass trombone, euphonium in B flat, E flat and B flat basses, and drums.

**Dedication:** To my friend Kenneth Wright.[29]

**Duration:** c. 17' 20" (4' 10"; 5' 25"; 4' 25"; 3' 20").

**First performance:** London, Crystal Palace, 1 October 1932 (the National Band Festival). The winning band was Foden's Motor Works Band, conducted by F. Mortimer. The adjudicators were Henry Gheel, J. Brier, and H. Bennett.

---

[29] Kenneth Wright (1899–1975): Assistant Director of Music at the BBC, 1935–7. Helped with the formation of the BBC Symphony Orchestra in 1930. He was acting Director of Music from 1946 to 1948, and later became Head of Music Programmes (TV) until 1959.

**Publication:** R. Smith & Co. Ltd. Full score © 1932.
**Location of manuscript:** Manuscript Collections, The British Library (Reference Division), Add. MS 52875 (condensed score).
**Bibliography:** W. A. Chislett, 'English Brass', *Gramophone*, 54/644 (Jan. 1977), 1193.
—— 'Ireland', *Gramophone*, 10/115 (Dec. 1932), 274.
J. H. Elliot, 'Interpretation and the New Repertoire: 3. Ireland's Downland Suite', *British Bandsman*, 22 May 1937, pp. 4–5.
H. Hughes, 'The British Band Festival', *Daily Telegraph*, 6 Sept. 1932, p. 8.
M. Macdonald, 'Bliss/Ireland', *Gramophone*, 54/640 (Sept. 1976), 410.
A. Mackler, 'Dr John Ireland's Downland Suite', *British Bandsman*, 24 Sept. 1932, p. 2.
G. Reynolds, 'British Music for Brass', *Gramophone*, 65/772 (Sept. 1987), 420.
A. Sanders, 'Compact Disc Round-Up', *Gramophone*, 66/786 (Nov. 1988), 878.
**Recordings:** Besses o'th'Barn Band/Ifor James *in* Pye TB 3012, ZCTP B 3012 (1977).
*Bickershaw Colliery Band, BBC Sound Archive 5906-8, BBC Transcription 13272/7.
Brighouse & Rastrick Band/Geoffrey Brand *in* Harlequin HAR 1122 CC (1990).
*Foden's Motor Works Band, Zonophone T 6228/9 (1932).
CWS (Manchester) Band/Alec Mortimer *in* Fontana TL 5466, STL 5466.
GUS (Kettering) Band/Geoffrey Brand *in* EMI Studio Two TWOX-1053 (1976).
London Brass Virtuosi/David Honeyball *in* Hyperion H 88013, KH 88013 (1988).
London Collegiate Brass/James Stobart *in* CRD digital CRDC 4144, CRD 3444 (1987).
No. 2:
Yorkshire Imperial Metals Band/Trevor Walmsley *in* CBS 62937 (1967).

## OTHER VERSIONS

### Two Pieces (Minuet and Elegy)

Freely adapted by the composer from *A Downland Suite* for string orchestra.
**Date of arrangement:** 1941.
**Instrumentation:** Violins I and II, violas, cellos, and double basses.
**Duration:** *c*.11'.
**Publication:** Hawkes & Co. Ltd. Score © 1942.
**Location of manuscript:** Manuscript Collections, The British Library (Reference Division), Add. MS 52875.

**Bibliography:** W. R. Anderson, 'Ireland', *Gramophone*, 17/204 (May 1940), 416–17.
W. A. Chislett, 'Yorkshire Brass', *Gramophone*, 45/529 (June 1967), 32.
T. Harvey, 'Contemporary Orchestral Works', *Gramophone*, 48/575 (Apr. 1971), 1632, 1637.
—— 'Elgar/Ireland', *Gramophone*, 46/552 (May 1969), 1595.
—— 'Festival of English Music', *Gramophone*, 50/592 (Sept. 1972), 550–1.
A. Robertson, 'Ireland', *Gramophone*, 44/520 (Sept. 1966), 157–8.
D.S., 'Ireland', *Gramophone*, 32/382 (Mar. 1955), 438.
A. Sanders, 'English Music for Strings', *Gramophone*, 66/784 (Sept. 1988), 432.
**Recordings:** LPO/Adrian Boult *in* Lyrita RCS 31, SRCS 31 (1966).
Minuet only:
*Boyd Neel Orchestra/Boyd Neel, Decca X 255 (1940).
Boyd Neel Orchestra/Boyd Neel *in* Decca LW5149 (1955), London LD 9170, Ace of Clubs ACL 316 (1969), Decca Eclipse ECS 648 (1972).
Guildhall String Ensemble/Robert Salter *in* RCA Victor Red Seal RL 87761, RK 87761, RD 87761 (1988).
Elegy only:
Leicester Schools Orchestra/André Previn *in* Argo 685 (1971).
**Notes:** A later reissue of the score (by the John Ireland Trust—selling agents R. Smith & Co. Ltd.) also contained the other two movements (Prelude and Rondo) arranged for string orchestra by Geoffrey Bush (1978). The following note appeared in the score:

It was John Ireland's intention to transcribe *A Downland Suite* for strings in its entirety; but he finished only the two middle movements which were published (in reverse order) as 'Minuet and Elegy'. In completing the transcription at the request of the John Ireland Trust I have reverted to the original order of movements; I have also followed the composer's example in reconceiving the music as a composition for string orchestra rather than making a literal re-arrangement of the brass band version.

**First performance:** London, BBC Studios, 17 June 1981. The BBC Concert Orchestra/Christopher Adey. This recording was subsequently broadcast in R3 on 27 July 1981.
**Bibliography:** M. Macdonald, 'Bridge/Ireland', *Gramophone*, 62/739 (Dec. 1984), 736.
A. Sanders, 'Bridge/Ireland', *Gramophone*, 65/768 (May 1987), 1546, 1550.
**Recordings:** ECO/David Garforth *in* Chandos ABRD 1112, ABTD 1112 (1984), CHAN 8390 (1987).

## A Downland Suite

Arranged for wind band by R. Steadman-Allen.
**Instrumentation:** 2 flutes and piccolo, 2 oboes, E flat clarinet, 3 clarinets in B flat, E flat alto clarinet, B flat bass clarinet, 2 bassoons, 2 alto saxophones in E flat, B flat tenor saxophones, E flat baritone saxophone, 3 cornets in B flat, 2 trumpets in B flat, 4 horns in F, 3 trombones, euphonium, tuba, string bass, and percussion.
**Duration:** 17' 30".
**Publication:** R. Smith & Co. Ltd. Full score © 1985.

**Elegy and Minuet**

From *A Downland Suite*, arranged for solo piano.
**Date of arrangement:**   1933.
**Publication:**   Ashdown & Co. Ltd. Score © 1933. Now Music Sales Ltd.

**Elegy**

From *A Downland Suite*, arranged for organ by Alec Rowley.
**Date of arrangement:**   1940.
**Publication:**   Ashdown & Co. Ltd. Score © 1940. Now Music Sales Ltd.

## Month's Mind

For solo piano.
**Duration:**   4' 30".
**First performance:**   London, BBC Studios, 2 April 1936. John Ireland (piano). (Broadcast in the National Programme.)
**Publication:**   Augener & Co. Ltd. Score © 1935. Now Stainer & Bell Ltd. Also included in volume iv of *The Complete Piano Works of John Ireland*, Stainer & Bell © 1976.
**Location of manuscript:**   Manuscript Collections, The British Library (Reference Division), Add. MS 52890. It is dated: for 25 May 1933.
**Bibliography:**   J. Brooke, 'Month's Mind', in his *The Dog at Clambercrown* (London, The Bodley Head, 1955), 99–101.
M. Harrison, 'Ireland: Piano Works', *Gramophone*, 56/661 (June 1978), 86.
M. Macdonald, 'Ireland', *Gramophone*, 42/497 (Oct. 1964), 201.
**Recordings:**   Eric Parkin (piano) *in* Argo RG 48 (1955), *in* Lyrita SRCS 89 (1979).
Alan Rowlands (piano) *in* Lyrita RCS 24 (1964).
**Notes:**   The score bears the following quotation from Brand's *Observations on Popular Antiquities* (1913): '. . . days which our ancestors called their "month's mind" as being the days whereon their souls (after death) were had in special remembrance: hence the expression of having a "month's mind" to imply a longing desire.'

## Legend

For piano and orchestra.
**Instrumentation:**   2 flutes, oboe, cor anglais, 2 clarinets in A, 2 bassoons, 4 horns in F, 2 tenor trombones, timpani, percussion (2 players: cymbals, triangle, tambourine, bass drum, and gong), and strings.
**Dedication:**   To Arthur Machen.
**Duration:**   15'.

**First performance:** London, Queen's Hall, Friday 12 January 1934. Helen Perkin (piano) and the BBC Symphony Orchestra, conducted by Adrian Boult.
**Publication:** Schott & Co. Ltd. Full score © 1938. Miniature score [© 1950].
**Location of manuscript:** Manuscript Collections, The British Library (Reference Division), Add. MS 52879A. The full score is dated and initialled: J.I. 1933. (The score was completed on 8 December 1933.)
**Bibliography:** R. Layton, 'Ireland', *Gramophone*, 64/764 (Jan. 1987), 1022.
W. McNaught, 'London Concerts', *Musical Times*, 75/1092 (Feb. 1934), 170.
M. E. Oliver, 'Ireland', *Gramophone*, 64/760 (Sept. 1986), 376.
A. Robertson, 'Ireland', *Gramophone*, 44/520 (Sept. 1966), 157–8.
**Recordings:** Eric Parkin (piano) and the LPO/Adrian Boult *in* Lyrita RCS 32, SRCS 32, Musical Heritage Society 1317 (1966).
Eric Parkin (piano) and the LPO/Bryden Thomson *in* Chandos ABRD 1174, ABTD 1174 (1986), CHAN 8461 (1987).
Kendall Taylor (piano) and London Chamber Players/Anthony Bernard, NSA tape M615W.
**Notes:** On 30 March 1932 Ireland wrote to Adrian Boult, 'I am at work on a *second piano concerto*, which will be ready for performance next season. [I am] anxious to write another work for the same combination in a totally different mood . . . I am writing again for a Beethoven orchestra with the solo instrument.' Three months later, on 25 June 1932, Ireland told Oliver Mase, 'I think it is safe to say it will be ready for performance by February or March next year.' Over a year later, it is obvious that Ireland had scaled the proposed concerto down: 'Queen Fridias, Prelude for orchestra and pianoforte', was mentioned as a possible title. However rehearsals for the 'second piano concerto' were arranged for 14 December 1933, but in a BBC memo, dated 12 December, the title of the new work is given as Prelude for piano and orchestra, 'Legend' being mentioned as a possible title and better than 'Prelude'.

OTHER VERSIONS

**Legend**

Arranged for two pianos by the composer.
**Date of arrangement:** [1933].
**Publication:** Schott & Co. Ltd. Score © 1938.
**Location of manuscript:** Manuscript Collections, The British Library (Reference Division), Add. MS 52879B.

## 1934

## Comedy Overture

For brass band.
**Commissioned by:** The National Brass Band Championships of Great Britain as the test piece for the 1934 contest.
**Instrumentation:** Solo cornet in B flat, soprano in E flat, ripieno and flugelhorn in B flat, 2nd and 3rd cornets in B flat, solo horn in E flat, 1st and 2nd horns in E flat, 1st and 2nd baritones in B flat, 1st and 2nd trombones in B flat, bass trombone, euphonium in B flat, E flat and B flat basses, drums and percussion (bass drum, cymbals, side-drum, triangle).
**Duration:** 11'.
**First performance:** London, Crystal Palace, 29 September 1934 (the National Band Festival). The winning band was Foden's Motor Works Band, conducted by F. Mortimer. The adjudicators were Henry Gheel, W. Reynolds, and F. Wright.
**Publication:** R. Smith & Co. Ltd. Full score © 1934.
**Bibliography:** T. Aitken, 'Mysterious Comedy', *Brass Band News* (Sept. 1984), 7–8.
    W. A. Chislett, 'Championship Brass', *Gramophone*, 46/548 (Jan. 1969), 1058, 1063.
    —— 'Music for Brass', *Gramophone*, 52/613 (June 1974), 116.
    J. H. Elliot, 'John Ireland's Comedy Overture', *British Bandsman*, 15 Sept. 1934, p. 5.
    G. Horn, 'British Music for Brass', *Gramophone*, 64/760 (Sept. 1986), 394, 398.
    M. Macdonald, 'Bliss/Ireland', *Gramophone*, 54/640 (Sept. 1976), 410.
    —— 'British Music for Brass', *Gramophone*, 63/754 (Mar. 1986), 1162.
    —— 'Classics for Brass Band', *Gramophone*, 54/648 (May 1977), 1703.
    R. Newsome and A. Hailstone, 'Comedy and its Composer', *British Bandsman*, 8 Sept. 1984, p. 10.
    A. Sanders, 'Compact Disc Round-Up', *Gramophone*, 66/786 (Nov. 1988), 878.
**Recordings:** Fairey Band/L. Lamb *in* Paxton LPT 1026 (1969).
    Foden's Motor Works Band/Rex Mortimer, NSA tape M327W.
    *Foden's Motor Works Band/Fred Mortimer, BBC Sound Archive 7702-4, BBC Transcription 255922/4.
    Grimethorpe Colliery Band/Elgar Howarth *in* Decca SXL 6820 (1977), KSXC 6820, 414 644-1DW, 414 644-4DW (1986).
    GUS (Kettering) Band/Geoffrey Brand *in* EMI Studio Two TWOX-1053 (1976).

London Brass Virtuosi/David Honeyball *in* Hyperion H88013, KH88013 (1988).
London Collegiate Brass/James Stobart *in* CRD/digital CRD 1134, CRDC 4134, CRD 3434 (1986).
Virtuoso Brass Band/Eric Ball *in* Virtuoso VR 7303 (1974).

## OTHER VERSIONS

### Comedy Overture

Arranged for wind band by R. Steadman-Allen.
**Date of arrangement:**   1986.
**Instrumentation:**   2 flutes and piccolo, 2 oboes, E flat clarinet, 3 clarinets in B flat, E flat alto clarinet, B flat bass clarinet, 2 bassoons, 2 alto saxophones in E flat, B flat tenor saxophone, E flat baritone saxophone, 3 cornets in B flat, 2 trumpets in B flat, 4 horns in F, 3 trombones, euphonium, tuba, string bass, and percussion (4 players).
**Publication:**   R. Smith & Co. Ltd. Full score © 1987.
**Bibliography:**   M. Macdonald, 'British Music for Concert Band', *Gramophone*, 67/802 (Mar. 1990), 1627.
**Recordings:**   City of London Wind Ensemble/Geoffrey Brand *in* LDR/Gamut LDRZC 1012, LDRCD 1012 (1990).

### A London Overture

For orchestra. A reworking of material from Comedy Overture (1934).
**Date of composition:**   1936.
**Instrumentation:**   2 flutes and piccolo, 2 oboes, 2 clarinets in B flat, 2 bassoons, 4 horns in F, 3 trumpets in B flat, 2 trombones, tuba, timpani, percussion (3 players: triangle, tambourine, glockenspiel, side-drum, bass drum, xylophone, gong, jingles, and cymbals), and strings.
**Dedication:**   In memory of Percy G. Bentham, Sculptor and Friend—died June 1936.[30]
**Duration:**   13'.
**First performance:**   London, Queen's Hall, Wednesday 23 September 1936. The BBC Symphony Orchestra, conducted by Henry J. Wood.
**Publication:**   Hawkes & Co. Ltd. Full and miniature scores © 1937. Boosey & Hawkes © 1942 (Hawkes Pocket Scores no. 16).

---

[30] Percy Bentham (1883–1936): A sculptor and friend of Ireland's who died tragically in a London heatwave when poison from a cheap Japanese imitation of a Panama hat was absorbed into his skin. Among his principal works were the Harbour Board Offices, Liverpool, a marble memorial to the 5th Earl of Harewood, two lions in bronze for Halifax, Nova Scotia, the figure of Navigation on the P. & O. Offices, London, and a bronze memorial to Thomas Weelkes in St Bride's Church, London. On 16 July 1936 Ireland wrote to Kenneth Thompson,

I have just lost my very best and most intimate friend—a man several years younger than myself—you met him—Bentham the sculptor. He was one of the most vital and energetic people I have ever met . . . a real man and a true friend—well, he died, in a few days, of blood poison.

I have not got over it—or shall never get over the loss of this friend.

**Location of manuscript:** RCM, London, RCM MS 4235. It is dated: A.M.D.G. 31 August, 1936. Errata in BL Add. MS 52900.
**Bibliography:** Anon., 'Promenade Concert', *The Times*, 24 Sept. 1936, p. 10.
D. Denton, 'Ireland', *Music Magazine*, 4 (Feb. 1991), 54.
T. Harvey, 'English Tone Pictures', *Gramophone*, 58/687 (Aug. 1980), 234.
—— 'Ireland, Bax, Delius', *Gramophone*, 44/525 (Feb. 1967), 424.
B. Jacobson, 'English Tone Poems', *High Fidelity*, 17 (May 1967), 69–70.
M. Kennedy, 'Elgar/Ireland . . .', *Gramophone*, 67/794 (July 1989), 174.
—— 'English Tone-Poems', *Gramophone*, 66/787 (Dec. 1988), 1016.
I. March, 'Cassette Commentary', *Gramophone*, 67/795 (Aug. 1989), 376.
A. Robertson, 'Ireland', *Gramophone*, 44/520 (Sept. 1966), 157–8.
**Recordings:** BBC Symphony Orchestra/?, BBC Sound Archives X 17434-6.
*Liverpool PO/Malcolm Sargent, Columbia DX 1155/6.
LPO/Adrian Boult *in* Lyrita RCS 31, SRCS 31 (1966), Musical Heritage Society 1498.
LPO/Adrian Boult (from the composer's collection), NSA tape M580W.
LSO/John Barbirolli *in* HMV ALP 2305, ASD 2305 (1967), Angel 36415, S36415, HMV Greensleeves ESD 7092, TC-ESD 7092 (1980), EMI CDC7 47984-2 (1988).
LSO/Richard Hickox *in* Chandos CHAN 8879, ABTD 1492 (1990).
Philharmonia Orch./Owain Arwel Hughes *in* ASV DCA 634, ZCDCA 634, CDDCA 634 (1989).
Yorkshire SO/Maurice Miles, BBC Transcription X13391-3.
**Notes:** Ireland told Kenneth Thompson, letter dated September 1936, that 'I have been working 12–16 hours a day for 6 weeks to complete my new orchestral work *A London Overture* which is to be played at the Prom concert at Queen's Hall on Wednesday next.'

In the original programme note, written by Ireland, it was stated:

The composer wishes this Overture to be regarded as no. 4 of his *London Pieces*, the first three, 'Chelsea Reach', 'Ragamuffin' and 'Soho Forenoons', having been written for piano in 1917 and 1918.

## OTHER VERSIONS

**A London Overture**

Arranged for brass band.
**Instrumentation:** Solo cornet in B flat, soprano in E flat, ripieno and flugelhorn in B flat, 2 and 3 cornets in B flat, solo horn in E flat, 1st and 2nd horns in E flat, 1st and 2nd baritones in B flat, 1st and 2nd trombones in B flat, bass trombone, euphonium in B flat and B flat basses, drums, and percussion.
Unpublished.
**Recordings:** *Black Dyke Mills Band/Alec Mortimer, Jamco BD 1206/7.

## 1936–1937

### These things shall be

Cantata for baritone (or tenor), mixed chorus (SATB), and orchestra. Text from *A Vista* by John Addington Symonds (1840–93).

**Commissioned by:** The BBC to celebrate the accession and coronation of HM King George VI in May 1937.

**Instrumentation:** 3 flutes, 2 oboes and cor anglais, E flat clarinet, 2 clarinets in E flat, 2 bassoons, double bassoon, 4 horns in F, 3 trumpets in C, 3 trombones, tuba, timpani, percussion (4 players: side-drum, bass drum, cymbals, gong, glockenspiel, triangle, xylophone, tubular bells), celesta, organ, and strings.

**Dedication:** To my friend Alan Bush.[31]

**Duration:** 22'.

**First performance:** London, BBC Studios, Thursday 13 May 1937. Dennis Noble (baritone)? and the BBC Chorus (Section A), and the BBC Orchestra (Section B), conducted by Adrian Boult. This concert featuring music 'for a royal occasion' was broadcast in the National Programme at 20.00 hours, on 13 May 1937.

**First public performance:** London, Queen's Hall, Wednesday 1 December 1937. Dennis Noble (baritone), the BBC Choral Society (chorus master: Leslie Woodgate), and the BBC Symphony Orchestra, conducted by Adrian Boult.

**Modern revival of the original version:** University Chapel, University of Keele, 18 June 1983. Barry Banks (tenor), University of Keele Choral Society and Orchestra, conducted by Stephen Banfield.

**Publication:** Winthrop Rogers & Co. Ltd. Vocal score © 1937. Now Boosey & Hawkes Ltd. Piano reduction by Eric Fenby.

**Location of manuscript:** Manuscript Collections, The British Library (Reference Division), Add. MS 52892. Sketches (52892A) and full score (52892B) in the hand of Alan Bush. The full score is signed and dated: 28 April 1937.

**Bibliography:** Anon., 'These things shall be', *The Times*, 2 July 1951, p. 7.

A. Bush, 'These things shall be', in J. Longmire, *Portrait of a Friend* (London, Baker, 1969), 149–51.

D. Denton, 'Ireland', *Music Magazine*, 4 (Feb. 1991), 54.

E. Evans, 'BBC Symphony Concerts', *Radio Times*, 26 Nov. 1937, p. 13.

---

[31] Alan Bush (1900– ): English composer, studied at the RAM and privately with Ireland. He taught at the Academy from 1925. A convinced communist, he was prominent in organizing the 'Festival of Music for the People' in April 1939 which included a performance of 'These things shall be'.

M. Harrison, 'English Music', *Gramophone*, 62/736 (Sept. 1984), 336.
T. Harvey, 'Ireland', *Gramophone*, 46/545 (Oct. 1968), 538–9.
W. McNaught, 'London Concerts: Ireland and Walton', *Musical Times*, 79 (Jan. 1938), 57.
A. Robertson, 'Ireland', *Gramophone*, 26/309 (Feb. 1949), 148.
A. Sanders, 'Bax/Ireland', *Gramophone*, 69/827 (Apr. 1992), 167.

**Recordings:** John Carol Case (baritone)/LP Choir and Orch./Adrian Boult *in* Lyrita SRCS 36 (1968), Musical Heritage Society 1429.

*Parry Jones (tenor)/Hallé Choir and Orch./John Barbirolli, HMV C3826/7 (1949), *in* HMV EX 290107-3, EX 290107-5 (1984), EMI CDH7 63910-2 (1992).

Redvers Llewellyn (baritone)/Luton CS/LPO/Adrian Boult, BBC Sound Archive T41731, NSA tape 931W.

René Soames (tenor)/BBCSO/Adrian Boult, BBC Transcription 40980/5.

Bryn Terfel (baritone)/LSC/LSO/Richard Hickox *in* Chandos CHAN 8879, ABTD 1492 (1990).

**Notes:** Ireland found himself short of time during the composition, and consequently requested the assistance of his former pupil and fellow-composer Alan Bush. Bush undertook much of the orchestral scoring from sketches of sections sent in by Ireland as soon as they were completed, with instructions for the orchestration.

In his programme note for the modern revival of the work at Keele in 1983, Stephen Banfield recounts:

At bar 278, after the end of stanza 7, Ireland became stuck. He pursued one possibility by phoning up Bush and arranging to meet him in the buffet of Charing Cross station. Did Bush know the famous revolutionary song (at that time the national anthem of the Soviet Union), the *Internationale*? He wanted to try quoting it. Bush wrote down the first two lines of melody on the back of an envelope, and the result was the wonderful poetic version of 'paradise' on earth expressed in the orchestral texture at that point. (Reproduced with kind permission.)

In later life Ireland came to hate the work, and this is evident in a letter he wrote to Dorothy Wood:

[I have an] urgent wish that there should be no mention of the following two points in the programme note:

(1) the name of Alan Bush
(2) the tune known as the 'Internationale', a phrase of which is still to be found in the vocal score, but which I removed from the orchestral score and parts some years ago. (Letter, dated 15 July 1957 now in the BBC Written Archives.)

## 1937

### Green Ways: Three Lyric Pieces

For solo piano.

1. The Cherry Tree (Moderato e con grazia)
2. Cypress (Andante mesto): original title was 'The Intruder' (Andante sostenuto)
3. The Palm and May (Con moto)

**Dedication:** 1—To Herbert S. Brown;[32] 2—To Alfred Chenhalls;[33] 3—For Harriet Cohen.

**Duration:** 1—3' 00"; 2—3' 30"; 3—3' 30".

**First performance:** Unable to trace. Helen Perkin may have given the first performance.

**Publication:** Winthrop Rogers Ltd. Score © 1938. Now Boosey & Hawkes Ltd. Each piece was also published separately. Also included in volume iv of *The Collected Piano Works of John Ireland*, Stainer & Bell © 1976. 'The Cherry Tree' is a slightly revised version of 'Indian Summer' (q.v. 1932), originally published in the Danish music journal *Pro musica* (1932).

**Location of manuscript:** Manuscript Collections, The British Library (Reference Division), Add. MS 52889. No. 3 is initialled and dated: J.I. Deal, 1937.

**Bibliography:** E. Blom, 'Green Ways', *Music and Letters*, 19 (1938), 360–1. M. Harrison, 'Ireland: Piano Works', *Gramophone*, 56/661 (June 1978), 86. J. Noble, 'Ireland', *Gramophone*, 38/449 (Oct. 1960), 228.

**Recordings:** Eric Parkin (piano) *in* Lyrita SRCS 89 (1978). Alan Rowlands (piano) *in* Lyrita RCS 15 (1960).

**Notes:** Each piece is prefaced by a quotation. No. 1 (A. E. Housman, *A Shropshire Lad*):

> And since to look at things in bloom
> Fifty springs are little room,
> About the woodlands I will go
> To see the cherry hung with snow.

No. 2 (William Shakespeare, *Twelfth Night*, act II, scene iv):

> Come away, come away, death,
> And in sad cypress let me be laid.

---

[32] Herbert S. Brown, a solicitor, lived in Deal and was Ireland's legal adviser and a gifted amateur musician.

[33] Alfred Chenhalls was Ireland's (and Sir William Walton's) accountant. He was also an outstanding amateur pianist. In June 1943 the plane on which he (and the actor Leslie Howard) was returning to London from Lisbon was shot down by German fighters in the mistaken belief that they were killing Churchill to whom Chenhalls bore a striking resemblance.

No. 3 (Thomas Nashe):

> The Palm and May
> make country houses gay.

## 1938

## Trio [No. 3] in E minor

For violin, cello, and piano.

1. Allegro moderato
2. Scherzo (Vivace)
3. Andante cantabile
4. Finale (Con moto)

**Dedication:**   To William Walton.[34]
**Duration:**   26′.
**First performance:**   London, BBC Studios, 4 April 1938. Antonio Broso (violin), Antonio Sala (cello), and John Ireland (piano).
**First public performance:**   London, Boosey & Hawkes Music Room (Regent Street), 20 June 1938. Frederick Grinke (violin), Florence Hooton (cello), and John Ireland (piano).
**Publication:**   Hawkes & Co. Ltd. Score © 1938.
**Location of manuscript:**   Manuscript Collections, The British Library (Reference Division), Add. MS 52886. Also included are the printed proofs.
**Bibliography:**   R. Fiske, 'Ireland', *Gramophone*, 42/501 (Feb. 1965), 384.
—— 'Ireland', *Gramophone*, 56/670 (Mar. 1979), 1580.
R. Hill, 'Ireland's Piano Trio', *Radio Times*, 18 Sept. 1942, p. 4.
A. Robertson, 'Ireland', *Gramophone*, 17/196 (Sept. 1939), 159.
—— *Trio 3: Prefatory Essay and Analytical Notes* (London, Decca (for the recording), 1939).
M.M.S., 'London Concerts', *Musical Times*, 79/1145 (July 1938), 536.
**Recordings:**   David Martin Trio *in* Saga XID 5230 (1965).
*Grinke Trio, Decca X 242/4 (1939), Z 799/801.
Yfrah Neaman (violin)/Julian Lloyd Webber (cello)/Eric Parkin (piano) *in* Lyrita SRCS 98 (1979).
**Notes:**   This trio is based on the Trio in D, originally written in 1912–13 (q.v.). It was completely rewritten with the exception of the Scherzo.

---

[34] William Walton (1902–83): English composer. Friend of Ireland. Indeed it was Ireland who suggested in 1935 that Walton should write a brass band work as a test piece for the brass band championships.

## Five Sixteenth-Century Poems

For voice and piano.
1. A Thanksgiving (With impulse and warmth), from William Cornish, in *Bassus* (1530).
2. All in a Garden Green (Leisurely and smooth), from Thomas Howell or Richard Edwardes, in *A Paradyse of Daynty Devises* (1576).
3. An Aside (Light and lively), from Anon., *temp.* Henry VIII; Harleian MS 7578.
4. A Report Song (Liltingly), from Nicholas Breton, in *England's Helicon* (1600).
5. The Sweet Season (With movement, but not fast), from Richard Edwardes, in *A Paradyse of Daynty Devises* (1576) (in the manuscript, this movement is marked 'with lilt').

**Dedication:** [To George Parker].[35]
**Duration:** 1—1' 35"; 2—1' 40"; 3—1' 05"; 4—1' 30"; 5—3' 00".
**First public performance:** London, Wigmore Hall, 31 October 1938. George Parker (baritone) and Norman Franklin (piano).
**Publication:** Hawkes & Co. Ltd. Vocal score © 1938. Copyright assigned to the John Ireland Trust in 1974 and reissued by Braydeston Press (Norwich) [© 1975]. Also included in volume iii of *The Complete Works for Voice and Piano*, Stainer & Bell © 1981.
**Location of manuscript:** Manuscript Collections, The British Library (Reference Division), Add. MS 52897. No. 2 is titled 'The Red Rose' and no. 3 'These Women'.
**Bibliography:** Anon., 'Concerts: John Ireland's Songs', *The Times*, 5 Nov. 1938, p. 8.
R. Fiske, 'Ireland: Songs', *Gramophone*, 53/626 (July 1975), 227–8.
A. Robertson, 'Ireland', *Gramophone*, 41/489 (Feb. 1964), 378–9.
J. B. Steane, 'An Anthology of English Song', *Gramophone*, 69/826 (Mar. 1992), 109.
**Recordings:** No. 1:
Janet Baker (mezzo-soprano) and Martin Isepp (piano) *in* Classics Club X541, Saga XIP 7013, XID 5213 (1964), STXID 5213 (1963), SAGA 5213, CA 5213, SCD9012 (1992).
Complete:
Benjamin Luxon (baritone) and Alan Rowlands (piano) *in* Lyrita SRCS 66 (1975).

---

[35] George Parker (1888–1970): English baritone. Lay clerk at Eton College and Manchester Cathedral; lay vicar at Westminster Abbey. Singing teacher. Created the part of Omar in Oscar Asche's production of *Chu Chin Chow*.

**Notes:** In April 1938 Ireland was asked by Ralph Hawkes for a fanfare, for performance by new trumpets recently manufactured by Boosey & Hawkes. Ireland declined, Arthur Bliss, Arthur Benjamin, Haydn Wood, and Frederick Curzon agreeing to write suitable pieces.

## 1939

## Concertino pastorale

For string orchestra.

1. Eclogue (Sostenuto)
2. Threnody (Lento espressivo)
3. Toccata (Allegro molto ma non troppo presto)

**Commissioned by:** The 1939 Canterbury Festival.
**Instrumentation:** Violins I and II, violas, cellos, and double basses.
**Dedication:** For Boyd Neel, Canterbury, 1939.
**Duration:** 19' (and with repeat in the last movement: 20').
**First performance:** Canterbury, cloisters of the Cathedral Church of Christ, Wednesday 14 June 1939. The Boyd Neel String Orchestra (leader: Frederick Grinke), conducted by Boyd Neel.
**First London performance:** Queen's Hall, 18 August 1939. Strings of the BBC Symphony Orchestra, conducted by Henry J. Wood.
**Publication:** Hawkes & Co. Ltd. Score © 1939. Boosey & Hawkes Ltd. Miniature score © 1942 (Hawkes Pocket Scores no. 30). It is initialled and dated: J.I. Deal, 1939.
**Location of manuscript:** Manuscript Collections, The British Library (Reference Division), Add. MS 52876. It is initialled and dated: J.I. May 1939. Toccata and 'Threnody' are also included in BL Add. MS 52900.
**Bibliography:** W. R. Anderson, 'Ireland', *Gramophone*, 17/204 (May 1940), 416–17.

T. Harvey, 'English Music for Strings', *Gramophone*, 55/652 (Sept. 1977), 438, 443.

—— 'English Music for Strings', *Gramophone*, 63/747 (Aug. 1985), 250.

W. McNaught, 'The Promenade Concerts', *Musical Times*, 80/1159 (Sept. 1939), 680–1.

A. Robertson, 'Ireland', *Gramophone*, 44/520 (September 1966), 157–8.
**Recordings:** Bournemouth Sinfonietta/George Hurst *in* Red Seal RL 25071 (1977), CHAN 8375 (1985), CBR 1020, CBT 1020.

*Boyd Neel String Orchestra/Boyd Neel, Decca X253/5 (1940).

LPO/Adrian Boult *in* Lyrita RCS 31, SRCS 31, Musical Heritage Society 1498 (1966).

MGM SO/Izler Solomon *in* MGM E 3074.

**Notes:** Serenade for strings has been used as an alternative title. In April 1940 Ireland told Kenneth Thompson that he was 'having a hellish time trying to concoct a suite for string orchestra, with no ideas at all'. Also in April 1939, Kenneth Wright at the BBC informed Ireland that he would like him to compose some pieces for solo violin and chamber orchestra for Liza Minghetti to play. Paul Sacher wanted the first world performance.

OTHER VERSIONS

**The Vagabonds**

See under *Mai-Dun* (1921) for full details.

## 1940

## Missa Sancti Stephani (in the Dorian Mode)

For 4-part unaccompanied chorus (SATB).

Kyrie (I)
Responses to the Commandments (III)
Sanctus and Benedictus (IV)
Agnus Dei
Gloria

**Dedication:** To Father Kenneth Thompson.[36]

**Location of manuscript:** Manuscript Collections, The British Library (Reference Division), Add. MS 52900.

**Notes:** It is unlikely that this Mass was ever completed: there is no Credo. It was written in 1940 when Ireland was organist at St Stephen's Church, Guernsey. (He played at his first service there on 28 April 1940.)

OTHER VERSIONS

**Missa Brevis (St Stephen's Mass)**

For unaccompanied mixed chorus, completed and edited by Geoffrey Bush (1991).

IA. Kyrie Eleison (Comodo: senza rigole)
IB. Lord have mercy (Comodo: senza rigole)
II. Sanctus and Benedictus (Molto moderato e sostenuto)
III. Agnus Dei (Molto moderato e sostenuto)
IV. Gloria (Comodo: senza rigole)

**Publication:** Braydeston Press Ltd. Vocal score © 1993.

[36] Kenneth Thompson (1904–91): Cleric and friend of the composer from the 1930s. Many of Ireland's letters to Thompson are now in the British Library.

**Notes:** In his introduction Geoffrey Bush recalls the history of the work and its rediscovery in 1989 by Vivien Laundon. He continues:

The manuscript contains a detailed rough sketch for the complete work, together with a fair copy of the Kyrie (Greek and English version), Sanctus and Benedictus. Only the Benedictus has the addition of performance directions; elsewhere these have been supplied by the editor. Of the two movements left in sketch form, the Agnus Dei merely needed transcription and a few minor revisions; the completion of the Gloria was a far more extensive task. Only the treble part is written out in full; the movement of the lower voices is partially indicated in the first and third sections but not at all in the second except at three of the four principal cadence points. The editor has supplied what is missing in accordance with what he believes to have been the composer's intentions. He has also made two omissions: (1) a third version of the Kyrie music cast in the form of responses to be used during the recitation of the Ten Commandments—not a present day liturgical practice, and (2) a monotone Amen, marked optional, between Sanctus and Benedictus.

### 1940–1941

## Sarnia: An Island Sequence

For solo piano.

1. Le Catioroc (Quasi lento)
2. In a May Morning (Con moto moderato)
3. Song of the Springtides (Allegro comodo)

**Dedication:** 1—to Alfred Sebire [a prominent Guernsey flautist]; 2—To Michael [Michael Rayson, son of the owner of Birnam Court Hotel in Guernsey]; 3—To Mrs Mignot [a clergy widow at whose invitation Ireland became organist at St Stephen's in Guernsey].

**Duration:** *c.* 20'.

**First performance:** London, Wigmore Hall, Saturday 29 November 1941. Clifford Curzon (piano). First broadcast from the BBC's Bedford Studios on 14 December 1941 with Curzon at the piano.

**Publication:** Winthrop Rogers Ltd. Score © 1941. Now Boosey & Hawkes Ltd. Also included in volume iv of *The Collected Piano Works of John Ireland*, Stainer & Bell © 1976.

**Location of manuscript:** Manuscript Collections, The British Library (Reference Division), Add. MS 52890. Each is dated as follows: 1—Fort Sausmarez, L'Erée, 1940; 2—Birnam Court, St Peter Port, May 1940; 3—J.I. April 1940—March 1941.

**Bibliography:** F. Bonavia, 'Boosey and Hawkes Concerts', *Musical Times*, 83/1188 (Feb. 1942), 62.

M. Harrison, 'Ireland: Piano Works', *Gramophone*, 56/661 (June 1978), 86.

—— 'Ireland: Piano Works', *Gramophone*, 57/674 (July 1979), 229–30.

E. Markham Lee, 'John Ireland's Sarnia', *Musical Opinion*, 65 (Apr. 1942), 231–2.

A. Robertson, 'Ireland', *Gramophone*, 41/482 (Aug. 1963), 111–12.

L. Salter, 'Ireland', *Gramophone*, 29/340 (Sept. 1951), 75.

**Recordings:** Daniel Adni (piano) *in* HMV HQS 1414 (1979).

*Graham Mitchell (piano), Argo AU 1001/3 (1951).

Eric Parkin (piano) *in* Argo RG 28, *in* Lyrita SRCS 89 (1978).

Alan Rowlands (piano) *in* Lyrita RCS 23 (1963).

**Notes:** Each movement is prefaced by a quotation. 'La Catioroc' is prefaced by a Latin quotation from *De situ orbis* by the Roman geographer Pomponius Mela which dates from about AD 50:

> Silet per diem universus, nec sine horrore secretus est; lucet nocturnis ignibus, chorus Aegipanum undique personatur; audiuntur et cantus tibiarum et tinnitus cymbalorum per oram maritimam.
>
> [All day long heavy silence broods, and a certain hidden terror lurks there. But at nightfall gleams the light of fires; the chorus of Aegipans resounds on every side: the shrilling of flutes and the clash of cymbals re-echo by the waste shores of the sea.]

'In a May Morning' is prefaced by a passage from Victor Hugo's *Les Travailleurs de la mer* [The Toilers of the Sea]. 'Song of the Springtides' is prefaced by a quotation from Swinburne's *Thalassius*:

> Upon the flowery forefront of the year
> One wondering by the grey-green April sea
> Breeze-brightened . . .

In a letter to Kenneth Thompson, dated September 1940, Ireland related that he wanted to call the first piece 'Boys' Love', which is a name of the plant Southernwood, the second 'Aegipaus' Headland', which was Fort Saumarez, and the third 'The Daffodil Field'. He told Edwin Evans that:

> the dates I have placed after numbers 1 and 2 actually refer to the inception of these pieces, not their completion, and 'April 1940–March 1941' really is meant to cover the whole period from the time when I first thought of this work till it was actually finished.
>
> You may like to know that my association with the Channel Islands began in 1908. In that year, and in every succeeding year till and including 1914 I spent 7 or 8 weeks there, also I was in Guernsey from June 1939 till 22 June 1940. The Germans bombed the Island on 28 June and occupied it on 30 June (1940). (Letter dated 1 December 1941.)

Documents, now in the BBC Written Archives Centre, reveal that Adrian Boult telegraphed the BBC on 23 June 1940: 'Have just heard John Ireland still at Courthouse Place, Guernsey but anxious [for] immediate evacuation. Could Corporation ask the Ministry of Information to press local authorities?' The following day B. E. Nicholls (BBC) telegraphed Major Beith at the War Office: 'Much like to secure your help in the evacuation of John Ireland from Courthouse Place, Guernsey ... Incidentally, we are thinking of commissioning him to compose a patriotic song.' Ireland later recalled the 'strenuous and painful experiences involved in my last-minute escape from Guernsey' in a letter to Kenneth Thompson (16 July 1940). In a postscript, he said he 'was obliged to leave behind ... the greater part of my orchestral accompaniment of *A Downland Suite* which in the process of adaptation I had considerably modified.'

Late in 1940, Ralph Hawkes, Ireland's publisher, suggested that he should write a cello concerto for Piatigorsky.

## 1941

### Morning Service in C major

For mixed chorus (SATB) and organ. Text from the Book of Common Prayer.

Te Deum Laudamus (With dignity and easy movement)
Benedictus (With moderate movement)
Jubilate Deo (Bright but not fast)

**Dedication:**   Te Deum: To Martin Shaw.[37]
**Publication:**   Novello & Co. Ltd. Vocal score © 1941. Te Deum: PCB 1247; Benedictus: PCB 1248; Jubilate Deo: PCB 1249.
**Location of manuscript:** Manuscript Collections, The British Library (Reference Division), Add. MS 52894—Te Deum only. It is initialled and dated: J.I. Banbury, February 1941. Fragments of the Jubilate also in BL Add. MS 52901D.
**Notes:**   This service (and the Evening Service) was inspired by St Stephen's Church, Guernsey.

### Ride a cock-horse

Unison song for equal voices and piano. Text from the nursery rhyme. Unpublished.
**Location of manuscript:** Manuscript Collections, The British Library (Reference Division), Add. MS 52896. It is initialled and dated: J.I. Banbury 6 February 1941.

---

[37] Martin Shaw (1875–1958): English organist and composer. Studied under Stanford at the RCM. Founded the Purcell Operatic Society. Collaborated with Ralph Vaughan Williams in the musical editorship of *Songs of Praise* and the *Oxford Book of Carols*.

## Evening Service in C major

For mixed chorus (SATB) and organ. Text from the Book of Common Prayer.
  Magnificat (With stately movement)
  Nunc Dimittis (Grave and sustained)
**Dedication:**   To the Rev. E. Howard Muncey, M.A. Precentor of Gloucester Cathedral.[38]
**Publication:**   Novello & Co. Ltd. Vocal score © 1941 (PCB 1252).
**Location of manuscript:**   Fragments of the Nunc Dimittis in BL Add. MS 52901D and sketches in Add. MS 52901B.

## Ninefold Kyrie in A minor

For mixed chorus (SATB) and organ (optional).
**Publication:**   Novello & Co. Ltd. Vocal score © 1941 (PCB 1246). It was intended for use with the Communion Service in C.

## O Happy Land

Song for voice and piano. Text by W. J. Linton (1812–98).
**Duration:**   2' 30".
**First performance:**   Bedford, BBC Studios, 18 April 1941. William Parsons (baritone) and John Ireland (piano). (Broadcast in the Home Service.)
**Publication:**   Winthrop Rogers Ltd. Vocal score © 1941. Now Boosey & Hawkes Ltd.

### OTHER VERSIONS

#### O Happy Land

Arranged as a unison song for equal voices and piano or string orchestra.
**Date of arrangement:**   1941.
**Instrumentation:**   Violins I and II, violas, cellos, and double basses.
**First performance:**   Bedford, BBC Studios, 8 February 1942. The BBC Chorus and BBC Orchestra (Section A), conducted by Adrian Boult.
**Publication:**   Winthrop Rogers Ltd. Vocal score © 1941 (Winthrop Rogers Edition Festival Series of Choral Music). Now Boosey & Hawkes Ltd.
**Location of manuscript:**   Manuscript Collections, The British Library (Reference Division), Add. MS 52896. 2 versions: with piano or string orchestra. It is initialled and dated: J.I. Banbury, July 1941.

---

[38] Edward H. Muncey (1886–1954): Curate of Chelsea, 1909. Assistant master at Wellington College, 1915. Headmaster of the King's School, Gloucester, and Precentor of Gloucester Cathedral, 1930–42.

## Boys' Names

Unison song for equal voices and piano. Text by Eleanor Farjeon (1881–1966), from *Over the Garden Wall*.
**Dedication:** To Peter Lihou [Peter Letson in a letter to Kenneth Thompson dated 8 March 1943. He was one of Ireland's choirboys in Guernsey].
**Publication:** J. Curwen & Co. Ltd. Vocal score © 1942 (Choruses of Equal Voices no. 2089). Now Music Sales Ltd.
**Location of manuscript:** Manuscript Collections, The British Library (Reference Division), Add. MS 52896 (2 versions: in A flat and A major). It is initialled and dated: J.I. July 1941. Sketches in BL Add. MS 52901B.

## Here be naked boys

**Date of composition:** c.1941.
Unpublished.
**Location of manuscript:** Manuscript Collections, The British Library (Reference Division), Add. MS 52901B.

## Three Pastels

For solo piano.
1. A Grecian Lad (Poco andante)
2. The Boy Bishop (Calmato e semplice sempre)
3. Puck's Birthday (Vivace e brioso)

**Dedication:** to [Evelyn] Howard-James for whom they were originally written in student days.
**Duration:** 1—3' 00"; 2—4' 00"; 3—1' 45".
**First performance:** Bedford, BBC Studios, 8 March 1942. John Ireland (piano). (Broadcast in the Home Service.)
**Publication:** Augener & Co. Ltd. Score © 1941. Now Stainer & Bell Ltd. Also included in volume iv of *The Collected Piano Works of John Ireland*, Stainer & Bell © 1976.
**Location of manuscript:** Manuscript Collections, The British Library (Reference Division), Add. MS 52891. No. 1 is initialled and dated: J.I. 1941. There is also a note at the end of the music which states that the piece was rewritten from an early manuscript (c.1906). Similarly nos. 2 and 3 are initialled and dated: J.I. August 1941.
**Bibliography:** M. Harrison 'John Ireland, his Friends and Pupils', *Gramophone*, 61/724 (Sept. 1983), 375.
R. Hill, 'Radio Music', *Radio Times*, 6 Mar. 1942, p. 5.

A. Robertson, 'Ireland: Piano Works', *Gramophone*, 48/566 (July 1970), 191–2.

**Recordings:** Eric Parkin (piano) *in* Chandos DBRD 2006, DBTD 2006 (1983). Alan Rowlands (piano) *in* Lyrita RCS 29 (1970).

**Notes:** Each piece is prefaced by a quotation. No. 1 (A. E. Housman, *A Shropshire Lad*):

> A Grecian lad, as I hear tell,
> One that many loved in vain,
> Looked into a forest well
> And never looked away again.

Ireland originally intended to call this piece 'Hyacinthus'.

No. 2 (Psalm 45):

> diffusa est gratia in labiis tuis.
>
> [Full of grace are thy lips.]

This second piece is also prefaced by the following note, taken from *Brand's Observations on Popular Antiquities*:

In Cathedrals, a Boy Bishop was wont to be elected from among the Children of the Choir on St. Nicholas' Day. In the Sarum Processional (1566) is printed the Service of the Boy Bishop, set to music, from which we learn that, on the Eve of the Holy Innocents' Day, the Boy Bishop went in solemn procession with his followers 'ad Altare Innocentium sive Sanctae Trinitatis' in their copes and with burning tapers in their hands ... And all this was done with solemnity of celebration, and under pain of anathema to any that should interrupt or press upon these Children ...

No. 3 (William Shakespeare, *A Midsummer Night's Dream*):

> I am that merry wanderer of the night.

Ireland told Julian Herbage at the BBC, letter dated 13 October 1941, that 'The first two (shorter piano pieces) are definitely re-written from pieces I wrote when I was 17 but beyond some re-shaping and polishing they are not harmonically altered. . . . They are the thoughts of an adolescent and rather naive mind.'

## A New Year Carol

For mixed chorus (SATB) and piano. Text: traditional from an anthology by W. H. Auden.

**Duration:** 0' 55".

**First performance:** Bedford, BBC Studios, 29 December 1941. The BBC Singers, conducted by Trevor Harvey. (Broadcast in the Home Service.)

**Publication:** Winthrop Rogers & Co. Ltd. Vocal score © 1942. Now Boosey & Hawkes Ltd.

**Location of manuscript:** Manuscript Collections, The British Library (Reference Division), Add. MS 52895. It is dated 'All Souls Day, 1941'.
**Bibliography:** T. Harvey 'Ireland: Choral Works', *Gramophone*, 57/673 (June 1979), 93–4.
**Recordings:** Gloucester Cathedral Choir/John Sanders *in* Abbey CACA 917, CDCA 917 (1991).
Worcester Cathedral Choir/Donald Hunt *in* Abbey LPB 803 (1979).

OTHER VERSIONS

A New Year Carol

Arranged for 2-part (SA) chorus or as a unison song for equal voices and piano.
**Date of arrangement:** 1941.
**Publication:** Winthrop Rogers Ltd. Vocal score © 1942 (Winthrop Rogers Edition Carol Series). Now Boosey & Hawkes Ltd.

## 1941–1942

# Epic March

For full orchestra.
**Commissioned by:** The BBC.
**Instrumentation:** 2 flutes (2nd doubling piccolo), 2 oboes, 2 clarinets in B flat, 2 bassoons, 4 horns in F, 2 trumpets in C, 3 trombones, tuba, timpani, percussion (2 players: side-drum, cymbal, bass drum, triangle, gong, xylophone, bells), organ, and strings.
**Duration:** 9'. (The composer authorized cuts: from 13 (p. 20 of the full score) to 15 (on p. 23), and from the last bar on p. 35 to the second bar on p. 42.)
**First performance:** London, Royal Albert Hall, Saturday 27 June 1942. The London Philharmonic Orchestra (leader: Jean Pougnet) and Berkeley Mason (organ), conducted by Henry J. Wood.
**Publication:** Hawkes & Co. Ltd. Full score © 1942. Boosey & Hawkes Ltd. Miniature score [© 1943] (Hawkes Pocket Score no. 55). It is initialled and dated: J.I. March 1942.
**Location of manuscript:** Unable to trace. There is a sketch in the BBC Written Archives.
**Bibliography:** Anon., 'The Promenade Concerts', *The Times*, 29 June 1942, p. 6.
  D. Denton, 'Ireland', *Music Magazine*, 4 (Feb. 1991), 54.
  T. Harvey, 'Ireland', *Gramophone*, 58/690 (Nov. 1980), 723.
  R. Hill, 'Heroic Music', *Radio Times*, 19 June 1942, p. 4.

W. McNaught, 'Promenade Concerts', *Musical Times*, 83/1192 (June 1942), 222–3.

A. Robertson, 'Ireland', *Gramophone*, 44/520 (Sept. 1966), 157–8.

**Recordings:** LPO/Adrian Boult *in* Lyrita RCS 31, SRCS 31, Musical Heritage Society 1498 (1966).

LPO/Henry Wood, BBC Archive LP 23936 (27 June 1942).

LSO/Richard Hickox *in* Chandos CHAN 8879, ABTD 1492 (1990).

*New Concert Orch./Stanford Robinson, Boosey & Hawkes OT 2081.

West Australian SO/David Measham *in* Unicorn-Kanchana KP 8001 (1980).

**Notes:** The score is prefaced by a definition of the word 'epic' from *Nuttalls's Standard Dictionary*: 'Concerning some heroic action or series of actions and events of deep and lasting significance in the history of a nation or a race.'

Letters, now in the BBC Archives, trace how the March was commissioned and written:

17 November 1940: A BBC memo reveals that 'the MoI has asked us to produce a patriotic march—in other words an alternative to "Land of Hope and Glory". Who do you suggest?'

28 November 1940: Letter to Ireland from Adrian Boult asking whether this idea would appeal to him.

30 November 1940: Reply from Ireland who accepts this commission.

20 December 1940: Letter from Boult offering a fee of 40 guineas (which is later increased to 60 guineas).

8 June 1941: Letter to Boult from Ireland telling him that he has sent a manuscript sketch to him for comment.

12 June 1941: 'Grim and Gay' (a Churchill quote) mentioned as a possible title.

14 July 1941: Letter to R. S. Thatcher at the BBC from Ireland with an enclosed sketch, the 'V' [for Victory] rhythm being indicated in red ink.

2 September 1941: Letter to Boult from Ireland informing him that he is hard at work on the March, and asking for his opinion about the Trio.

8 September 1941: Letter to Julian Herbage at the BBC from Ireland saying that he intends to call the March 'The Liberators'.

14 September 1941: More variations on the title: 'Calling all Shirkers' or 'Ussia (USSR) v. Prussia'.

14 September 1941: Letter to Boult from Ireland: 'The March is now completed to the end of Trio section, and I can see my way clearly to the close. I have only just commenced the full score . . .'

5 March 1942: Letter to Thatcher from Ireland: 'I am inclined to call it EPIC MARCH. (Ireland had already jettisoned Heroic March and March in C minor before finally settling on this title.)

31 March 1942: Letter to Boult from Ireland: 'At last the new March is finished ...'

## OTHER VERSIONS

**Epic March**

Arranged for symphonic wind band by Geoffrey Brand.
**Date of arrangement:** 1989.
**Instrumentation:** 2 concert flutes and piccolo, 2 oboes, E flat clarinet, solo B flat clarinet, 3 B flat clarinets, E flat alto clarinet, B flat bass clarinet, E flat alto saxophone, B flat tenor saxophone, E flat baritone saxophone, B flat bass saxophone and B flat contrabass clarinet, 2 bass, 4 horns in F, solo and first B flat cornet, 2nd B flat cornet, 2 B flat trumpets, 2 tenor trombones, bass trombone, euphonium (baritone), basses, string bass, timpani, and percussion.
**Publication:** R. Smith & Co. Ltd. Full score © 1990.

**Epic March**

Arranged for solo piano by the composer.
**Date of arrangement:** 1942.
**Publication:** Hawkes & Co. Ltd. Score © 1942.

**Epic March**

Arranged for organ by Robert Gower.
**Date of arrangement:** 1988.
**Publication:** Hawkes & Co. Ltd. Score © 1988. Included in *Processionals for Organ*, Novello & Co. Ltd. © 1988.

## 1942

## The Boy

Unison song for equal voices and piano. Text by Eleanor Farjeon (1881–1966).
**Publication:** J. Curwen & Co. Ltd. Vocal score © 1942. Now Music Sales Ltd.
**Location of manuscript:** Manuscript Collections, The British Library (Reference Division), Add. MS 52896.

## The Bell in the Leaves

Unison song for equal voices and piano. Text by Eleanor Farjeon (1881–1966).
**Publication:** Winthrop Rogers Ltd. Vocal score © 1942. Now Boosey & Hawkes Ltd.

## Joseph fell a-dreaming

Unison song for equal voices and piano. Text by Eleanor Farjeon (1881–1966).
**Dedication:** To my friend Thomas Dunhill.
**Publication:** Winthrop Rogers & Co. Ltd. Vocal score © 1942 (Winthrop Rogers Edition of Choral Music for Festivals). Now Boosey & Hawkes Ltd.

## Looking on

Unison song for equal voices and piano. Text by Eleanor Farjeon (1881–1966).
**Dedication:** For John Longmire.[39]
**Publication:** J. Curwen & Co. Ltd. Vocal score © 1949 (Choruses for Equal Voices no. 2092). Now Music Sales Ltd.

## Immortality

Song for unaccompanied mixed chorus (SATB). Sonnet by Henry P. Crompton.
**Date of composition:** June 1942.
**Dedication:** To Leslie Woodgate[40] and the BBC Chorus.
**Duration:** 3' 45".
**First performance:** Bedford, BBC Studios, 22 February 1943. The BBC Chorus, conducted by Leslie Woodgate. (Broadcast in the Home Service.)
**Publication:** Winthrop Rogers & Co. Ltd. Vocal score © 1942 (part of the Winthrop Rogers Edition of Choral Music for Festivals). Now Boosey & Hawkes Ltd.
**Recordings:** Louis Halsey Singers, BBC LP 33249.

## Julius Caesar

Music for the play by William Shakespeare (1564–1616).
**Date of composition:** 1942.
**Commissioned by:** The BBC.
**Music written for the following:** (1) Opening Fanfare; (2) Overture (Serioso); (3) Fanfare: Caesar's Ceremonial Trumpets; (4) Lupercalia Music (Animato); (5) Entr'acte: Storm Music; (6) Caesar's Triumphant March (Alla marcia); (7) Caesar's Trumpets (Bold); (8) Short Tragic March

---

[39] John Longmire (1902–86): Composer, educationist, and examiner at Trinity College of Music. Scholar and Exhibitioner, RCM, from 1923. Composer of many well-known piano albums, choral works, operettas, and school songs.

[40] Leslie Woodgate (1902–61): Joined the BBC in 1929 and became chorus master. Wrote several songs, chamber music, orchestral works, and an oratorio.

(Solemn); (9) Entr'acte II; (10) Military March; (11) Brutus' Theme; (12) Cassius' Theme (with mute); (13) Lucius' Song; (13A: Lucius' music was omitted); (14 and 14A) Ghost Music (Poco lento); (15) Brutus' and Cassius' Music; (16) Military March (as 10); (17) Brutus' and Cassius' Music (as 15); (18) [Battle Music]—see notes below; (19) Funeral March (Solemn).

**Instrumentation:** 2 flutes and piccolo, 2 oboes and cor anglais, 2 clarinets in B flat, clarinet in E flat, 2 bassoons, 3 horns in F, 3 trumpets in B flat, 3 trombones, tuba, bass tuba, bass, timpani, percussion (2 players: bass drum, cymbals, tambourine, large triangle, side-drum), and piano (in no. 4 only).

**First performance:** London, Broadcasting House, Monday 28 September 1942. Broadcast in the Home Service at 20.00 hours. Music played by 24 players of the Royal Artillery Band, Woolwich, conducted by Charles Groves. Cast included Marius Goring, Eric Portman, and Valentine Dyall. Unpublished.

**Location of manuscript:** Manuscript Collections, The British Library (Reference Division), Add. MS 52880. The score is initialled and dated: J.I. 12 September 1942. Ireland's attempts at the Battle Music can also be found in BL Add. MS 52900. Part (0' 45") of Honegger's music to *The Tempest* (on record) was substituted for Ireland's Battle Music in the broadcast.

**Notes:** In a letter to John Longmire, dated 11 September 1942, Ireland wrote: 'I suddenly got saddled with the job of writing incidental *orchestral* music for a BBC production of 'Julius Caesar' and the score has to be delivered in 10 days . . . I have to orchestrate 19 numbers. Some of these are quite short . . . but others are not so short.'


## OTHER VERSIONS

**Scherzo and Cortège on themes from Julius Caesar**

Arranged for orchestra by Geoffrey Bush.
**Date of arrangement:** 1970, for the Lyrita recording.
**Instrumentation:** 2 flutes and piccolo, 2 oboes and cor anglais, 2 clarinets and bass clarinet, 2 bassoons, 3 horns, 2 trumpets, 3 trombones, tuba, timpani, percussion (2), and 2 or more double basses.
**Duration:** 6' 30".
**Publication:** Boosey & Hawkes Ltd. Score [© 1971] (Hawkes Pocket Scores no. 867).
**Bibliography:** M. Jameson, 'Ireland: Orchestral Works', *Gramophone* 69/825 (Feb. 1992), 35–6.
  A. Robertson, 'Ireland: Orchestral Works', *Gramophone*, 48/573 (Feb. 1971), 1310, 1315.
**Recordings:** LPO/Adrian Boult *in* Lyrita SRCS 45, Musical Heritage Society 1481 (1971).
  LSO/Richard Hickox *in* CHAN 8994 (1991).

**Notes:** In a letter to Ireland from Denis Wright, dated 10 November 1942, he wrote: 'I am sending you an official invitation to write either a March (not over 4 minutes) or a *fantasy* of about 6 to 8 minutes, and I think your idea of drawing material from Playford would be an excellent one.'

## 1943

### Fantasy Sonata

For clarinet (in B flat) and piano.
**Date of composition:** Autumn and winter 1943.
**Dedication:** For Frederick Thurston.[41]
**Duration:** *c.* 15'.
**First performance:** London, Wigmore Hall, Saturday 5 February 1944. Frederick Thurston (clarinet) and Kendall Taylor (piano). First broadcast the following day from the BBC's Bedford Studios with Thurston and Ireland playing the piano.
**Publication:** Hawkes & Sons Ltd. Score © 1945. The printed copy is initialled and dated: J.I. June–December 1943.
**Bibliography:** Anon., 'Boosey and Hawkes Concert', *The Times*, 1 Feb. 1944, p. 8.

Anon., 'John Ireland', *Tempo*, 6 (1944), 20.

Anon., 'Wigmore Hall Concert', *The Times*, 11 Oct. 1944, p. 6.

S. Goddard, 'John Ireland's Fantasy Sonata for Clarinet and Piano', *Tempo*, 8 (Sept. 1944), 6–9.

R. Hill, 'Clarinet and Harp', *Radio Times*, 4 Feb. 1944, p. 4.

R. Layton, 'English Wind Music', *Gramophone*, 49/584 (Jan. 1972), 1233.

M. Macdonald, 'English Music for Clarinet and Piano', *Gramophone*, 65/774 (Nov. 1987), 772.

A. Robertson, 'Ireland', *Gramophone*, 40/477 (Feb. 1963), 391.

E. Warr, 'Ireland', *Gramophone*, 49/588 (May 1972), 1902, 1907.

**Recordings:** John Denman (clarinet) and Hazel Vivienne (piano) *in* Revolution RCF 009 (1972).

Thea King (clarinet) and Alan Rowlands (piano) *in* Saga XIP 7008 (1963), XID 5206.

Gervase de Peyer (clarinet) and Eric Parkin (piano) *in* Lyrita SRCS 59 (1972).

—— (clarinet) and Geoffrey Pryor (piano) *in* Chandos ABRD 1237, ABTD 1237 (1987), CHAN 8549.

*Frederick Thurston (clarinet) and Kendall Taylor (piano), BBC Transcription 32994/7.

---

[41] Frederick Thurston (1901–53): Clarinet soloist and professor at the RCM. Made many recordings and gave the first performances of many important works for the clarinet.

**Notes:** In the summer of 1943, Ireland was seriously considering writing another piano concerto at the invitation of Moiseiwitsch. According to John Longmire, Ireland attended a Promenade concert on 8 July 1943 to hear him play Rachmaninov's Third Piano Concerto.

## 1944

### Ex ore innocentium

Motet for treble voices (SA) and piano (or organ). Text by Bishop W. W. How.
**Commissioned by:** Sir Sydney H. Nicholson.[42]
**Dedication:** To Sydney H. Nicholson.
**Duration:** 3' 35".
**First performance:** Durham, Cathedral Church of Christ and Blessed Mary the Virgin, 18 August 1944. The School of English Church Music Cathedral Course choir, conducted by Sydney Nicholson.
**Publication:** Winthrop Rogers & Co. Ltd. Vocal score © 1944. Now Boosey & Hawkes Ltd.
**Location of manuscript:** Manuscript Collections, The British Library (Reference Division), Add. MS 52894 (2 versions: motet with organ or piano accompaniment). It is initialled and dated: J.I. June 1944. According to the Revd Kenneth Thompson, 'It is a thing' was a text that Ireland had, for years, been meaning to set for boys' voices. Sketches can also be found in BL Add. MS 52900, Add. MS 52901B, Add. MS 52901D.
**Bibliography:** J. Chissell, 'Ireland', *Gramophone*, 46/550 (Mar. 1969), 1318.
T. Harvey, 'Ireland: Choral Works', *Gramophone*, 57/673 (June 1979), 93–4.
S. Webb, 'Choral Works', *Gramophone*, 52/620 (Jan. 1975), 1380.
**Recordings:** Choir of the School of St Mary and St Anne, Abbots Bromley/ Barry Draycott (organ)/Llywela Harris *in* Argo ZRG 785 (1975).
Leeds Parish Church Choir/Anthony Cooke (organ)/Paul Dutton (treble)/ Donald Hunt *in* Morgan MR 1138 (1969).
Worcester Cathedral Choir/Donald Hunt *in* Abbey LPB 803 (1979).
York Minster Choir/Francis Jackson (organ) *in* Abbey E 7620, E 7620 (stereo).
**Notes:** A letter, now in the Ireland Trust Archives, is signed by all the choirboys (from various church choirs) who took part in the first performance whilst on a School of English Church Music (later the Royal School of Church Music) holiday course at Durham.

---

[42] Sidney H. Nicholson (1875–1947): Founder and Director of the Royal School of Church Music. Organist of various churches and cathedrals including Carlisle, Manchester, and Westminster Abbey, 1918–27. Composer of cantatas, church music, and light operas.

## 1944–1946

## Satyricon

Overture for orchestra (after Petronius).
**Commissioned by:** The BBC.
**Instrumentation:** 2 flutes (2nd doubling piccolo), 2 oboes, 2 clarinets in A, 2 bassoons, 4 horns in F, 2 trumpets in C, 2 tenor trombones, bass trombone, tuba, timpani, percussion (2 players: xylophone, whip, tambourine, glockenspiel, cymbals), harp, and strings.
**Dedication:** To Julian and Anna [Herbage].[43]
**Duration:** *c.*8'.
**First performance:** London, Royal Albert Hall, Wednesday 11 September 1946. The BBC Symphony Orchestra, conducted by Basil Cameron.
**Publication:** J. Williams & Co. Ltd. Full score © 1949. Miniature score © 1950 (William's Music Scores no. 1). Now Stainer & Bell Ltd.
**Location of manuscript:** Manuscript Collections, The British Library (Reference Division), Add. MS 52877. It is initialled and dated: J.I. 19 August 1946.
**Bibliography:** Anon., 'Orchestral', *Monthly Musical Record*, 79 (Nov. 1949), 246.
   J. Ireland, Programme note for the first performance, 11 Sept. 1946, p. 6 in the programme.
   M. Jameson, 'Ireland: Orchestral Works', *Gramophone*, 69/825 (Feb. 1992), 35–6.
   I. Keys, 'Overture: Satyricon', *Music and Letters*, 32 (1951), 194.
   R. Layton, 'John Ireland: Overture—Satyricon', *Musical Survey*, 2 (1949), 105.
   W. McNaught, 'London Concerts', *Musical Times*, 87/1244 (Oct. 1946), 316.
   A. Robertson, 'Ireland', *Gramophone*, 44/520 (Sept. 1966), 157–8.
   H. Rutland, 'Reviews of Music', *Music Review*, 12 (1951), 241–2.
**Recordings:** *BBC SO/Adrian Boult, BBC Transcription 41748/9.
   BBC SO/Adrian Boult, NSA tape M567W.
   BBC SO/Malcolm Sargent, BBC Sound Archive T45257 (2 Aug. 1949).
   LPO/Adrian Boult *in* Lyrita RCS 32, SRCS 32, Musical Heritage Society 1317 (1966).
   LSO/Richard Hickox *in* CHAN 8994 (1991).
**Notes:** The score is prefaced by a quote from Burnaby's translation of the *Satyricon* of T. Petronius Arbiter:

---

[43] Julian L. Herbage (1904–76): Musicologist, writer, and broadcaster. Assistant Director of Music at the BBC 1940–4. Editor with Anna Instone, his wife, of the BBC radio programme *Music Magazine* from 1944 to 1973.

I... am resolved to be as good as my Word, being so met to our Desires; not only to improve our Learning, but to be merry, and put life in our Discourse with pleasanter Tales.

In a letter to Ireland dated 7 September 1944, Julian Herbage at the BBC wrote, 'you were unable to complete anything in time for Sir Henry Wood's Jubilee Proms but I believe you were at work on the *Variations on Paul's Steeple*.' (Sketch in Manuscript Collections, British Library (Reference Division) at Add. MS 52901.)

Almost two years later, letter dated 22 June 1946, Ireland told Kenneth Thompson that 'two years ago, I began an orchestral work based on The Satyricon of Petronius'. He had informed Victor Hely-Hutchinson, Director of Music at the BBC, on 17 February 1946 that 'I think I can have my new overture *Satyricon* ready...'. It was not however until August that the score was delivered to the BBC, in time for the Promenade concert rehearsals. (Letter to Julian Herbage, dated 14 August 1946.)

1946–1947

## The Overlanders

Music for the film. Ealing Studios. Producer: Michael Balcon. Director: Harry Watt.

**Music composed for the following episodes:** Main Titles (Allegro maestoso); Scorched Earth; Departure of Ship (Malincolico); Roll Up (start of trek); Open Country (Broad and noble); Start of Trek; River Crossing (horses): A (Lento); Cattle in River: C (Comodo); Cart Music (Whimsically); Cheer up tune (based on the music of no. 4) (all orchestrated by Ernest Irving); Catching the Brumbies; Breaking the Brumbies (orchestrated by Alan Rawsthorne); Love Theme (Andantino, con sentimento); Night Stampede (Allegro marcato); Finding Sailor (Moderato); Cart Music (orchestrated by Irving); Mountain Crossing (Moderato); Water Stampede (Slow) (orchestrated by Irving and Roy Douglas); End Titles.

**Instrumentation:** 2 flutes and piccolo, 2 oboes and cor anglais, 2 clarinets in B flat and A, bass clarinet in B flat, 2 bassoons, 4 horns in F, 2 trumpets in B flat and A, cornet, 3 trombones, tuba, timpani, percussion (3 players: bass drum, side-drum, cymbals, triangle, tenor drum, xylophone, glockenspiel), piano, harp, and strings.

**Duration of film:** 91'.

**Film first shown:** Trade shown 19 September 1946: London, Odeon Theatre, Leicester Square. General release *c*.3 October 1946. Music played by the Philharmonia Orchestra, conducted by Ernest Irving. The film, starring Chips Rafferty, describes how a group of north Australian herdsmen, finding themselves and their cattle threatened during World War II by the prospect of a Japanese invasion, trekked across mountains, rivers, and deserts to safety hundreds of miles further south.

Unpublished.

**Location of manuscript:** Manuscript Collections, The British Library (Reference Division), Add. MS 52881. A fragment can also be found in BL Add. MS 52900.

**Bibliography:** Anon., 'The Overlanders', *Kinematograph Weekly*, 26 Sept. 1946, p. 21.

Anon., 'The Overlanders: Box-Office Winner in all Theatres', *Today's Cinema*, 20 Sept. 1946, pp. 3, 18.

K.F.B., 'The Overlanders', *Monthly Film Bulletin*, 13/154 (1946–7), 135.

H. Crosland, 'The Overlanders', *Soundtrack*, 24 (1980/1), 17–19.

'Harlequin', 'Ireland', *Gramophone*, 25/291 (Aug. 1947), 42.

A. Vesselo, 'British Films of the Quarter', *Sight and Sound* (Winter 1946–7), 155–6.

**Recordings:** Excerpts:

*LSO/Muir Mathieson, Decca K1602 (1947), London T5055, *in* set LA48.

The film is not available on home video. A copy (16 mm.) can however be hired from the National Film Archive.

**Notes:** Ireland told John Longmire, letter dated 16 January 1946, that the film company 'had moved heaven and earth to get me to do it and have given me an excellent contract—every obstacle I raised, they gave way.... The film itself is of an exceptional character, which presents nothing I should dislike writing music about. They clearly thought I am the *only* composer who could provide really suitable music.' In another letter, dated 10 April 1946, Ireland wrote,

> The episodes in the film are long and extremely strenuous, and exhausting to conceive, and they keep on altering the 'timings' which involves a lot more needless and difficult work—I had to work 4 *hours* till 2am the other night (after working all day) to put straight something they had altered—in all only about 50" of music. I will never undertake anything of this sort again unless ample time is available.

Ireland was later approached for another film score: Cavalcanti's *Toilers of the Sea*. However this came to nothing when Cavalcanti left Ealing Studios.

## OTHER VERSIONS

### The Overlanders

Suite for orchestra, selected and edited from the film by Charles Mackerras.

1. March: Scorched Earth (Allegro maestoso) (consisting of the Main Titles and Scorched Earth music);

2. Romance: Mary and the Sailor (Andante) (Love theme);
3. Intermezzo: Open Country (Allegretto amabile) (Open Country);
4. Scherzo: Brumbies (Allegro vivace) (Catching the Brumbies);
5. Finale: Night Stampede (Allegro marcato) (Night Stampede).

**Date of arrangement:** 1965.
**Instrumentation:** 2 flutes and piccolo, 2 oboes and cor anglais, 2 clarinets in A, 2 bassoons, 4 horns in F, 3 trumpets in A (3rd doubling cornet), 3 trombones, tuba, timpani, percussion (3 players: bass drum, side-drum, cymbals, triangle, xylophone, glockenspiel), harp, and strings.
**Duration:** c. 22' (5' 24"; 4' 20"; 3' 30"; 4' 14"; 3' 54").
**Publication:** Boosey & Hawkes Ltd. Full score © 1971. Miniature score [© 1971] (Hawkes Pocket Scores no. 869). The March (no. 1) was also published separately.
**Bibliography:** T. Harvey, 'Ireland', *Gramophone*, 58/690 (Nov. 1980), 723.
 M. Jameson, 'Ireland: Orchestral Works', *Gramophone*, 69/825 (Feb. 1992), 35–6.
 I. March, 'British Music for Film and TV', *Gramophone*, 57/679 (Dec. 1979), 1024.
 A. Robertson, 'Ireland: Orchestral Works', *Gramophone*, 48/573 (Feb. 1971), 1310, 1315.
**Recordings:** LPO/Adrian Boult *in* Lyrita SRCS 45, Musical Heritage Society 1481 (1971).
 LSO/Richard Hickox *in* Chandos CHAN 8994 (1991).
 West Australian SO/David Measham *in* Unicorn-Kanchana KP 8001 (1980).
 No. 2 only:
 CBSO/Marcus Dods *in* HMV ASD 3797, TC-ASD 3797 (1979).

**Two Symphonic Studies**

For orchestra, arranged by Geoffrey Bush from material taken from unpublished sections of the film.

1. Fugue (Pesante)
2. Toccata (Lento)

**Date of arrangement:** 1969 (July–October), for the Lyrita recording.
**Commissioned by:** Norah Kirby[44] and the John Ireland Trust, to whom it is dedicated.
**Instrumentation:** 2 flutes, 2 oboes, 2 clarinets, 2 bassoons, 4 horns, 3 trumpets, 3 trombones, tuba, timpani, percussion (2), and strings.
**Duration:** 10'–11'.
**Publication:** Boosey & Hawkes Ltd. Full score © 1971 (Hawkes Pocket Scores no. 868).
**Bibliography:** A. Robertson, 'Ireland: Orchestral Works', *Gramophone*, 48/573 (Feb. 1971), 1310, 1315.
**Recordings:** LPO/Adrian Boult *in* Lyrita SRCS 45, Musical Heritage Society 1481 (1971).

---

[44] Norah Kirby (1895–1982): Personal secretary and companion to John Ireland. Introduced to Ireland by Ralph Hill.

## 1947

### Man in his labour rejoiceth

Choral song for mixed chorus (SATB) and brass band. Text by Robert Bridges (1844–1930), from *A Hymn of Nature*.

**Commissioned by:** The *Daily Herald* in co-operation with the National Coal Board.

**Instrumentation:** Solo cornet in B flat, soprano in E flat, ripieno and flugelhorn in B flat, 2nd and 3rd cornets in B flat, solo horn in E flat, 1st and 2nd horn in E flat, 1st and 2nd baritones in B flat, 1st and 2nd trombones in B flat, bass trombone, euphonium in B flat and B flat basses, drums, and percussion.

**Dedication:** To the Mineworkers of Britain.

**Duration:** 2' 45".

**First performance:** London, Harringay Arena, 1 May 1948. Choirs conducted by Leslie Woodgate and bands conducted by Adrian Boult.

**Publication:** J. Williams & Co. Ltd. Vocal score © 1947 (St Cecilia Series 26 no. 16). Now Stainer & Bell Ltd.

**Bibliography:** Anon., 'Colliery Music Festival', *Coal* (Jan. 1948), 13.
Anon., 'Folk Dancers at Pit Festival', *Daily Herald*, 3 May 1948, p. 3.
Anon., 'National Colliery Music Festival', *Colliery Guardian*, 7 May 1948, p. 636.
W. M. Harman, 'Harringay Impressed the Experts', *Coal* (June 1948), 20–1.

**Recordings:** Choir and organ, BBC Sound Archive 13403.

**Notes:** Ireland told Kenneth Thompson, letter dated 30 December 1947, that the Coal Board seemed quite pleased with the piece. He added, 'my days of inspired music are over'.

## 1948

### Sampford

Hymn tune for mixed chorus (SATB) and organ. Text ('Christ the Lord is risen today') by Jane E. Leeson. Written for *Hymns Ancient and Modern Revised*.

**Commissioned by:** Sir Sydney Nicholson.

**Publication:** William Clowes & Sons © 1950.

## 1949

## Columbine

For solo piano.
**Date of composition:** 1949; revised 1951.
**Duration:** 2' 30".
**Publication:** The British and Continental Music Agencies Ltd. Score © 1951. (Included in *Down the Centuries*, an anthology of piano pieces, ed. Leonard Isaacs, pp. 20–4.) Also included in volume iv of *The Collected Piano Works of John Ireland*, Stainer & Bell © 1976.
**Location of manuscript:** Manuscript Collections, The British Library (Reference Division), Add. MS 52889 (both versions). It is dated May 1949.
**Bibliography:** M. Harrison, 'Ireland: Piano Works', *Gramophone*, 57/674 (July 1979), 229–30.
—— 'John Ireland, his Friends and Pupils', *Gramophone*, 61/724 (Sept. 1983), 375.
A. Robertson, 'Ireland: Piano Works', *Gramophone*, 48/566 (July 1970), 191–2.
**Recordings:** Daniel Adni (piano) *in* HMV HQS 1414 (1979).
Eric Parkin (piano) *in* Chandos DBRD 2006, DBTD 2006 (1983).
Alan Rowlands (piano) *in* Lyrita RCS 29 (1970).
**Notes:** Ireland told Professor Beedle, letter dated Good Friday 1949, that 'I have accepted a commission to write a piano piece for an unusual purpose—some man who is a friend of the Agent I went to (over Williams & Co) wants to give his wife, on her birthday, a piano piece specially written for the occasion—by me—he is prepared to pay £50.00 so I can't turn that down!'

Ireland was asked for another piano concerto as part of the musical celebrations marking the Festival of Britain in 1951 but refused.

## 1952

## Piece for oboe and piano

Unpublished.
**Location of manuscript:** Manuscript Collections, The British Library (Reference Division), Add. MS 52901E. These incomplete sketches were for a combination of instruments for which Ireland never published any music. He was said to be working on the piece as early as October 1952, and had these forces in mind when endeavouring to compose a work for Evelyn Rothwell (Lady Barbirolli) to play at a recital in February 1953 but found them uncongenial.

## 1953

### The Hills

Song for unaccompanied mixed chorus (SATB). Text by James Kirkup (1923– ).
**Date of composition:** January 1953.
**Commissioned by:** The Arts Council of Great Britain (for the anthology *A Garland for the Queen*) to mark the occasion of the coronation of HM Queen Elizabeth II.
**Dedication:** [To HM Queen Elizabeth II, by gracious permission].
**Duration:** 2' 15".
**First performance:** London, Royal Festival Hall, Monday 1 June 1953. The Cambridge University Madrigal Society and the Golden Age Singers, conducted by Boris Ord.
**Publication:** Stainer & Bell Ltd. Vocal score © 1953 (composite), © 1956 (separate) (Choral Library no. 347).
**Location of manuscript:** Unable to trace. Sketches in BL Add. MS 52900.
**Bibliography:** R. Fiske, 'A Garland for the Queen', *Gramophone*, 55/649 (June 1977), 90.
   H. Keller, 'The Half-Year's New Music', *Music Review*, 14 (1953), 209–19.
   H. Ottaway, 'A Garland for the Queen', *Musical Times*, 118/1618 (Dec. 1977), 1017.
   A. Robertson, 'A Garland for the Queen', *Gramophone*, 31/366 (Nov. 1953), 203.
   J. Steane, 'A Garland for the Queen', *Gramophone*, 69/827 (Apr. 1992), 150.
**Recordings:** Cambridge University Chamber Choir/Timothy Brown *in* Gamut Classics GAM CD 529 (1991).
   CUMS and the Golden Age Singers/Boris Ord *in* Columbiua CX 1063 (1953).
   Exultate Singers/Garrett O'Brien *in* RCA Gold Seal GL 25062, GK 25062 (1977).

## 1956

### Adam lay ybounden

Carol for unaccompanied mixed chorus (SATB). Text from a fifteenth-century manuscript.
**Duration:** 1' 27".
**Publication:** E. H. Freeman & Co. Ltd. (Brighton). Vocal score © 1956 (University Part Songs and Anthems no. 115). Now EMI Music Publishing Ltd.

**Bibliography:** T. Harvey, 'Ireland: Choral Works', *Gramophone*, 57/673 (June 1979), 93–4.
**Recordings:** Christ College Chapel Choir, Brecon/Jonathan Leonard *in* Abbey CAPS 407 (1991).
Worcester Cathedral Choir/Donald Hunt *in* Abbey LPB 803 (1979).

## 1958

## Psalm 23

Unaccompanied setting (omitting verse 5) for baritone. Text from the Book of Common Prayer.
**Dedication:** For George Parker.
Unpublished.
**Location of manuscript:** The John Ireland Trust, London. It is initialled and dated: J.I. 1958 A.M.D.G. Mention of the piece can also be found in Ireland's notebooks (Manuscript Collections, British Library, Add. MS 52901A).
**Notes:** In a letter to George Parker, dated 22 March 1958, Ireland insisted that this was not a song, 'only inflected speech' (Ireland Trust Archive).

## Meditation on John Keble's Rogation Hymn

For organ.
**Commissioned by:** Unable to trace, although the request is said to have come from the United States.
**Duration:** 7'.
**Publication:** B. Feldman & Co. Ltd. (E. H. Freeman, Brighton). Score © 1959. Now EMI Music Publishing Ltd. Also included in *The Organ Music of John Ireland* (ed. Robert Gower), Novello © 1983.
**Location of manuscript:** Manuscript Collections, The British Library (Reference Division), Add. MS 52890. It is initialled and dated: J.I. 29 May 1958.
**Bibliography:** M. Rochester, 'Great European Organs', *Gramophone*, 68/816 (May 1991), 2047.
S. Webb, 'Howells/Ireland', *Gramophone*, 57/676 (Sept. 1979), 487.
**Recordings:** Robert Gower (organ) *in* Wealdon Studios WS 179 (1979).
Jonathan Bielby (organ) *in* Priory PRCD 298 (1991).
A. Sievewright (organ) *in* APS 319, CAPS 319.
**Notes:** The hymn tune by John Keble (1792–1866) is 'For Rogation: Lord, in thy name thy servants plead'.

## OTHER VERSIONS

**Elegiac Meditation**

Arranged for string orchestra by Geoffrey Bush.
**Date of arrangement:** 1982, for the Chandos recording (see below).
**Publication:** Novello & Co. Ltd. Score © 1988.
**Bibliography:** M. Macdonald, 'Bridge/Ireland', *Gramophone*, 62/739 (Dec. 1984), 736. A. Sanders, 'Bridge/Ireland', *Gramophone*, 65/768 (May 1987), 1546, 1550.
**Recordings:** English Chamber Orchestra/David Garforth *in* Chandos ABRD 1112, ABTD 1112 (1984), CHAN 8390 (1987).
**Notes:** Geoffrey Bush put the following quotation from J. B. Priestley's play *The Linden Tree* at the head of the score:

> Listen—he's remembering the earlier themes now . . . and saying goodbye to them.
>   Wandering through the darkening house of life—touching all the things he loved—crying Farewell—for ever—for ever.

## 1961

## Cupid

Song for unaccompanied mixed voices (SATB). Text by William Blake (1757–1827).
**Publication:** Augener & Co. Ltd. Vocal score © 1961. Now Stainer & Bell Ltd.
**Location of manuscript:** Manuscript Collections, The British Library (Reference Division), Add. MS 52895.

# BIBLIOGRAPHY
## (including Ireland's writings)

《》

### 1915

Anon., 'John Ireland', *Monthly Musical Record*, 45/45 (July 1915), 192.

### 1918

Evans, E., 'Mr Edwin Evans on Eugene Goossens and John Ireland', *Musical Times*, 59/905 (July 1918), 321–2.

### 1919

Eaglefield Hull, A., 'A Modern English Classicist', *Musical Opinion and Music Trade Review*, 42/497 (Feb. 1919), 281–2.
—— 'John Ireland's Songs', *Musical Opinion and Music Trade Review*, 42/498 (Mar. 1919), 350–1.
—— 'The Instrumental Music of John Ireland', *Musical Opinion and Music Trade Review*, 42/499 (Apr. 1919), 415–17.
Evans, E., 'John Ireland', *Musical Quarterly*, 5 (1919), 213–20.
—— 'Modern British Composers: V—John Ireland' (part 1), *Musical Times*, 60/918 (Aug. 1919), 394–6.
—— 'Modern British Composers: V—John Ireland' (part 2), *Musical Times*, 60/919 (Sept. 1919), 457–62.
Gatti, G. M., 'John Ireland', *Organist and Choirmaster*, 27/314 (June 1919), 10 (part of a translation of an article by Gatti in *La critica musicale*).

### 1922

Anderton, H. O., 'Cameo Portraits: No. 22—Ariel Enmeshed', *Musical Opinion and Music Trade Review*, 45 (Aug. 1922), 953–5.
Eggar, K. E., 'The Pianoforte Music of John Ireland', *Music Teacher*, 14 (June 1922), 465–7.
Lyle, W., 'The Songs of John Ireland', *Sackbut*, 2 (July 1922), 27–30.

## 1923

Anon., *Miniature Essays: John Ireland* (London, J. & W. Chester, 1923).
Moeran, E. J., 'Introductions: X—John Ireland', *Music Bulletin*, 5/10 (Oct. 1923), 300–3.

## 1924

Evans, E., 'John Ireland', in *A Dictionary of Modern Music and Musicians* (London, J. M. Dent, 1924), 252–3.

## 1925

Holbrooke, J., 'John Ireland', in his *Contemporary British Composers* (London, Palmer, 1925), 72–82.

## 1927

Ireland, J., 'A Speech for the Opposition', *Music and Letters*, 8/2 (Apr. 1927), 109–10.
Ould, H., 'British Song-Writers of Today: VI—John Ireland', *Musical News and Herald*, 72/15 (Aug. 1927), 312–13.

## 1928

Anon., 'Less Sheet Music Sold', *The Times*, 4 Apr. 1928, p. 9.
Bedford, H., 'Stereoscopic Views—II: John Ireland', *Dominant* (Oct.–Nov. 1928), 25–7.

## 1929

Foss, H. J., 'The Later Works of John Ireland', *Gamut* (1929), 24–8.
Gray, C., 'Modern Works', *Gamut* (1929), 39–?.

## 1930

Evans, E., 'John Ireland', *Chesterian*, 11/85 (Mar. 1930), 133–40.
Maine, B., 'The British Composers—5: John Ireland', *Morning Post*, 2 Oct. 1930, p. 5.

## 1931

Moeran, E. J., 'John Ireland as Teacher', *Monthly Musical Record*, 61 (Mar. 1931), 67–8.

## 1936

Dunhill, T., 'The Piano' (Letter to *The Times*), *The Times*, 12 Sept. 1936, p. 8.

## 1937

Hull, R., 'Music of John Ireland', *Radio Times*, 22 Jan. 1937, p. 12.

## 1939

J.A.W., 'John Ireland's Songs', *Radio Times*, 3 Mar. 1939, p. 13.

## 1940

Dickinson, A. E. F., 'The Progress of John Ireland', *Music Review*, 1/4 (Nov. 1940), 343–53.

## 1943

Townshend, N., 'The Achievement of John Ireland', *Music and Letters*, 24/2 (Apr. 1943), 65–74.

## 1944

Blom, E., 'Some New Ireland Works', *Tempo*, 6 (Feb. 1944), 2–3.

## 1945

Herbage, J., 'Four Works by Ireland', *Listener*, 33, 5 Apr. 1945, p. 389.
Hill, R., 'John Ireland: His Music', *Radio Times*, 6 Apr. 1945, p. 72.
Rees, C. B., 'John Ireland: The Man', *Radio Times*, 6 Apr. 1945, p. 5.

## 1946

Brook, D., 'John Ireland', in his *Composer's Gallery* (London, Rockcliff, 1946), 78–81.
Goddard, S., 'Composers of Today—I: John Ireland', *Our Time*, 5/6 (Jan. 1946), 116.
Hill, R., 'John Ireland', in A. L. Bacharach, *British Music of our Time* (Harmondsworth, Pelican Books, 1946), 99–112.

## 1949

Anon., 'Editorial Notes', *Strad*, 60 (Oct. 1949), 163.

## 1950

Ireland, J. '[Alan Bush]: The Student', in *Tribute to Alan Bush on his 50th Birthday: A Symposium* (London, WMA, 1950), 15–16.

## 1951

Anon., 'Composer of Today: John Ireland', *Music Parade*, 2 (1951), opposite p. 1.
Foss, H., 'John Ireland: Born 13 August 1879', *Hallé*, 39 (Aug. 1951), 4–7.

## 1952

Barnard, L. S., 'Philip Dore's English Organ Music Lectures', *Musical Opinion*, 75 (July 1952), 621, 623.
Frank, A. C., 'Contemporary Portraits—no. 10: John Ireland', *Music Teacher and Piano Student*, 31 (Jan. 1952), 23–4 (reprinted and expanded in his *Modern British Composers* (London, Dennis Dobson, 1953), 15–20).

## 1953

Ireland, J., 'My Introduction to Beethoven', in *Music Magazine*, chosen and edited by Anna Instone and Julian Herbage (London, Rockcliff, 1953), 26–31.
Suckling, N., 'John Ireland and the Piano', *Listener*, 50 (24 Dec. 1953), 1101.

## 1954

Anon., 'John Ireland: An Endearing Composer', *The Times*, 13 Aug. 1954, p. 9.
Anon., 'Promenade Concert: Ireland's Birthday', *The Times*, 14 Aug. 1954, p. 6.
Anon., 'Profile: Dr John Ireland', *Observer*, 15 Aug. 1954, p. 3.
Crossley-Holland, P., 'John N. Ireland', in *Grove's Dictionary of Music and Musicians*, 5th edn., ed. E. Blom (London, Macmillan, 1954), iv. 533–44. See also supplementary volume (no. 10) (1961), 231–2.
Holland, A. K., 'John Ireland at 75: An Appreciation', *Tempo*, 32 (Summer 1954), 7–8.
Martin, J. M., 'John Ireland', *Chesterian*, 29 Oct. 1954, pp. 35–8.
Ottaway, H., 'The Piano Music of John Ireland', *Monthly Musical Record*, 84 (Dec. 1954), 258–66.

Rees, C. B., 'Musical Roundabout', *Music Teacher and Piano Student*, 33 (July 1954), 323.
Rutland, H., 'John Ireland's 75th Birthday', *Radio Times*, 6 Aug. 1954, p. 7.

## 1956

Ireland, J., Obituary of C. à Becket Williams (1890–1956) (English composer and writer), unpublished. MS in John Ireland Trust Archives.

## 1957

Anon., 'Composer's Home Invaded by Sounds from the Sand Pits', *Southern Weekly News*, 6 Sept. 1957, p. 8.
Anon., 'No Peace for a Composer', *The Times*, 29 Aug. 1957, p. 4.
Demuth, N., 'John Ireland', *Musical Opinion*, 81 (Oct. 1957), 21.
Ireland, J., 'Albert Sammons: A Tribute', *Musical Times*, 98/1376 (Oct. 1957), 548.
Stiles, H. D. S., 'Broken Idyll' (Letter to *The Times*), *The Times*, 31 Aug. 1957, p. 7.

## 1958

Brooke, J., 'The Music of John Ireland', *Musical Times*, 99/1389 (Nov. 1958), 600–2.
Ireland, J., 'Tribute to Ralph Vaughan Williams', *Musical Times*, 99/1388 (Oct. 1958), 535–6.

## 1959

Anon., 'Birthday Tribute to Dr Ireland', *The Times*, 15 Aug. 1959, p. 3.
Anon., 'Dr Ireland Misses Birthday Prom', *The Times*, 15 Aug. 1959, p. 6.
Anon., 'Dr Ireland Reviews his Long Career', *The Times*, 3 Aug. 1959, p. 10.
Anon., 'Intimate Poetic Lyricism', *The Times*, 3 Oct. 1959, p. 4.
C.G.-F., 'Macnaghten Concerts', *Musical Opinion*, 83 (Nov. 1959), 81.
—— 'Promenade Concerts', *Musical Opinion*, 82 (Sept. 1959), 783.
Goddard, S., 'Music: John Ireland', *Listener*, 62 (16 July 1959), 112, 114.
Herbage, J., 'John Ireland and the Orchestra', *Listener*, 61 (4 June 1959), 1001.
Howes, F., 'Ave John Ireland', *RCM Magazine*, 55 (Nov. 1959), 105–6.
Hull, R., 'Macnaghten Concert: John Ireland's Music', *Musical Times*, 100/1401 (Nov. 1959), 609.
Jacobs, A., 'Passing Notes', *Gramophone*, 37 (Sept. 1959), 137.
Ottaway, H., 'Ireland's Shorter Piano Pieces', *Tempo* 52 (Autumn 1959), 3–6, 17.
Rutland, H., 'The Achievement of John Ireland', *Musical Times*, 100/1398 (Aug. 1959), 421–2.

## 1960

Anon., 'For Ireland Music', *Music and Musicians*, 8 (May 1960), 23.
Anon., 'John Ireland Society: Inaugural Concert', *Musical Times*, 101/1408 (June 1960), 368.
Anon., 'Too Much of Himself!', *Music and Musicians*, 8 (June 1960), 22.
C.G.-F., 'John Ireland Society', *Musical Opinion*, 83 (June 1960), 600.
—— 'John Ireland Society', *Musical Opinion*, 84 (Dec. 1960), 143.
Howes, F., 'John Ireland', *Canon*, 14 (Sept.–Oct. 1960), 42–3.
Senior, E., 'John Ireland', *Music and Musicians*, 8 (June 1960), 28.

## 1961

Anon., 'Concert of John Ireland's Works', *The Times*, 18 May 1961, p. 17.
Anon., 'Evangelists for Ireland', *Music and Musicians*, 9 (Jan. 1961), 20–1.
Anon., 'Finest Writer of Songs', *The Times*, 9 Oct. 1961, p. 16.
Chaffer, J., 'An Introduction to the Piano Music of John Ireland', *Chesterian*, 36/207 (1961), 22–5.
Scott-Sutherland, C., 'Nationalism and John Ireland', *Music Review*, 22/3 (1961), 195–7.
Waterhouse, J. F., 'Views of Ireland', *Birmingham Post*, 30 Oct. 1961, p. 6.

## 1962

Anon., 'Dr John Ireland: A Composer of Solid Achievement', *Guardian*, 13 June 1962, p. 8.
Anon., 'Dr John Ireland: A Fastidious Composer', *The Times*, 13 June 1962, p. 12.
Anon., 'Funeral: Dr John Ireland', *The Times*, 18 June 1962, p. 14.
Anon., 'Ireland in the Round', *The Times*, 15 Oct. 1962, p. 14.
Anon., 'John Ireland Memorial Concert', *Strad*, 73 (Nov. 1962), 265.
Anon., 'Loss to Music', *Music and Musicians*, 10 (July 1962), 39.
Anon., 'Obituary: John Ireland', *Canon*, 15 (June 1962), 23.
Anon., 'Obituary: John Ireland', *Musica d'oggi*, 5 (1962), 248.
Arnell, R., 'John Ireland 1879–1962', *Tempo*, 61–2 (Spring–Summer 1962), 39–40.
Cooper, M., 'John Ireland: Fine Composer of Solo Songs', *Daily Telegraph*, 13 June 1962, p. 14.
Foss, H., 'John Ireland', *Musical TImes*, 103/1434 (Aug. 1962), 536–7.
Longmire, J., 'John Ireland: An Appreciation', *Music Teacher and Piano Student*, 41 (Aug. 1962), 361.
—— 'Obituary: John Ireland', *Musical Opinion*, 85/1018 (July 1962), 599.
Rees, C. B., 'John Ireland: In Memoriam', *Musical Events*, 17 (Aug. 1962), 4–5.
Robertson, A., 'Obituary', *Gramophone*, 40 (Aug. 1962), 95.

Rutland, H. and Rowlands, A., 'John Ireland 1879–1962', *RCM Magazine*, 58/3 (1962), 69–71.
Simmons, D., 'Polite Tribute', *Music and Musicians*, 11 (Dec. 1962), 59.

## 1963

Payne, A., 'Ireland the Inhibited', *Music and Musicians*, 1 (Aug. 1963), 46.
Schafer, M., 'John Ireland: Interview', in his *British Composers in Interview* (London, Faber & Faber, 1963), 24–35.

## 1964

Anon., 'John Ireland Memorial Window in the Musicians' Chapel', *Music Teacher*, 43 (Feb. 1964), 85.
Brooke, J., *The Birth of a Legend: A Reminiscence of Arthur Machen and John Ireland* (London, B. Rota, 1964) (limited edition of 65 signed and numbered copies).
L.N. 'John Ireland Memorial Window', *Musical Times*, 105/1451 (Jan. 1964), 38.
Payne, A., 'For Devotees Only', *Music and Musicians*, 12 (Mar. 1964), 41.

## 1965

Brooke, J., 'John Ireland: A Reminiscence', *London Magazine* (Apr. 1965), 75–80.
Bush, G., 'A Real Live Composer', *Performing Right*, 43 (Oct. 1965), 27–9, 32.

## 1966

Chapman, E., 'John Ireland Programme', *Musical Events*, 21 (Jan. 1966), 14.

## 1968

Chapman, E., *John Ireland: A Catalogue of Published Works and Recordings* (London, The John Ireland Trust, 1968).
Kirby, N., 'Appreciation and Biographical Sketch', in *John Ireland: A Catalogue* (London, The John Ireland Trust, 1968), 8–11.

## 1969

Le Fleming, C., 'John Ireland: An Appreciation', *Musical Opinion*, 93 (Oct. 1969), 19, 21.
Longmire, J., 'Bax and John Ireland', *Bax Society Bulletin* (Aug. 1969), 99–100.
—— *John Ireland: Portrait of a Friend* (London, J. Baker, 1969).

Mann, W., 'John Ireland's New Appeal', *The Times*, 15 Aug. 1969, p. 9.
Pitfield, T., 'Ireland in Bowden', *Cheshire Life* (Oct. 1969), 95.
Scott, C., 'John Ireland: A Short Study', in J. Longmire, *John Ireland: Portrait of a Friend* (London, Baker, 1969), 144–8.
Yenne, V. L., 'Three Twentieth Century English Composers: Peter Warlock, E. J. Moeran and John Ireland', thesis submitted in partial fulfilment of the requirements for the degree of DMA, University of Illinois, 1969.

## 1970

Rankin, W. D., 'The Solo Piano Music of John Ireland', thesis submitted in partial fulfilment of the requirements for the degree of DMA, University of Boston, 1970.

## 1972

Cooke, M. W., 'John Ireland: A Biographical and Critical Study, with Special Reference to the Works involving Piano', thesis submitted for the degree of Master of Arts, University College of North Wales, Bangor, 1972.

## 1973

Rutland, H., 'John Ireland', *Recorded Sound*, 50–1 (Apr.–July 1973), 190–8.

## 1974

Hughes, E., 'John Ireland Discography', *Recorded Sound*, 53 (1974), 258–62.
Parkin, E., 'John Ireland and the Piano—1', *Music Teacher*, 53 (June 1974), 11–12.
—— 'John Ireland and the Piano—2', *Music Teacher*, 53 (July 1974), 15–16.
—— 'John Ireland and the Piano—3', *Music Teacher*, 53 (Aug. 1974), 12–13.
—— 'John Ireland and the Piano—4', *Music Teacher*, 53 (Sept. 1974), 13.

## 1975

Scott, S., 'The Chamber Music of John Ireland', *Composer*, 54 (Spring 1975), 23–5.

## 1977

Webber, J. L., 'The Piano Trios of John Ireland', *Strad*, 88 (June 1977), 137, 139.

## 1979

Gower, R., 'John Ireland's Organ Music', *Musical Times*, 120/1638 (Aug. 1979), 682–3.
Larner, G., 'The Poet who Painted in Music', *Guardian*, 26 June 1979, p. 8.
Pirie, P. J., 'A Vision Dimly Seen', *Music and Musicians*, 27 (Aug. 1979), 18–20.
Rennert, J., 'The Church and Organ Music of John Ireland', *English Church Music* (1979), 8–16.
Scott, S., *The Chamber Music of John Ireland* (London, S. Scott, 1979).
—— *John Ireland and the Church* (London, S. Scott, 1979).
Searle, M., *John Ireland: The Man and his Music* (Tunbridge Wells, Midas Books, 1979).

## 1980

Ottaway, H., 'John Nicholson Ireland', in *Grove's Dictionary of Music and Musicians*, 6th edn., ed. S. Sadie (London, Macmillan, 1980), ix. 325–7.
Scott-Sutherland, C., *John Ireland* (Rickmansworth, Triad Press, 1980).

## 1981

Byfield, D., 'Musical Reflections', *Musical Opinion*, 104 (Apr. 1981), 246–8.

## 1983

Bush, G., [John Ireland], in his *Left, Right and Centre* (London, Thames Publishing, 1983), 100–12.

## 1986

Dawney, M., 'Music Born High on the South Downs', *Sussex Life* (Aug. 1986), 18–19.

## 1987

Renouf, D. F., 'Thomas Hardy and the English Musical Renaissance', thesis submitted for the degree of Doctor of Philosophy, Trent Polytechnic, 1987.

## 1988

Palmer, C. (ed.), *The Collected Arthur Machen* (London, Duckworth, 1988).

## 1989

Laudon, V., 'British Library Additional MSS 52900–52901: A Survey of the Compositional Process and Some Unpublished Works of John Ireland', thesis submitted for the degree of Master of Arts, University of London, August 1989.

Pilkington, M., *Gurney, Ireland, Quilter and Warlock* (London, Duckworth, 1989).

## 1990

Keir, P., 'John Ireland: A Practical Guide to Selected Works for Piano', thesis submitted for the degree of Master of Music, Royal College of Music, 1990.

APPENDIX 1

# Ireland as Conductor, Performer, and Speaker

《》

### Ireland as Conductor

*The Forgotten Rite* (incomplete)
BBC Symphony Orchestra, conducted by Ireland. Queen's Hall, London, 10 January 1935. BBC Sound Archive T45273.

### Ireland as Performer (piano)
(Arranged alphabetically by title of composition)

*Amberley Wild Brooks*
BBC Sound Archive T42800 (recorded 28 May 1948), NSA tape M618W.
*April*
Columbia L 2317 (1929), HMV DB 9651 (1951), EMI CDH7 63910-2 (1992), BBC Sound Archive T42799, BBC Sound Archive T42800 (recorded 28 May 1948), BBC Transcription 42816, NSA tape M618W.
*Fantasy Sonata for clarinet and piano*
Frederick Thurston (clarinet) and John Ireland (piano). BBC Sound Archive T41822 (recorded 8 Jan. 1948).
Frederick Thurston (clarinet) and John Ireland (piano), NSA tape M577W.
*Green Ways*
NSA tape M616W.
*London Pieces*
BBC Sound Archive T42800 (recorded 28 May 1948), NSA tape M617W.
*Sonata for cello and piano*
Antonio Sala (cello) and John Ireland (piano). Columbia L 2314/7 (1929).
Anthony Pini (cello) and John Ireland (piano). BBC Sound Archive T42799 (recorded 28 Mar. 1947), BBC Transcription 42810/4.
*Sonata No. 1 for violin and piano*
Frederick Grinke (violin) and John Ireland (piano). Decca K 1400/3 (1948).
*Sonata No. 2 for violin and piano*
Albert Sammons (violin) and John Ireland (piano). NSA tape 935W.
*The Towing Path*
BBC Sound Archive T42800 (recorded 28 May 1948), NSA tape M613W.
*The Undertone* (No. 1 of Four Preludes)
BBC Sound Archive T42799 (recorded 28 Mar. 1947), BBC Transcription 42817.

*Various songs*
Peter Pears (tenor) and John Ireland (piano). BBC Sound Archive T41844 (recorded 14 May 1951 in the Wigmore Hall at the London Festival of the Arts).

## Ireland as speaker (Arranged in chronological order)

On first attempts to play Beethoven, *Music Magazine*, 16 Dec. 1945, BBC Sound Archive 20601.

Recollections of C. V. Stanford, *Music Magazine*, 24 Mar. 1949, BBC Sound Archive 9846, MT 41747.

Interviewed by Julian Herbage, *Music Magazine*, 9 Oct. 1954, BBC Sound Archive LP 38127.

Interviewed by Joseph Cooper, *The Composer Speaks*, 5 July 1957, BBC Sound Archive 23704.

Interviewed for series *Town and Country*, 15 July 1958, BBC Sound Archive LP/24590.

Interviewed by Arthur Jacobs, 11 Aug. 1959, BBC Sound Archive LP/25900.

Interviewed by Murray Schafer in early 1960s for his book *British Composers in Interview* (London, Faber, 1963). Material deposited at the NSA by the John Ireland Trust.

# APPENDIX 2
# Alphabetical List of Compositions

《》

Adam lay ybounden, 120
Adoration, The (*Three Songs*, 1918–19), 56
Advent, The (*Songs Sacred and Profane*, 1929–31), 81
Aegipaus' Headland *see* Sarnia (1940–1), 102
Alla marcia for organ, 20
All in a Garden Green (*Five Sixteenth-Century Poems*, 1938), 98
Almond Trees, The, 33
Alpine Song, 24
Amberley Wild Brooks (*Two Pieces* for piano, 1921), xi, 65
Annabel Lee (Poe), 20
April (*Two Pieces* for piano, 1925), 73
Aside, An (*Five Sixteenth-Century Poems*, 1938), 98
At Early Dawn, 25
Aubade, 29
Aubade (*Two Pieces* for piano, 1929–30), 80

Baby (*Mother and Child*, 1918), 54
Bagatelle for violin and piano, 21
Ballade for piano, xv, 80
Ballade of London Nights, 84
Beckon to Me (*Five Poems by Thomas Hardy*, 1926), 75
Bed in Summer, 32
Bell in the Leaves, The, 109
Bells of San Marie, The, 50
Benedicite in F (1919), 58
Benedictus in F (1912), 29
Berceuse for violin and piano, 10
Bergomask (*Two Pieces* for piano, 1925), 73

Billee Bowline (written under the pseudonym Turlay Royce), 24
Blind (*Two Songs*, 1916), 46
Blind Boy, The (*Mother and Child*, 1918), 54
Blow out, you bugles (*Two Songs*, 1917–18), 48
Boy, The, 109
Boy Bishop, The (*Three Pastels*, 1941), 105
Boys' Love *see* Sarnia (1940–1), 102
Boys' Names, 105
Brumbies (*The Overlanders*, Suite, 1965), 117
By the Mere (*Leaves from a Child's Sketchbook*, 1918), 53

Calling all Shirkers *see* Epic March, 108
Capriccio for organ, 22
Carol *see* Preludes for piano (1913–15), 41
Catioroc, Le (*Sarnia*, 1940–1), 101
Cavatina for violin and piano, 14
Chelsea: hymn tune, 72
Chelsea Reach (*London Pieces*, 1917–20), xii, 48
Cherry Tree, The (*Green Ways*, 1937), 96
Cherry Tree, The *see* Indian Summer (1932), 85
Child's Song, 33
Columbine, 119
Comedy Overture, 91
Communion Service in A flat (1896), 4
Communion Service in C (1913), 33
Concertino pastorale, xv, 65, 99
Concerto for cello and orchestra, 103
Concerto for piano and orchestra, xii, xv, 82

## Appendix 2

Concerto for piano and orchestra (1933), 90
Concerto for piano and orchestra (1943), 113
Concerto for piano and orchestra (1951), 119
Concerto for viola and orchestra arr. for viola and piano (Forsyth), 14
Cost, The (*Two Songs*, 1916), 46
Country Dance (*Three Dances*, 1913), 39
Cradle Song, A, 28
Cupid, 122
Cypress (*Green Ways*, 1937), 96

Daffodil Field, The *see* Sarnia (1940–1), 102
Darkened Valley, The, 61
Daydream (*In Those Days*, 1895), 3
Dear, think not that they will forget you (*Five Poems by Thomas Hardy*, 1926), 75
Death-Parting (*Mother and Child*, 1918), 54
Decorations, xi, xiv, 30
Downland Suite, A, xv, 86, 88
During Music (*Two Songs*, 1928), 79

Earth's Call (A Sylvan Rhapsody), 49
Eastgate: hymn tune, 15
East Riding, The, 62
Echoing Green, The, 36
Eclogue (*Concertino pastorale*, 1939), 99
Elegiac Meditation, 122
Elegiac Romance for organ, 10
Elegy (*A Downland Suite*, 1932), 86, 87, 89
Encounter, The (*The Land of Lost Content*, 1920–1), 63
English May (*Songs of a Wayfarer*, 1903–11), 11
Epic March, xv, 107
Epilogue (*The Land of Lost Content*, 1920–1), 63
Equinox, xi, 69
Evening Service in A (1905), 15
Evening Service in C (1941), 104
Evening Service in F (1915), 44

Evening Song, 30
Ex ore innocentium, 113

Fain would I change, 67
Fanfare, 99
Fantasy for band (1942), 112
Fantasy Sonata for clarinet and piano, x, 112
February's Child (*Two Pieces* for piano, 1929–30), 80
Ferry, The, 67
Fire of Spring (Preludes for piano, 1913–15), 40
First Rhapsody in C sharp minor for piano, 15
Five Poems by Thomas Hardy, 75
Five Sixteenth-Century Poems, 98
For Remembrance (*Two Pieces* for piano, 1921), 65
Forgotten Rite, The, xiv, 35
Fraternity: hymn tune, 60
Friendship in Misfortune (*Three Songs*, 1926), 76
Frog and the Crab, The, 20
Full Fathom Five, 18

Garland, The (*Mother and Child*, 1918), 54
Garrison Churchyard, A, 46
Goal and Wicket (*The Land of Lost Content*, 1920–1), 63
Graduation Song, A, 76
Greater love hath no man, 26
Great Things, 73
Grecian Lad, A (*Three Pastels*, 1941), 105
Green Ways: Three Lyric Pieces, 96
Grim and Gay *see* Epic March, 108
Gypsy Dance (*Three Dances*, 1913), 39

Hawthorn Time, 59
Heart's Desire, The, 47
Here be naked boys, 105
Here's to the Ships!, 29
Heroic March *see* Epic March, 108
Her Song (*Three Songs to Poems by Thomas Hardy*, 1925), 74
Hillo, My Bonny (written under pseudonym Turlay Royce), 25

## Alphabetical List of Compositions

Hills, The, xv, 120
Holy Boy, The (Preludes for piano, 1913–15), 40
Hope (*Mother and Child*, 1918), 54
Hope the Hornblower, 22
How Jubilant the Summer Sky, 25
Hunt's Up, The (*Leaves from a Child's Sketchbook*, 1918), 53
Hyacinthus see Three Pastels, 106
Hymn for a Child (*Songs Sacred and Profane*, 1929–31), 81
Hymn to Light, 23

If there were dreams to sell, 51
If we must part, 79
I have twelve oxen, 50
Immortality, 110
In a May Morning (*Sarnia*, 1940–1), 101
In Boyhood (*We'll to the Woods no more*, 1926–7), 78
Indian Summer, 85
In my Sage Moments (*Five Poems by Thomas Hardy*, 1926), 75
In Praise of May, 20
In Praise of Neptune, 25
In Summer Woods, 28
Intermezzo see Sextet, 6
In the Meadow (*Leaves from a Child's Sketchbook*, 1918), 53
In Those Days, 3
Intrada for organ, 12
 see also Miniature Suite; Three Pieces for organ
Intruder, The see Cypress (*Green Ways*, 1937), 96
Irene: hymn tune, 56
Island Hymn, An, 44
Island Praise, 45
Island Spell, The (*Decorations*, 1912–13), xi, xiv, 30
It was what you bore with you, woman (*Five Poems by Thomas Hardy*, 1926), 75
I was not sorrowful (*Songs of a Wayfarer*, 1903–11), 11
I will walk on the earth (*Songs of a Wayfarer*, 1903–11), 11

J'ai douze bœufs, 51
Joseph fell a-dreaming, 110
Journey, The, 62
Jubilate in F (1914), 43
Julius Caesar: incidental music, 110

Kishmul's Gallery, 147

Ladslove (*The Land of Lost Content*, 1920–1), 63
Land of Lost Content, The, xi, xiv, 63
Laughing Song, A, 20
Leaves from a Child's Sketchbook, 53
Legend, xi, 89
Lent Lilly, The (*The Land of Lost Content*, 1920–1), 63
Liberators, The see Epic March, 108
London (3 pianos), 49
London: Impressions for piano see London Pieces, 49
London Overture, A, xii, xv, 92
London Pieces, xii, 48
Looking on, 110
Love and Friendship (*Three Songs*, 1926), 76
Love is a sickness, 66
Love's Window (written under the pseudonym Turlay Royce), 24
Love Unknown: hymn tune, 58

Mai-Dun, xiv, 64, 65
Man in his labour rejoiceth, 118
March in C minor see Epic March, 108
Marcia popolare for organ, 14
 see also Three Pieces for organ
Marigold, 34
Maritime Overture, A, 8
Mary and the Sailor (*The Overlanders*, Suite, 1965), 117
Mass in the Dorian Mode, 147
May Flowers, 58
Meditation on John Keble's Rogation Hymn, xv, 121
Meine Seele erhebt der Herren arr. for solo piano (J. S. Bach), 85
Memory (*Songs of a Wayfarer*, 1903–11), 11

Menuetto-impromptu for organ, 13
  see also Miniature Suite; Three Pieces for organ; Two Pieces for orchestra
Meridian (*In Those Days*, 1895), 3
Merry Andrew, 53
Merry Month of May, The, 66
Mighty Father: hymn tune, 59
Miniature Suite, 12, 13
Minuet (*A Downland Suite*, 1932), 86, 87, 89
Missa Brevis, 100
Missa Sancti Stephani, 100
Month's Mind, 89
Moon-Glade (*Decorations*, 1912–13), 30
Morning Service in C (1941), 103
Mother and Child, 54
My Fair (*Songs Sacred and Profane*, 1929–31), 81
My song is love unknown, 59
My true love hath my heart (*Two Songs*, 1920), 60

Newborn (*Mother and Child*, 1918), 54
New Prince, New Pomp: carol, 79
New Year Carol, A, 106
Night Stampede (*The Overlanders*, Suite, 1965), 117
Ninefold Kyrie in A minor, 104
Nurses' Song, 36

Obsession (Preludes for piano, 1913–15), 40
O Happy Land, 104
On a Birthday Morning, 67
One Hope, The (*Three Songs*, 1926), 76
Only Child, The (*Mother and Child*, 1918), 54
Open Country (*The Overlanders*, Suite, 1965), 117
Overlanders, The, xv, 115
Overture for Henry Wood's Jubilee, 115

Palm and May, The (*Green Ways*, 1937), 96
Pater Noster, 17
Patriotic Song, 103
Peaceful Western Wind, The, 3

Pelléas et Mélisande, 147
Penumbra (*Marigold*, 1913), 34
  see also Prelude in E flat for piano
Phantasie-Trio in A minor, x, xiv, 16
Piano Piece (no title): theme (1897), 4
Piece for oboe and piano, 119
Poem in A minor, 10
Porto Rico (written under the pseudonym Turlay Royce), 39
Prelude (*A Downland Suite*, 1932), 86
Prelude in E flat, 71
Prelude: Midsummer, 147
Preludes for solo piano, 40
Princess Maleine, The, 147
Psalm 23, 121
Psalm 42, 17
Psalm Chant, 15
Puck's Birthday (*Three Pastels*, 1941), 105

Quartet No. 1 for strings in D minor, 4
Quartet No. 2 for strings in C minor, 5
Queen Fridias, Prelude for orchestra and piano, 90

Ragamuffin (*London Pieces*, 1917–20), 48
Rat, The (*Three Songs*, 1918–19), 56
Reapers' Dance (*Three Dances*, 1913), 39
Red Rose, The see Five Sixteenth-Century Poems, 98
Remember, 54
Report Song, A (*Five Sixteenth-Century Poems*, 1938), 98
Rest: Respos (*Three Songs*, 1918–19), 56
Rhapsody, 44
Ride a cock-horse, 103
River, The see Chelsea Reach (*London Pieces*, 1917–20), 49
Rosebud see Preludes for piano (1913–15), 41
Round (*A Downland Suite*, 1932), 86

Sacred Flame, The, 52
Salley Gardens, The (*Songs Sacred and Profane*, 1929–31), 81
Sampford: hymn tune, 118
Santa Chiara (Palm Sunday: Naples), 74
Sarnia: An Island Sequence, xii, xv, 101

## Alphabetical List of Compositions

Satyricon, xv, 114
Scapegoat, The (*Songs Sacred and Profane*, 1929–31), 81
Scherzo and Cortège (*Julius Caesar*), 111
Scorched Earth (*The Overlanders*, Suite, 1965), 116
Sea Fever, 36
Sea Idyll, A, 9
Secret Ceremonies, The (*Decorations*, 1912–13), xi, 30
See how the morning smiles, 30
Serenade for Strings *see* Concertino pastorale, 100
Sextet, x, 6
Skylark and Nightingale (*Mother and Child*, 1918), 54
Slumber Song, 28
Soho Forenoons (*London Pieces*, 1917–20), 48
Soldier, The (*Two Songs*, 1917–18), 48
Soldier's Return, The (*Songs Sacred and Profane*, 1929–31), 81
Soliloquy, 68
Sonata in C minor for piano, 147
Sonata in C minor for violin and piano, 147
Sonata in D minor for violin and piano, 147
Sonata in E minor-major for piano, 57
Sonata in G minor for cello and piano, x, 69
Sonata in G minor for violin and piano, 147
Sonata No. 1 in D minor for violin and piano, x, xiv, 19
Sonata No. 2 in A minor for violin and piano, x, xiv, 45
Sonatina for piano, xv, 77
Song from o'er the Hill, 39
Song of March, A, 55
Song of the Springtides (*Sarnia*, 1940–1), 101
Songs of a Wayfarer, 11
Songs Sacred and Profane, 81
Spleen (*Marigold*, 1913), 34
  *see also* Preludes for piano (1913–15)
Spring, 28

Spring goeth all in white, 147
Spring Sorrow, 50
Spring, the Sweet Spring, 18
Spring will not wait (*We'll to the Woods no more*, 1926–7), 78
Summer Evening, 60
Summer Schemes (*Three Songs to Poems by Thomas Hardy*, 1925), 74
Sunset Play *see* Nurses' Song, 36
Sursum Corda for organ, 22
Sweet Season, The (*Five Sixteenth-Century Poems*, 1938), 98
Sylvan Rhapsody, A ('Earth's Call', 1918), 49

Te Deum (19 bars), 147
Te Deum in F (1907), 17
Thanksgiving, A (*Five Sixteenth-Century Poems*, 1938), 98
Theme—juvenile piano piece, 4
There is a garden in her face, 18
These things shall be, xii, xv, 94
These Women *see* Five Sixteenth-Century Poems, 98
They told me, Heraclitus, 72
Three Dances for piano, 39
Three Pastels for piano, 105
Three Pieces for organ, 13
Three Ravens, The, 62
Three Rustic Dances *see* Three Dances for piano
Three Songs (1918–19), 56
Three Songs (1926), 76
Three Songs to Poems by Thomas Hardy (1925), 74
Three Variations on 'Cadet Rousselle', 55
Threnody (*Concertino pastorale*, 1939), 65, 99
Toccata (*Concertino pastorale*, 1939), 99
Toilers of the Sea, 116
Towing Path, The, 55
Tragedy of the Moment, The (*Five Poems by Thomas Hardy*, 1926), 75
Trellis, The (*Two Songs*, 1920), 60
Trio for piano, violin, and cello in A minor, 147

Trio in D (1912–13), 32
Trio in E minor (1917), 47
Trio in E minor (1938), 97
Tritons, 7
Tryst (*Two Songs*, 1928), 79
Tutto e sciolto, 85
Twilight Night, 69
Two Pieces for orchestra, 13, 14
Two Pieces for piano (1921), 65
Two Pieces for piano (1925), 73
Two Pieces for piano (1929–30), 80
Two Songs (1916), 46
Two Songs (1917–18), 48
Two Songs (1920), 60
Two Songs (1928), 79
Two Symphonic Studies (*The Overlanders*, 1946–7), 117

Undertone, The (Preludes for piano, 1913–15), 40
Ussia (USSR), v. Prussia *see* Epic March, 108

Vagabond, The, 68
Vagabonds, The (ballet), 65, 100
Vain Desire, The (*The Land of Lost Content*, 1920–1), 63
Variations in E flat for piano, 147

Variations in F sharp minor for piano, 148
Variations on an Irish tune for piano, 148
Variations on 'Cadet Rousselle', 55
Variations on 'Paul's Steeple', 115
Vesper Hymn, 28
Vexilla Regis, 6
Villanella for organ, 12
    *see also* Miniature Suite; Two Pieces for orchestra
Vocal Rhapsody, 148

Weathers, 74
We hardly see the sunbeam yet, 25
We'll to the Woods no more, xi, 78
What are you thinking of?, 72
When daffodils begin to peer (*Songs of a Wayfarer*, 1903–11), 11
When I am dead, my dearest, 71
When lights go rolling round the sky, 23
When May is in her prime, 61
Work for solo violin and chamber orchestra, 100

Your brother has a falcon *see* Newborn (*Mother and Child*, 1918), 54
Youth's Spring-Tribute (*Marigold*, 1913), 34

APPENDIX 3

# Classified List of Compositions

«◊»

## Arrangements and Transcriptions of Music by Other Composers

BACH, J. S.: Meine Seele erhebt der Herren
  arr. for piano, 85
FORSYTH, C.: Concerto for viola and orchestra
  arr. for viola and piano, 14

## Ballets

Vagabonds, The
  see Mai-Dun (1920–1); Concertante pastorale (1939), 65

## Brass, Military, and Symphonic Wind Band

Bagatelle
  arr. for military band, 21
  see also Chamber Music
Comedy Overture
  for brass band, 91
  arr. for wind band, 92
  see also Orchestral
Downland Suite, A, xv, 86
  arr. for wind band, 88
  see also Keyboard (Elegy and Minuet); Orchestral
Holy Boy, The (Preludes for piano)
  arr. for brass ensemble, 41
  see also Chamber Music; Choral Music; Keyboard; Orchestral; Songs and Song Cycles
London Overture, A
  arr. for brass band, 93
  see also Orchestral
Maritime Overture, A (based on Tritons)
  arr. for military band, 8
  arr. for wind band, 8
  see also Orchestral

## Chamber Music

Bagatelle for violin and piano, 21
  see also Orchestral
Berceuse for violin and piano, 10
Cavatina for violin and piano, 14
  see also Keyboard
Fantasy Sonata for clarinet and piano, x, 112
Holy Boy, The
  arr. for cello and piano, 42
  arr. for flute and piano, 42
  arr. for two descant recorders and piano, 42
  arr. for viola, 42
  arr. for violin and piano, 42
  see also Brass, Military, and Symphonic Wind Band; Choral Music; Keyboard; Orchestral; Songs and Song Cycles
Phantasie-Trio in A minor, x, xiv, 16
Piece for oboe and piano (1952), 119
Quartet No. 1 for strings in D minor, 4
Quartet No. 2 for strings in C minor, 5
Sextet, x, 6
Sonata in G minor for cello and piano, x, 69
  cello part arr. for viola, 70
Sonata No. 1 in D minor for violin and piano, x, xiv, 19
Sonata No. 2 in A minor for violin and piano, x, xiv, 45
Trio in D (1912–13), 32

Trio in E minor (1917), 47
Trio in E minor (1938), 97

## Choral Music

Alpine Song, 24
At Early Dawn, 25
Aubade, 29
Bed in Summer, 32
   see also Songs and Song Cycles
Bell in the Leaves, The, 109
Boy, The, 109
Boys' Names, 105
Child's Song, 33
Cradle Song, A, 28
Cupid, 122
Echoing Green, The, 36
Evening Song, 30
Fain would I change, 67
Ferry, The, 67
Frog and the Crab, The, 20
Full Fathom Five, 18
Graduation Song, A, 76
Here be naked boys, 105
Hills, The, xv, 120
Holy Boy, The
  arr. for mixed chorus, 43
  see also Brass, Military, and
    Symphonic Wind Band; Chamber
    Music; Keyboard; Orchestral; Songs
    and Song Cycles
How Jubilant the Summer Sky, 25
Immortality, 110
In Praise of May, 20
In Praise of Neptune, 25
In Summer Woods, 28
Island Hymn, An (1915), 44
  see also Island Praise (1955)
Island Praise (1955), 45
  see also An Island Hymn (1915)
Joseph fell a-dreaming, 110
Laughing Song, A, 20
Looking on, 110
Man in his labour rejoiceth, 118
May Flowers, 58
New Year Carol, A, 106
  see also Church Music

Nurses' Song, 36
O Happy Land, 104
  see also Songs and Song Cycles
Peaceful Western Wind, The, 3
Ride a cock-horse, 103
Sea Fever, 36
  see also Songs and Song Cycles
See how the morning smiles, 30
Slumber Song, 28
Song of March, A, 55
Spring, 28
Spring, the Sweet Spring, 18
There is a garden in her face, 18
These things shall be, xii, xv, 94
They told me, Heraclitus, 72
Twilight Night, 69
We hardly see the sunbeam yet, 25
When May is in her prime, 61

## Church Music

Adam lay ybounden, 120
Benedicite in F (1919), 58
Benedictus in F (1912), 29
Chelsea: hymn tune, 72
Communion Service in A flat (1896), 4
Communion Service in C (1913), 33
Eastergate: hymn tune, 15
Evening Service in A (1905), 15
Evening Service in C (1941), 104
Evening Service in F (1915), 44
Ex ore innocentium, 113
Fraternity: hymn tune, 60
Greater love hath no man, 26
Irene: hymn tune, 56
Jubilate in F (1914), 43
Love Unknown: hymn tune, 58
Mighty Father: hymn tune, 59
Missa Brevis, 100
  see also Missa Sancti Stephani
Missa Sancti Stephani, 100
Morning Service in C (1941), 103
New Prince, New Pomp: carol, 79
New Year Carol, A, 106
  see also Choral Music
Ninefold Kyrie in A minor, 104
Pater Noster, 17

Psalm 23, 121
Psalm 42, 17
Psalm Chant, 15
Sampford: hymn tune, 118
Te Deum in F (1907), 17
Vesper Hymn, 28
Vexilla Regis, 6

Film Music

Overlanders, The, xv, 115
  see also Orchestral

Keyboard

Alla marcia for organ, 20
Almond Trees, The, 33
Ballade for piano, xv, 80
Ballade of London Nights, 84
Capriccio for organ, 22
Cavatina, 14
Columbine, 119
Concerto for piano and orchestra
  arr. for 2 pianos, 84
  see also Orchestral
Darkened Valley, The, 61
Decorations, xi, xiv, 30
Elegiac Romance for organ, 10
Elegy
  arr. for organ, 89
  see also Brass, Military, and
    Symphonic Wind Band; Orchestral
Elegy and Minuet (Downland Suite)
  arr. for piano, 89
  see also Brass, Military, and
    Symphonic Wind Band; Orchestral
Epic March
  arr. for piano, 109
  arr. for organ, 109
  see also Orchestral
Equinox, xi, 69
First Rhapsody in C sharp minor for
    piano, 15
Forgotten Rite, The
  arr. for piano duet, 36
  see also Orchestral
Green Ways: Three Lyric Pieces, 96

Holy Boy, The
  arr. for organ, 42
  see also Brass, Military, and
    Symphonic Wind Band; Chamber
    Music; Choral Music; Orchestral;
    Songs and Song Cycles
In Those Days, 3
Intrada for organ, 12
Leaves from a Child's Sketchbook, 53
Legend
  arr. for 2 pianos, 90
  see also Orchestral
London (3 pianos), 49
London Pieces, xii, 48
Mai-Dun
  arr. for piano duet, 65
  see also Orchestral
Marcia popolare for organ, 14
Meditations on John Keble's Rogation
    Hymn, xv, 121
  see also Orchestral (Elegiac
    Meditation)
Menuetto-impromptu for organ, 13
  see also Orchestral
Merry Andrew, 53
Miniature Suite for organ (Intrada;
    Villanella; Menuetto-impromptu),
    12, 13
  see also Orchestral
Month's Mind, 89
On a Birthday Morning, 67
Prelude in E flat, 71
Preludes for piano (The Holy Boy), 40–3
  see also Brass, Military, and
    Symphonic Wind Band; Chamber
    Music; Choral Music; Orchestral;
    Songs and Song Cycles
Rhapsody, 44
Sarnia: An Island Sequence, xii, xv, 101
Sea Idyll, A, 9
Soliloquy, 68
Sonata in E minor-major for piano, 57
Sonatina for piano, xv, 77
Summer Evening, 60
Sursum Corda for organ, 22
Theme—juvenile piano piece, 4
Three Dances for piano, 39

Three Pastels for piano, 105
Three Pieces for organ (Intrada;
  Villanella; Menuetto-impromptu),
  12, 13
  see also Orchestral
Towing Path, The, 55
Two Pieces for piano (1921), 65
Two Pieces for piano (1925), 73
Two Pieces for piano (1929–30), 80
Villanella for organ, 12
  trans. for piano, 13
  see also Orchestral

Orchestral

Bagatelle
  arr. for small orchestra, 21
  see also Chamber Music
Comedy Overture, 91
  see also A London Overture
Concertino pastorale, xv, 65, 99
  see also Ballets
Concerto for piano and orchestra, xii,
  xv, 82
  see also Keyboard
Downland Suite, A, 87
  see also Brass, Military, and
  Symphonic Wind Band; Keyboard
  (Elegy and Minuet)
Elegiac Meditation, 122
  see also Keyboard (Meditations on
  John Keble's Rogation Hymn)
Epic March, xv, 107
  see also Keyboard
Forgotten Rite, The, xiv, 35
  see also Keyboard
Holy Boy, The
  arr. for string orchestra, 41
  see also Brass, Military, and
  Symphonic Wind Band; Chamber
  Music; Choral Music; Keyboard
  (Preludes for piano); Orchestral;
  Songs and Song Cycles
Legend, xi, 89
  see also Keyboard
London Overture, A, xii, xv, 92
  see also A Comedy Overture

Mai-Dunn, xiv, 64
  see also Ballets; Keyboard
Menuetto-impromptu, 14
  see also Keyboard
Merry Andrew, 53
  see also Keyboard
Overlanders The: Suite, 116
  see also Film Music
Poem in A minor, 10
Satyricon, xv, 114
Scherzo and Cortège, 111
  see also Radio Incidental Music
Tritons, 7
  see also Brass, Military, and
  Symphonic Wind Band (Maritime
  Overture)
Two Pieces for orchestra (Villanella;
  Menuetto-impromptu), 13, 14
  see also Keyboard
Two Pieces (Minuet and Elegy:
  Downland Suite) for string
  orchestra, 87
  see also Brass, Military, and
  Symphonic Wind Band; Keyboard
Two Symphonic Studies (The
  Overlanders), 117
  see also Film Music
Variations on 'Cadet Rousselle', 56
  see also Songs
Villanella, 13
  see also Keyboard


Projected Works (including those
pieces with alternative titles)

Aegipaus' Headland see Sarnia, 102
Boys' Love see Sarnia, 102
Calling all Shirkers see Epic March, 108
Carol see Preludes for piano, 41
Cherry Tree, The see Green Ways, 96
  see also Indian Summer
Concerto for cello and orchestra, 103
Concerto for piano and orchestra,
  (1933), 90
Concerto for piano and orchestra (1943),
  113

## Classified List of Compositions

Concerto for piano and orchestra (1951), 119
Daffodil Field, The *see* Sarnia, 102
Fanfare, 99
Fantasy for band (1942), 112
Grim and Gay *see* Epic March, 108
Heroic March, *see* Epic March, 108
Hyacinthus *see* Three Pastels, 106
Indian Summer *see* Green Ways, 85
Intermezzo *see* Sextet, 6
Intruder, The *see* Green Ways, 96
Liberators, The *see* Epic March, 108
London: Impressions for piano *see* London Pieces, 49
March in C minor *see* Epic March, 108
Overture for Henry Wood's Jubilee, 115
Patriotic Song, 103
Penumbra *see* Marigold, 34
   *see also* Prelude in E flat
Queen Fridias, Prelude for orchestra and piano, 90
Red Rose, The *see* Five Sixteenth-Century Poems, 98
Rosebud *see* Preludes for piano, 41
Serenade for Strings *see* Concertino pastorale, 100
Spleen *see* Marigold, 34
   *see also* Preludes for piano
Sunset Play *see* Nurses' Song, 36
These Women *see* Five Sixteenth-Century Poems, 98
Three Rustic Dances *see* Three Dances for piano, 39
Toilers of the Sea (music for the film), 116
Ussia (USSR) v. Prussia *see* Epic March, 108
Variations on 'Paul's Steeple', 115
Work for solo violin and chamber orchestra, 100

## Radio Incidental Music

Julius Caesar, 110
   *see also* Orchestral

## Recitation

Annabel Lee (Poe), 20

## Songs and Song Cycles

Bed in Summer
   arr. for voice and piano (Stevenson), 32
   *see also* Choral Music
Bells of San Marie, The (Masefield), 50
Billee Bowline (Weatherly), 24
Earth's Call (A Sylvan Rhapsody) (Monro), 49
East Riding, The (Chilman), 62
Five Poems by Thomas Hardy, 75
Five Sixteenth-Century Poems (Cornish; Howell; Anon.; Breton; Edwards), 98
Garrison Churchyard, A (Cooper) 46
Great Things (Hardy), 73
Hawthorn Time (Housman), 59
Heart's Desire, The (Housman), 47
Here's to the Ships! (O'Reilly), 29
Hillo, My Bonny (J. V. Blake), 25
Holy Boy, The
   arr. for voice and piano/organ/strings (Brown), 43
   *see also* Brass, Military, and Symphonic Wind Band; Chamber Music; Choral Music; Keyboard (Preludes for piano); Orchestral; Songs and Song Cycles
Hope the Hornblower (Newbolt), 22
Hymn to Light (James Blake), 23
If there were dreams to sell (Beddoes), 51
If we must part (Dowson), 79
I have twelve oxen (Anon.), 50
   *see also* J'ai douze bœufs
J'ai douze bœufs (Anon.), 51
   *see also* I have twelve oxen
Journey, The (E. Blake), 62
Land of Lost Content, The (Housman), xi, xiv, 63
Love is a sickness (Daniel), 66
Love's Window (Banning), 24

Marigold (Rossetti; Dowson), 34
Merry Month of May, The (Dekker), 66
Mother and Child (C. Rossetti), 54
O Happy Land (Linton), 104
  see also Choral Music
Porto Rico (Weatherly), 39
Remember (M. Coleridge), 54
Sacred Flame, The (M. Coleridge), 52
Santa Chiara (Symons), 74
Sea Fever (Masefield), 36
  see also Choral Music
Song from o'er the Hill (O'Reilly), 39
Songs of a Wayfarer (Blake;
  Shakespeare; Rossetti; Dowson;
  James Blake), 11
Songs Sacred and Profane (Meynell;
  Warner; Yeats), 81
Spring Sorrow (Brooke), 50
Three Ravens, The (Anon.), 62
Three Songs (1918–19) (Symons), 56
Three Songs (1926) (E. Brontë; Anon.;
  D. G. Rossetti), 76
Three Songs to Poems by Thomas
  Hardy, 74
Three Variations on 'Cadet Rousselle'
  (Anon.), 55
  see also Orchestral
Tutto e sciolto (Joyce), 85
Two Songs (1916) (Cooper), 46
Two Songs (1917–18) (Brooke), 48
Two Songs (1920) (Sidney; Huxley), 60
Two Songs (1928) (Symons; D. G.
  Rossetti), 79
Vagabond, The (Masefield), 68

Variations sur 'Cadet Rousselle'
  (Anon.), 55
We'll to the Woods no more (Housman),
  xi, 78
What are you thinking of? (C. Rossetti),
  72
When I am dead, my dearest
  (C. Rossetti), 71
When lights go rolling round the sky
  (James Blake), 23

Works and Sketches, Lost or
  Undated

Kishmul's Gallery, 147
Mass in the Dorian Mode, 147
Pelléas et Mélisande, 147
Prelude: Midsummer, 147
Princess Maleine, The, 147
Sonata in C minor for piano, 147
Sonata in C minor for violin and piano,
  147
Sonata in D minor for violin and piano,
  147
Sonata in G minor for violin and piano,
  147
Spring goeth all in white, 147
Te Deum (19 bars), 147
Trio for piano, violin, and cello in
  A minor, 147
Variations in E flat for piano, 147
Variations in F sharp minor for piano,
  148
Variations on an Irish tune for piano, 148
Vocal Rhapsody, 148

## APPENDIX 4
# Works and Sketches, Lost or Undated

《》

Sources of information

MMR   Anon., 'John Ireland', *Monthly Musical Record*, 1 July 1915, p. 192.

MT   E. Evans, 'Modern British Composers: V—John Ireland', *Musical Times*, 1 Sept. 1919, p. 462.

### Kishmul's Gallery

For baritone and orchestra.
**Reference:** S. Aronowsky, *Performing Times of Orchestral Works* (London, Benn, 1959), 370, where the timing is given as 2' 30".

### Mass in the Dorian Mode

For 4 voices (strict style of Palestrina).
**Reference:** MMR.

### Pelléas et Mélisande

Overture for orchestra.
**Reference:** MT.

### Prelude: Midsummer

For orchestra.
**Reference:** MMR and MT.

### The Princess Maleine

Poem for orchestra.
**Reference:** MMR.

### Sonata in C minor for piano

**Reference:** MMR and MT.

### Sonata in C minor for violin and piano

**Reference:** MMR and MT.

### Sonata in D minor for violin and piano

First movement only (undated).
**Reference:** Manuscript Collections, British Library (Reference Division), Add. MS 52901.

### Sonata in one movement for violin and piano in G minor

**Reference:** MMR and MT.

### Spring goeth all in white

Unpublished song with text by Robert Bridges (undated).
**Reference:** Manuscript Collections, British Library (Reference Division), Add. MS 52901E (notebooks).

### Te Deum (19 bars)

**Reference:** Manuscript Collections, British Library (Reference Division), Add. MS 52900. Also part in Add. MS 52901A (notebooks).

### Trio for piano, violin, and cello in A minor

**Reference:** MMR.

### Variations in E flat for piano

**Reference:** MMR.

**Variations in F sharp minor for piano**

**Reference:** *MMR*.

**Variations on an Irish tune for piano**

**Reference:** *MMR*.

**Vocal Rhapsody**

**Reference:** A letter (dated 25 Dec. 1913) from John Ireland to Edwin Evans (John Ireland Trust Archive).

## APPENDIX 5

# Index of Song Titles and First Lines

《 》

A birdless heaven ('Tutto e sciolto'), 85
A churchyard by a road side bend ('A Garrison Churchyard'), 46
Adoration, The (*Three Songs, 1918–19*), 56
Advent, The (*Songs Sacred and Profane*), 81
All in a Garden Green (*Five Sixteenth-Century Poems*), 98
All suddenly the wind comes soft ('Spring Sorrow'), 50
Around were all the roses red ('Spleen'), 34
Aside, An (*Five Sixteenth-Century Poems*), 98
A song came over the hill to me ('A song from o'er the Hill'), 39

Baby (*Mother and Child*), 54
Because it is the day of Palms ('Santa Chiara'), 74
Beckon to me to come (*Five Poems by Thomas Hardy*), 75
Billee Bowline (Turlay Royce), 24
Blind (*Two Songs, 1916*), 46
Blind Boy, The (*Mother and Child*), 54
Blind from my birth ('The Blind Boy'), 54
Blow out, ye bugles (*Two Songs to Poems by Rupert Brooke*), 48

Cadet Rousselle a trois garçons (*Variations sur 'Cadet Rousselle'*), 56
Cost, The (*Two Songs, 1916*), 46
Crying, my little one? ('The Only Child'), 54

Dear, think not that they will forget you (*Five Poems by Thomas Hardy*), 75
Death-Parting (*Mother and Child*), 54
Down by the salley gardens (*Songs Sacred and Profane*), 81
Do you see the road awinding? ('The Journey'), 62
Dunno a heap about what and why ('The Vagabond'), 68
During Music (*Two Songs, 1928*), 79

Encounter, The (*The Land of Lost Content*), 63
English May (*Songs of a Wayfarer*), 11
Epilogue (*The Land of Lost Content*), 63

Fair, no beauty of thine will last (*Songs Sacred and Profane*), 81
Flocking to the temple (*Songs Sacred and Profane*), 81
Friendship in Misfortune (*Three Songs, 1926*), 76

Garland, The (*Mother and Child*), 54
Give me the depth of love ('Friendship in Misfortune'), 76
Goal and Wicket (*The Land of Lost Content*), 63
God, who gave the world its fairness ('Blind'), 46
Goodbye in fear, goodbye in sorrow ('Death-Parting'), 54

Hark ye, hark to the winding horn ('Hope the Hornblower'), 22
Here's to the ships, the grey ships, 29

Her Song (*Three Poems by Thomas Hardy*), 74
Hillo, My Bonny (Turlay Royce), 25
Hope (*Mother and Child*), 54
Hymn for a Child (*Songs Sacred and Profane*), 81

I did not look upon her eyes ('Penumbra'), 34
I do defy ye, crabbed age ('Hillo, My Bonny'), 25
I dug and dug amongst the snow ('Hope'), 54
If I should die, think only this of me ('The Soldier'), 48
If there were dreams to sell, 51
If truth in hearts that perish (*The Land of Lost Content*), 63
If we must part, 79
I have twelve oxen that be fair and brown, 50
I must go down to the seas again ('Sea Fever'), 36
In Boyhood (*We'll to the Woods no more*), 78
In my Sage Moments (*Five Poems by Thomas Hardy*), 75
In the morning let me face ('Hymn to Light'), 23
In winter I get up at night ('Bed in Summer'), 32
I sang that song on Sunday ('Her Song'), 74
It's pleasant in Holy Mary ('The Bells of San Marie'), 50
It was many a many a year ago ('Annabel Lee'), 20
It was what you bore with you, woman (*Five Poems by Thomas Hardy*), 75
I was not sorrowful (*Songs of a Wayfarer*), 11
I will walk on the earth (*Songs of a Wayfarer*), 11

Jump through the hedge, lass! (*Songs Sacred and Profane*), 81

Ladslove (*The Land of Lost Content*), 63
Lent Lilly, The (*The Land of Lost Content*), 63
Look not in my eyes, for fear (*The Land of Lost Content*), 63
Love and Friendship (*Three Songs*, 1926), 76
Love is a sickness full of woes, 66
Love is like the wild rose-briar ('Love and Friendship'), 76
Love me, I love you ('Baby'), 54
Love's Window (Turlay Royce), 24
Lowly, laid in a manger ('The Holy Boy'), 43

Memory, hither come, and tune your merry note (*Songs of a Wayfarer*), 11
My Fair (*Songs Sacred and Profane*), 81
My true love hath my heart (*Two Songs*, 1920), 60

Newborn (*Mother and Child*), 54
No sudden thing of glory or fear (*Songs Sacred and Profane*), 81

O cool unto the sense of pain ('During Music'), 79
O happy land half-hid in the dewy grass, 104
One Hope, The (*Three Songs*, 1926), 76
Only Child, The (*Mother and Child*), 54
On this sweet bank ('Youth's Spring-Tribute'), 34
O Rico is a bully place ('Porto Rico'), 39
O, the month of May ('The Merry Month of May'), 66
O 'twas Monday in the morn ('Billee Bowline'), 24

Pain gnaws at my heart ('The Rat'), 56
Penumbra (*Marigold: An Impression*), 34
Pleasure it is to hear, iwis, the birdes sing ('A Thanksgiving'), 98
Porto Rico (Turlay Royce), 39

Rat, The (*Three Songs*, 1918–19), 56
Report Song, A (*Five Sixteenth-Century Poems*), 98
Rest (*Three Songs*, 1918–19), 56
Roses blushing red and white ('The Garland'), 54

Salley Gardens, The (*Songs Sacred and Profane*), 81
Salt-laden, sad with cry of ships ('The East Riding'), 62
Scapegoat, The (*Songs Sacred and Profane*), 81
See the scapegoat, happy beast (*Songs Sacred and Profane*), 81
Shall we go dance the hay, the hay? ('A Report Song'), 98
Skylark and Nightingale (*Mother and Child*), 54
Soldier, The (*Two Songs to Poems by Rupert Brooke*), 48
Soldier's Return, The (*Songs Sacred and Profane*), 81
Spleen (*Marigold: An Impression*), 34
Spring will not wait [piano solo] (*We'll to the Woods no more*), 78
Summer Schemes (*Three Poems by Thomas Hardy*), 74
Sweet cyder is a great thing ('Great Things'), 73
Sweet Season, The (*Five Sixteenth-Century Poems*), 98

Take back the honour and the fame ('The Cost'), 46
Thanksgiving, A (*Five Sixteenth-Century Poems*), 98
The boys are up the wood with day ('The Heart's Desire'), 47
The fountain murmuring of sleep ('Tryst'), 79
The fresh air moves like water round a boat ('Earth's Call'), 49
The peace of a wandering sky ('Rest'), 56
There were three ravens sat on a tree ('The Three Ravens'), 62

These women all both great and small ('An Aside'), 98
The street sounds to the soldier's tread (*The Land of Lost Content*), 63
The Tragedy of that Moment (*Five Poems by Thomas Hardy*), 75
Thick-flowered is the trellis ('The Trellis'), 60
This is the weather the cuckoo likes ('Weathers'), 74
Thy hand is mine ('The Sacred Flame'), 52
Time brought me many another friend ('Remember'), 54
'Tis spring, come out to ramble (*The Land of Lost Content*), 63
'Tis time, I think, by Wenlock town ('Hawthorne Time'), 59
Trellis, The (*Two Songs*, 1920), 60
Tryst [In Fountain Court] (*Two Songs*, 1928), 79
Twice a week the winter through (*The Land of Lost Content*), 63

Up to the top of the trees ('I will walk on the earth'), 11

Vain Desire, The (*The Land of Lost Content*), 63

Weathers (*Three Poems by Thomas Hardy*), 74
We'll to the Woods no more, 78
Were there a little lamp ('Love's Window'), 24
What art thou thinking of? (*Mother and Child*), 54
When a mounting skylark sings ('Skylark and Nightingale'), 54
Whenas the mildest month of jolly June ('All in a Garden Green'), 98
When daffodils begin to peer (*Songs of a Wayfarer*), 11
When friendly summer calls again ('Summer Schemes'), 74
When I am dead, my dearest, 71

When I would muse in boyhood ('In Boyhood'), 78
When lights go rolling round the sky, 23
When May is in his prime ('The Sweet Season'), 98
When vain desire at last ('The One Hope'), 76
Why have you brought me myrrh' ('The Adoration'), 56
Would God your health were as this month of May ('English May'), 11

Your brother has a falcon ('Newborn'), 54
You smile upon your friend today (*The Land of Lost Content*), 63
Youth's Spring-Tribute (*Marigold: An Impression*), 34

# GENERAL INDEX

«‹›»

Adami, Mme 52
Adey, Christopher 58
Adni, Daniel 31, 33, 39, 40, 73, 102, 119
Aitken, T. 91
Akerman, Martin 33
Alcock, Walter 6, 7
Alexander, Arthur 80
Alington, C. A. 72
Alison, Richard 18
Allbright, Terence 27
Allen, Hugh xv
Allen, Thomas 37
*Amoris victima* (Symons) 56
Anderson, R. 70
Anderson, W. R. 19, 35, 88, 99
Anderton, H. O. 123
Antheil, George 86
Archer, J. Stuart 45
Armstrong, John 81, 86
Arnell, Richard, xv, 128
Aronowsky, S. 147
Arts Council of Great Britain 3, 120
Asche, Oscar 98
Auden, W. H. 106
Austin, E. 40

Bach, J. S. 85, 141
*Bach Book for Harriet Cohen, A* 85
Bach Choir 3, 5
Bacharach, A. L. 125
Backhouse, J. 27
Baker, George 52
Baker, Janet 75, 82, 98
Balcon, Michael 115
*Balder* (Dobell) 29
Balfour, H. L. 22 45
Ball, Eric 92
*Ballads and Poems* (Masefield) 50
Banfield, Stephen 94, 95
Banks, Barry 94
Banning, H. D. 24
Barbican Piano Trio 16
Barbirolli, Evelyn (née Rothwell) 119
Barbirolli, John 35, 64, 93, 95
Barnard, L. S. 126

Bartok, Bela ix
*Bassus* (Cornish) 98
Baulard, Valerie 50, 75
Bax, Arnold 56, 85, 86, 93, 95, 129
BBC Choral Society 94
BBC Chorus 94, 104, 110
BBC Concert Orchestra 88
BBC Singers 43, 106
BBC Symphony Orchestra 83, 86, 89, 92, 93, 94, 95, 99, 104, 114, 133
Beddoes, Thomas Lowell 51
Bedford, H. 124
Beecham Orchestra 45
Beedle, Professor 119
Beethoven, Ludwig van 90, 134
Beith, Major 103
Belchamber, F. W. 45
Benjamin, Arthur 99
Bennett, H. 86
Bennson, G. 58
Benson, Lionel S. 18
Bentham, Percy G. 92
Bernard, Anthony 90
Berry, Mary 26
Besses o'th 'Barn Band 87
Bevan, Ven. Henry E. J. 17
Bianca, Sandra 83
Bickershaw Colliery Band 87
Bielby, Jonathan 10, 12, 13, 21, 22, 34, 42, 121
Binge, Ronald 13
Birch, John 27
Black Dyke Mills Band 93
Blackmore, George 43
Blake, Ernest 62
Blake, James Vila 11, 23, 24, 25, 28, 30, 55
Blake, William 11, 20, 28, 36, 61, 122
Bliss, Arthur ix, 86, 87, 91, 99
Blom, Eric 83, 96, 125
Blyth, Alan 51, 82
Blyth, Ethel Mary 18
Bolton, R. 37
Bonavia, F. 101
*Book of Common Prayer* 15, 17, 29, 43, 44, 58, 103, 104, 121
Bott, Paula 7, 27

Boughton, Rutland ix, 76
Boulding, K. R. R. 38
Boult, Adrian 7, 35, 41, 64, 84, 88, 89, 93, 94, 95, 99, 102, 104, 108, 109, 111, 114, 117, 118
Bournemouth Municipal Orchestra 35
Bournemouth Sinfonietta 99
Bowen, York 53
Boyce, Frederick 12
Boyd Neel Orchestra 41, 88, 99
Brae, June 65
Brahms, Johannes x
Brand, Geoffrey 8, 87, 91, 92, 109
Brand, John 89, 106
Brash, James 53
Breton, Nicholas 98
Bridge, Frank ix, 16, 41, 56, 88, 122
Bridges, Robert 118, 147
Bridgewater, Leslie 13, 14, 21
Brier, J. 86
Brighouse and Rastrick Band 87
British Broadcasting Corporation (BBC) xv, 59, 77, 81, 84, 86, 90, 94, 100, 101, 102, 103, 106, 107, 108, 110, 114, 115
Britten, Benjamin ix, x, xv, 8, 49, 51, 61, 63, 70, 77, 84
Brontë, Emily 76
Brook, Donald 125
Brook, Jocelyn 70, 89, 127, 129
Brooke, Rupert 48, 50
Broso, Antonio 97
Brown, Herbert S. 43, 96
Brown, Laurence 37
Brown, Timothy 120
Brownlee, John 37
Brymbo Male Choir 39
Bülow, Hans von 57
Burchill, M. 38
Burden, John 6
Burke, Anthony 65
Burnaby, F. G. 114
Busch, William 86
Bush, Alan xv, 16, 70, 94, 95, 126
Bush, Geoffrey 19, 88, 100, 101, 111, 117, 122, 129, 131
Bye, Frederick 23, 52
Byfield, D. 131

Cambridge University Chamber Choir 120
Cambridge University Madrigal Society 120
Cameron, Basil 83, 114
Campion, Thomas 3, 25, 30
Canterbury Cathedral Choir 27
Canterbury Festival (1939) 99
Carducci, Edgardo 86
Carlisle Cathedral Choir 27
Carter, Alan 65

Case, John Carol 43, 95
Cassini, Leonard 19, 70
Catterall, Arthur 46
Cavalcanti, Alberto 116
Chaffer, J. 128
Chapman, Ernest 6, 129
Chenhalls, Alfred 96
Chester, Betty, 37
Chester, J. & W. 9
*Chesterian, The* 57
Chichester Cathedral Choir 27
Child, M. 57
*Child's Garden of Verses, A* (Stevenson) 32
Chilman, Eric 62
Chislett, W. A. 37, 38, 87, 88, 91
Chissell, Joan 26, 113
Choir of the School of St Mary and St Anne (Abbots Bromley) 131
Chrimes, Pamela 65
Christ College Chapel Choir (Brecon) 121
*Chu Chin Chow* (Norton) 98
Church of the Holy Trinity (Sloane Street) xi, xiv, 4, 6, 17, 22, 28
Church of St Jude (Chelsea) xiv, 12
Church of St Luke (Chelsea) xii, xiv, 12, 15, 17, 40, 68, 81
Church of St Sepulchre (London) xv
Church of St Stephen (St Peter Port) xi, 100, 101, 103
Churchill, W. S. 96, 108
City of Birmingham Symphony Orchestra 117
City of London Sinfonia 23, 52
City of London Wind Ensemble 8, 92
Clark, Edward 77, 81, 84
Clarke, R. 16
Clegg, John 66
Cliffe, Frederick ix, xiv, 3
Clutsam, G. H. 33, 54
Coates, Albert 64
Cobbett, W. W. x, 16
Cobbett Chamber Music Competition x, xiv, 16, 19
Cohen Harriet 55, 85, 96
Coleridge, Mary 52, 54
Coleridge, Samual Taylor ix
Collignon, Raimond 55
Collinge, Jack 37
Collins, A. 83
*Composer Speaks, The* 134
*Concerto No. 3 for Piano and Orchestra* (Rachmaninov) 113
Constable, John 37
Cooke, Anthony 117
Cooke, M. W. 130
Cooper, Eric Thirkell 46
Cooper, Joseph 134

*General Index* 155

Cooper, Martin 128
Cornish, William 98
Cory, William 72
*Countess of Pembrokes's Arcadia, The* (Sydney) 60
Cousins, M. 27
Coyle, Edgar 37
Crabtree, C. M. 37
Craggs, Stewart R. xii
Cranko, John 65
Crompton, Henry P. 110
Crosland, H. 116
Crossley-Holland, P. 126
Crossman, Samuel 58
*Crossways* (Yeats) 81
Curror, Ian 27
Curzon, Clifford 84, 101
Curzon, Frederick 99
CWS (Manchester) Band 87

*Daily Herald* 118
d'Alvarez, Marguerite 56
Daniel, Samuel 66
Darlow, D. 24
David Martin Trio 16, 47, 97
Dawes, F. 77
Dawney, Michael 131
Dawson, Peter 51
De Reszke Singers 72
Dearth, Harry 29
Debussy, Claude x
*Decorations: In Verse and Prose* (Verlaine) 34
Deering, Richard 81
Dekker, Thomas 66
Delius, Frederick 3, 93
Demuth, Norman 127
Denman, John 112
Denton, D. 7, 27, 41, 93, 94, 107
Devon County Library 18
Dickinson, A. E. F. 125
Dilkes, Neville 41
Dobell, Sydney 29
Dods, Marcus 117
Dohnányi, Ernst von 84
Douglas, Roy 115
Dowson, Ernest 11, 34, 79
Draper, Charles 32
Draycott, Barry 113
Drinkwater, John 76
Duckworth, Gerald & Co. xi
Dunhill, Thomas 5, 19, 29, 33, 110, 125
Dutton, Paul 113
Dyall Valentine 111

Eaglefield Hull, A. 123
Ealing Studios 115, 116
Edward VII, King 7

Edwardes, Richard 61, 98
Edwards, Gwynne 5
Eggar, K. E. 123
Elgar, Edward 9, 76, 93
Elizabeth II, Queen xv, 120
Elizabethan Madrigal Society 18
Elliot, J. H. 87, 91
Elm Park Mansions (Chelsea) xiv, 15, 18, 30
Elms, Roderick 7, 27
Elwes, Gervase Henry 64
*England's Helicon* (Breton) 98
English Chamber Orchestra 41, 88, 122
*English Hymnal* 15
English Sinfonia 41
*Espalier, The* (Warner) 81
Etches, Mathilda 65
Evans, Edwin 55, 56, 94, 102, 123, 124, 147, 148
Exeter Cathedral Choir 27
Exultate Singers 120

Fairey Band 91
Farjeon, Eleanor 105, 109, 110
Fearn, Lillian 51
Fenby, Eric 94
Festival of Britain (1951) 119
*First Part of Airs, The* (Hume) 67
Fiske, Roger 11, 16, 19, 23, 24, 34, 37, 47, 48, 50, 51, 52, 61, 62, 63, 67, 68, 70, 71, 73, 74, 75, 76, 78, 79, 80, 82, 86, 97, 98, 120
Flood, David 27
Foden's Motor Works Band 86, 87, 91
Folkening, John 59
Forsyth, Cecil 14, 141
Fortunatus, Bishop Venantius 6
Foss, Hubert J. 124, 126, 128
Foster, Ivor 22
Foster, Muriel 46, 47, 48
Frank, Alan, C. 126
Franklin, Norman 98
Fricker, Peter Racine 85
Froggatt, Alan 17
Frohnmayer, Ellen 49
Frohnmayer, Philip 46

Galway, James 42
Gange, Fraser 37
Garforth, David 41, 88, 122
*Garland for the Queen, A* xv, 120
Gatti, G. M. 123
George V, King 7, 44
George, VI, King xv, 7, 94
Gheel, Henry 86, 91
Gideon, Melville 37
Glasby, Bobby 40, 81
Glock, W. G. 36
Gloucester Cathedral Choir 107

## General Index

*Goblin Market and Other Poems* (Rossetti) 71
Goddard, Scott 112, 125, 127
Godfrey, Dan 35
Golden Age Singers 120
Goldstone, Alan 85
Goodwin, Amina 16
Goossens, Eugene ix, 56, 64, 86, 123
Goossens Symphony Orchestra 64
Goring, Marius 111
Goss, John 75
Goss-Custard, Reginald 12
Gower, Robert 10, 12, 13, 21, 22, 42, 109, 121, 131
Grailville College Singers 79
Gray, Cecil 124
Greenfield, Edward 41, 47, 50, 51, 52, 67, 73, 74, 76, 82
Griffiths, E. 52
Grimethorpe Colliery Band 91
Grinke, Frederick 97, 99, 133
Grinke Trio 16, 97
Groves, Charles 111
*Grove's Dictionary of Music* 10
Grundting, Mary 81
Guest, George 27
Guest, Helen 84
Guildford Cathedral Choir 27
Guildhall String Ensemble 88
Gunter Grove (Chelsea) xii, xiv, 30, 41, 81
Gurney, Ivor 132
GUS (Kettering) Band 87, 91

Hailstone, A. 91
Hale, Paul 59
Hallé Choir 95
Hallé Orchestra 35, 64, 83, 95
Halling, Patrick 5
Halling, Peter 5
Hamburg, Boris 42
Hamburg Philharmonic Orchestra 83
Hamburger, Paul 82
Hampton Music Club 6
Handel, G. F. x
Handley, Vernon 84
Hardy, Thomas x, xiv, xv, 73, 74, 75
Harewood, Earl of 92
'Harlequin' 116
Harman, W. M. 118
Harris, Llywela 113
Harrison, Beatrice 69, 70
Harrison, Max 31, 33, 35, 39, 40, 57, 60, 61, 64, 66, 67, 68, 69, 70, 73, 77, 80, 84, 89, 95, 96, 101, 105, 119
Hartley Trio 16
Harvey, Frederick 24, 38
Harvey, Trevor 7, 17, 26, 32, 41, 43, 44, 47, 49, 52, 54, 55, 57, 58, 59, 61, 62, 63, 66, 72, 74, 83, 88, 93, 95, 99, 106, 107, 113, 117, 121
Hattey, Philip 82
Hawkes, Ralph 8, 99, 103
Haywood, Marjorie 19, 21
Headington, Christopher 31
Headmasters' Conference 58, 60
Hely-Hutchinson, Victor 115
Henderson, Roy 37, 48
Herbage, Anna 114
Herbage, Julian 106, 108, 114, 115, 125, 127, 134
Herbert, A. P. 29
Herincx, Raimund 37
Heward, Leslie 83
Hickox, Richard 7, 23, 27, 35, 41, 52, 93, 95, 108, 111, 114, 117
Hill, Ralph 65, 71, 97, 105, 107, 112, 117, 125
Hindemith, Paul ix
HM's Chapels Royal 6
HMS *Archilles* 44
Hodge, Herbert 45
Hodgson, Alfreda 32, 49, 54, 57, 62, 72, 75
Holbrooke, Joseph 124
Holland, A. K. 126
Holst, Gustav ix, x, 76
Honegger, Arthur 111
Honeyball, David 41, 87, 92
Hooton, Florence 42, 97
Horn, G. 91
Horsley, Colin 83
*House of Life, The* (D. G. Rossetti) 34, 76
*House of Souls* (Machen) xi, 31,
Housman, A. E. x, 47, 59, 63, 78, 96, 106
How, Bishop W. W. 113
Howard, Leslie 96
Howard-Jones, Evelyn 3, 69, 105
Howarth, Elgar 91
Howell, Thomas 98
Howells, Herbert ix, 10, 21, 22, 86, 121
Howes, Frank 127, 128
Hughes, Clifford 43
Hughes, Eric 130
Hughes, G. 39
Hughes, Herbert 72, 85, 86, 87
Hughes, Owain Arwel 93
Hugo, Victor 102
Hull, Robin 125, 127
*Human Shows* (Hardy) 75
Hume, Tobias 67
Hunt, Donald 7, 17, 27, 43, 44, 59, 107, 113, 121
Hurlstone, William ix
Hurst, George 99
Huxley, Aldous 60
*Hymen's Triumph* (Daniel) 66
*Hymn of Nature, A* (Bridges) 118

*Images of Good and Evil* (Symons) 74
Instone, Anna (Mrs Anna Herbage) 114
International Society for Contemporary Music (ISCM) 55, 77
*Internationale* xii, 95
*Ionica* (Cory) 72
Ireland, Alexander (father) xiv
Ireland, Annie (mother) xiv
Ireland, John:
  as arranger 13, 14, 17, 26, 36, 41, 43, 65, 87, 90, 109
  as conductor 6, 84, 133
  as performer 5, 9, 11, 19, 32, 46, 47, 48, 63, 70, 77, 78, 81, 89, 97, 104, 105, 112, 133
  as a writer 5, 7, 9, 16, 45, 83, 114, 124, 126, 127, 148
Irish Folksong Society 72
Irving, Ernest 115
Irwin, Robert 37
Isaacs, Leonard 119
Isepp, Martin 75, 98

Jackson, Francis 113
Jacob, Gordon ix
Jacobs, Arthur 127, 134
Jacobson, Bernard 93
James, Ifor 87
Jameson, M. 7, 35, 111, 114, 117
Jean-Aubry, G. 57
John Ireland Memorial Window (St Sepulchre's Church) xv
John Ireland Trust xv, 36, 38, 51, 88, 98, 117, 121, 134
John Ireland Trust Archive 4, 5, 7, 9, 16, 43, 45, 56, 83, 113, 127, 148
Johnson, Anthony Rolfe 11, 63
Johnson, Graham 11
Jones, Parry 95
Joyce, Eileen 83, 84
Joyce, James 85
*Joyce Book, The* 85, 86

Kalisch, A. 53, 57
Kamaran Trio 47
Keble, John 121
Keir, P. 132
Keller, Hans 120
Kennedy, Michael 16, 23, 24, 31, 37, 52, 83, 93
Kernot, Vivienne 65
Kersey, Eda 46
Kersley, Leo 65
Keys, Ivor 114
Kilgare Presyterian Church Choir 27
Kimmins, ? 18
King, Thea 6, 112
Kirby, Norah xv, 68, 117, 129

Kirkup, James 120
Konrath, Anton J. 84

Lamb, A. 38
Lamb, L. 91
Lambert, H. 83
Lamond, Frederic 57, 58
*Land of Hope and Glory* (Elgar) 108
Larner, Gerald 131
*Last Poems* (Houseman) 78
*Late Lyrics and Earlier* (Hardy) 74, 75
Laundon, Vivien 101, 132
Lawrenson, John 38
Layton, Robert 19, 64, 70, 83, 90, 112, 114
Le Fleming, C. 129
League of the Arts for National and Civic Ceremony 60
Leeds Festival 5
Leeds Parish Church Choir 113
Leeson, Jane E. 118
*Left, Right and Centre* (Bush) xii
Leicester Schools Orchestra 88
Lemare, E. H. 10
Leonard, Jonathan 121
*Les Travailleurs de la Mer* (Toilers of the Sea) (Hugo) 102, 116
Lewis, Ivor 39
Liddle, S. 22, 29
Lihou, Peter 105
*Linden Tree, The* (Priestley) 122
Linton, W. J. 104
Liszt, Franz 57
Liverpool Philharmonic Orchestra 93
Llewellyn, Redvers 95
Lloyd Webber, Julian 16, 42, 47, 70, 97, 130
Logan, Sinclair 86
London Ballad Concerts 22, 29
London Brass Virtuosi 41, 87, 92
London Chamber Players 90
London Collegiate Brass 87, 92
London Festival of the Arts (1951) 134
London Philharmonic Choir 95
London Philharmonic Orchestra 7, 35, 41, 64, 84, 88, 90, 93, 95, 99, 107, 108, 111, 114, 117
London Symphony Chorus 7, 27, 95
London Symphony Orchestra 7, 27, 35, 41, 64, 93, 95, 108, 111, 114, 116, 117
London Trio 16
Long, Katherine 46
Longmire, John xv, 23, 36, 50, 60, 63, 68, 72, 73, 74, 76, 79, 83, 94, 110, 111, 116, 128, 129
*Loom of Dreams, The* (Symons) 56
Louis Halsey Singers 110
Loveday, Alan 19
Lucas, Andrew 27

## 158  General Index

Lunn, Kirby 23
Luton Choral Society 95
Lutyens, Elisabeth 77
Luxon, Benjamin 11, 23, 24, 34, 37, 48, 50, 51, 52, 62, 67, 68, 71, 74, 75, 77, 78, 79, 80, 82, 86, 98
Lyle, W. 123
Lympany, Moira 44
Lyrita Ltd. 111, 117

McCabe, John 42, 70, 77
Macdonald, Malcolm 8, 41, 44, 55, 58, 61, 87, 88, 89, 91, 92, 112, 122
Machen, Arthur xi, xiv, 31, 35, 89, 129, 131
McKellar, Kenneth 37
Mackenzie-Rogan Symphony Orchestra 38
Mackerras, Charles 116
Mackler, A. 87
Macmillan, Kenneth 65
McNaught, William 90, 95, 99, 108, 114
Macpherson, Charles 26, 76
Magpie Madrigal Society 18
Maine, Basil 124
Mann, William 83, 130
Manuscript Collections (British Library) 3, 4, 5, 6, 7, 8, 9, 10, 11, 12, 13, 15, 18, 20, 26, 29, 30, 32, 34, 35, 36, 40, 43, 46, 47, 48, 49, 55, 57, 61, 63, 64, 65, 66, 67, 68, 69, 70, 71, 72, 73, 74, 75, 76, 78, 79, 80, 81, 83, 84, 87, 89, 90, 93, 94, 96, 97, 98, 99, 100, 101, 103, 104, 105, 106, 109, 111, 113, 114, 115, 116, 119, 120, 121, 122, 132, 147
March, Ivan 93, 117
Markham Lee, E. 53, 66, 102
Marks, Charles 4, 5
Marshall, Lois 51
Martin, J. M. 126
Mase, Oliver 90
Masefield, John 36, 50, 68
Mason, Berkeley 107
Mathieson, Muir 116
Measham, David 84, 108, 117
Melbourne Symphony Orchestra 84
Melos Ensemble 6
Mendelssohn, Felix x
Merrick, Frank 40, 58
*Methodist Hymn Book* 15
Meynell, Alice 81
MGM Symphony Orchestra 99
*Midsummer Night's Dream, A* (Shakespeare) 106
Mignot, Mrs 101
Miles, Maurice 93
Milhaud, Darius 86
Miller, Arthur, G. xv, 68, 71, 76, 78, 80
Millington, Andrew 27
Minghetti, Liza 100

Ministry of Information (MoI) 102, 108
Mischa-Léon, Harry H. 36
Mitchell, Donald 49, 70
Mitchell, Graham 55, 66, 69, 101
Mitchinson, John 47, 52, 55, 59, 61, 62, 63, 66
Moeran, Ernest, J. ix, xv, 70, 86, 124, 130
Moiseiwitsch, Benno 113
*Moments of Vision* (Hardy) 73
Moore, Gerald 24, 37, 42, 82
Moore, Thomas 33
Morales, Pedro G. 30
Morgan, Paul 27
Morley, Thomas 20
Morris, G. O'Connor 45
Morrison, Angus 84
Mortimer, Alec 87, 93
Mortimer, Fred 86, 91
Mortimer, Rex 91
Moss, Alfred 56
*Mother and Child* (Rossetti) 72
*Motherland Song Book, The* 60
Moulton, Dorothy 86
Muckle, May 32
Muncey, Revd. E. Howard 104
Munro, Harold 49
Murdoch, William 45, 46, 53, 77
Music Magazine 114, 134
*Musical Times* 67, 69

Nashe, Thomas 18, 97
National Brass Band Championships of Great Britain 86, 91
National Coal Board 118
National Film Archive 116
National Sound Archive 134
Navarra, André 70
Neale, J. M. 6
Neaman, Yfrah 16, 19, 46, 47, 97
Neel, Boyd 41, 88, 99
Neighbour, O. W. 85
Nethsingha, Lucian 27
Nevinson, Bernard 9
New Concert Orchestra 108
New Queen's Hall Orchestra 64
Newbolt, Henry 22, 52
Newby, N. 48
Newsome, Roy 91
Newton, Ivor 37, 48
Nicholas, M. 27
Nicholls, B. E. 103
Nicholson, Sydney H. 113, 118
*1914 and Other Poems* (Brooke) 48
Noble, Denis 94
Noble, Jeremy 49, 67, 68, 69, 77, 96
*Not Yet in Fancy's Following* (Coleridge) 54
*Nuttall's Standard Dictionary* 108

## General Index

O'Brien, Garrett 120
*Observations on Popular Antiquities* (Brand) 89
Ogdon, John 40, 73
Oliver, Michael 41, 64, 83, 90
Ord, Boris 120
O'Reilly, P. J. 29, 39
Orr, C. W. 86
Ottaway, Hugh 120, 126, 127, 131
Ould, H. 124
*Over the Garden Wall* (Farjeon) 105
*Oxford Book of Carols* (1928) 79, 103
*Oxford Poetry* (Huxley) 60
Oxford University Press 86
Oxley, James 7

Palestrina, G. x, 147
Palmer, C. xi, 31, 40, 44, 49, 53, 55, 71, 131
*Paradyse of Daynty Devices, A* (Edwardes) 98
Parker, George 23, 37, 38, 47, 50, 51, 52, 71, 74, 77, 82, 98, 121
Parkin, Eric 3, 16, 19, 31, 33, 40, 44, 46, 47, 49, 50, 51, 52, 53, 55, 58, 60, 61, 66, 67, 68, 69, 70, 71, 73, 74, 75, 77, 80, 82, 84, 85, 89, 90, 96, 97, 102, 106, 112, 119, 130
Parrott, Walter 3, 20, 22
Parry, Hubert x, 14
Parsons, William 104
Partridge, Ian 55
Partridge, Jennifer 55
Paul, Reginald 84
Payne, A. 129
Pears, Peter 51, 61, 63, 74, 77, 134
Pengelly, Albert 51
Perkin, Helen xv, 81, 82, 83, 90, 96
Perry, Roy 27
Petronius (T. Petronius Arbiter) 114, 115
Peyer, Gervase de 112
*'Phantasy' Piano Trio* (Bridge) 16
Philharmonia Orchestra 35, 93, 115
Philip Jones Brass Ensemble 27
Phillips, Dorothy xv
Piatigorsky, Gregor 103
Pilkington, M. 132
Pini, Anthony 133
Pirie, Peter J. 84, 131
Pitfield, Thomas 130
Platts, Harry 65
Poe, Edgar Alan 20
*Poems New and Old* (Newbolt) 22
*Poems*, 1907 (Coleridge) 52
*Poems 1911–1914* (Brooke) 50
*Poetical Sketches* (Blake) 11
*Pomes Penyeach* (Joyce) 85
Pomponius Mela 102
Porter, Andrew 51
Portman, Eric 111
Portsmouth Cathedral Choir 17

Pougnet, Jean 107
Pratt, R. 42
*Preludes* (Meynell) 81
Previn, André 88
Priestley, J. B. 122
*Pro Musica* 85, 96
Pryor, Geoffrey 112
Pulkingham, Betty 59
Purcell, Henry x
Purcell Operatic Society 103

Quartet Pro Musica 5, 6
Queen's Hall Orchestra 14, 35
Quilter, Roger 132
Quinn, R. 8
*Quintet for Clarinet and Strings* (Brahms) 6

Rachmaninov, Serge 113
Radford, Robert 11
Rafferty, Chips 115
Rankin, W. D. 130
Ravel, Maurice x
Rawsthorne, Alan 115
Rayson, Michael 101
Read, Alfred 73
Reed, Philip 49, 70
Rees, Clifford B. 125, 127, 128
Reiss, Thelma 70
Rennert, Jonathan 131
Renouf, D. F. 131
Reynolds, Gordon 87
Reynolds, W. 91
Richardson, Norman 8
*Rite of Spring* (Stravinsky) xi
Robbins, Tessa 46
Robertson, Alec 3, 7, 9, 16, 26, 31, 33, 35, 37, 40, 41, 42, 45, 51, 53, 58, 60, 64, 66, 71, 73, 75, 78, 80, 83, 84, 88, 90, 93, 95, 97, 98, 99, 102, 106, 108, 111, 112, 114, 117, 119, 120, 128
Robertson, Stuart 24, 37, 38, 50, 51
Robeson, Paul 37
Robinson, Stanford 108
Rochester, M. 10, 12, 13, 21, 22, 42, 121
Rock Lodge (Sussex) xv
Rodney Christian Fellowship Choir 58
Roper, E. Stanley 45
Rossetti, Christina 54, 58, 67, 69, 71, 72
Rossetti, Dante Gabriel 11, 34, 76, 79
Roston, R. 42
Rousell, Albert 86
Rowlands, Alan 3, 7, 9, 11, 23, 24, 31, 32, 33, 34, 37, 40, 44, 46, 47, 48, 49, 50, 51, 52, 53, 54, 55, 57, 58, 59, 60, 61, 62, 63, 66, 67, 68, 69, 71, 72, 73, 74, 77, 78, 79, 80, 82, 84, 85, 86, 89, 96, 98, 102, 106, 112, 119, 129

Rowley, Alec 89
Royal Academy of Music xv, 3, 11, 21, 26, 85, 94
Royal Artillery Band, Woolwich 8, 111
Royal Choral Society 22
Royal College of Music ix, xiv, xv, 3, 4, 5, 6, 7, 8, 9, 11, 14, 29, 30, 45, 53, 70, 72, 82, 93, 103, 110, 112
Royal College of Music Student Orchestra 5, 7
Royal College of Organists xiv
Royal Corps of Signals Band 38
Royal Marines Band 38
Royal Philharmonic Orchestra 41, 45, 83, 84
Royal School of Church Music Choir 58, 113
Royce, Turlay (pseud.) 24, 25, 39
Ruckert, Fredrich 30
Runnett, Brian 27
Russell-Smith, Geoffrey 42
Rutland, Harold 31, 49, 114, 127, 129, 130

Sacher, Paul 100
Sadler's Wells Theatre Ballet 65
St Edmundsbury Cathedral Choir 27
St George's Chapel (Windsor) 3
St John's College, Cambridge 27
St Matthew's Church Choir (Northampton) 27
St Paul's Cathedral Choir 26, 27
Sala, Antonio 70, 97, 133
Salter, Lionel 31, 49, 58, 64, 102
Salter, Robert 88
*Saltwater Ballads* (Masefield) 36, 68
Sammons, Albert 45, 47, 53, 127, 133
Sanders, A. 35, 37, 41, 42, 83, 87, 88, 91, 95, 122
Sanders, Francis G. 45
Sanders, John 107
Sargent, Malcolm 93, 114
Sauret, Emile 21
Schafer, Murray 129, 134
Schiller, Alan 31
Schoenberg, Arnold ix
Scott, C. 130
Scott, Ernest 5
Scott, John 27
Scott, S. 130, 131
Scott-Sutherland, C. 128, 131
Scottish Junior Singers 79
Scottish National Academy of Music 57
Seal, Richard 27
Searle, Humphrey xv, 70
Searle, Muriel 83, 131
Sebire, Alfred 101
Sellick, Phyllis 66
Senior, Eric 128
Sessions, Roger 86
Ševčik, Otakar 21
Sewell, Frederick A. 22, 29, 45

Shakespeare, William xii, 11, 18, 96, 106, 110
Shaw, Geoffrey 60
Shaw, Martin 103
Shaw, Teresa 7
Shirley-Quirk, John 37, 47, 50, 51, 52, 67, 74, 77, 82
*Shoemaker's Holiday, The* (Dekker) 66
*Shropshire Lad, A* (Housman) 47, 59, 63, 78, 96, 106
Sievewright, A. 12, 27, 121
*Silhouettes* (Symons) 79
Simmons, D. 129
Simonetti, Signor 16
Simpson, Derek 70
*Sing-Song: A Nursery Rhyme Book* (Rossetti) 54
Skelton, Logan 46, 49
Smith-Bishton, R. 58
Smyly, C. F. 21
Soames, Rene 95
*Soliloquies of a Subaltern* (Cooper) 46
Solomon, Izler 99
*Sonata for Violin and Piano in C minor* (Beethoven) 5
*Songs of Experience* (Blake) 28
*Songs of Innocence* (Blake) 36
*Songs of Praise* (BBC) 59
Sons of the Clergy Festival 27
Sotherby's (London) 9, 25, 34, 35, 38
Southwell, Robert 79
Stacey, G. 23, 24
Stainer, John 22
Standen, Richard 38
Stanford, Charles V. ix, x, xii, xiv, 5, 6, 7, 14, 16, 103, 134
Steadman-Allen, R. 88, 92
Steane, John B. 11, 26, 37, 46, 49, 75, 82, 98, 120
Stepp, Robert E. 41
Stevenson, Isabella S. 15
Stevenson, Robert Louis 32
Stewart, Robert 59
Stiles, H. D. S. 127
Stobart, James 87, 92
Stone, Frederick 38, 75
Stott, Katherine 84
Stravinsky, Igor ix, xi
Suckling, Norman 126
Sullivan, Arthur 22
Swinburne, Algernon 102
Sydney, Philip 60
Sylvan Press 86
Symons, Arthur 11, 31, 56, 74, 79
Symonds, John Addington 60, 94

Taylor, Kendall 90, 112
*Tempest, The* (Honegger) 111

## General Index

Terfel, Bryn 7, 27, 95
Tertis, Lionel 42, 70
*Thalassius* (Swinburne) 102
Thatcher, R. S. 108
Thibault, Conrad 38
Thomas, Mansel 39
Thompson, Revd. Kenneth 4, 92, 93, 100, 102, 103, 105, 113, 115, 118
Thomson, Bryden 64, 84, 90
Thorne, D. 17
Three Arts Club 38
*Three Character Pieces* (Britten) 49
*Three Hymns for the Celebration of Peace* 56
Thurston, Frederick 112, 133
Toms, Sydney 45
*Town and Country* 134
Townshend, N. 125
Tozer, Geoffrey 84
Trepte, Paul 7, 17, 27, 44, 59
Trew, Graham 47
*Trio in B major* (Brahms) 5
Tunnard, Viola 37, 74
Twelfth Night (Shakespeare) 96
Twemlow, Sydney 23, 37, 47, 50, 51, 52, 71, 74, 77, 82

University of Cambridge 5
University of Durham xiv, xv, 18
University of Keele 94
University of Keele Choral Society 94
University of Keele Orchestra 94
University of London 76

Valois, Ninette de 65
Van Dieren, Bernard 86
Varcoe, Stephen 23, 52
Vasari Singers 27
Vaughan Williams, Ralph ix, x, 85, 103
Verlaine, Paul 34
*Verses* (Dowson) 11, 79
Vesselo, A. 116
Vignoles, Roger 37, 47
Vinden, Maurice 45
Virtuoso Brass Band 92
*Vista, A* (Symonds) 94
Vivienne, Hazel 112

Wakefield Cathedral Choir 34
Walmsley, Trevor 87
Walsh, Stephen 10, 21, 22
Walther, Hans-Jürgen 83
Walton, William 86, 95, 96, 97
Waring, Holburt 76
Warlock, Peter 130, 132

Warner, Sylvia Townsend 81
Warr, E. 6, 19, 45, 70, 112
Warrack, John 77
Warrick-Evans, C. 47
Waterhouse, J. F. 128
Watt, Harry 115
Watts, Helen 75
Watts, L. 48
Weatherly, Frederick E. 24, 39
Webb, S. 27, 113, 121
Webern, Anton von 82
Webster, John xii
*Weekend* (Munro) 49
Weelkes, Thomas 92
Wesley, Charles 59
Westbrook, F. B. 37
Western Australia Symphony Orchestra 108, 117
Wetton, H. Davan 45
Whipp, Ivy Mason 51
Whitehouse, W. E. 16
Whittall, Arnold 84
Wicks, Alan 27
Widicombe, T. 28
Wilbur, Jay 41
Willcocks, David 41
Williams, C. à Becket 127
Williams, G. 38
Williams, Harold 23
Williams, Norman 51
Willison, David 37, 63
*Winter's Tale, A* (Shakespeare) 11
Wood, Dorothy 95
Wood, Haydn 99
Wood, Henry J. 35, 64, 83, 92, 99, 107, 108, 115
Woodgate, Leslie 94, 110, 118
Woolford, Denis 37
Woolley, Kitty 5
Worcester Cathedral Choir 7, 17, 27, 43, 44, 59, 107, 113, 121
Worcester Festival Choral Society 7, 59
Worcester Sinfonia Brass Ensemble 7
Worshipful Company of Musicians 16
Wright, Denis 112
Wright, Kenneth 86, 100
Wright, P. 27, 91
Wright, Simon 50, 75

Yaro, R. 37
Yeats, Y. B. 81
Yenne, V. L. 130
York Minster Choir 113
Yorkshire Imperial Metals Band 87
Yorkshire Symphony Orchestra 93